Creating Value

Creating Value

Shaping tomorrow's business

Shiv S. Mathur

and

Alfred Kenyon

Butterworth-Heinemann
Linacre House, Jordan Hill, Oxford OX2 8DP
A division of Reed Educational and Professional Publishing Ltd

℞ A member of the Reed Elsevier plc group

OXFORD   BOSTON   JOHANNESBURG
MELBOURNE   NEW DELHI   SINGAPORE

First published 1997
Reprinted 1997

© Shiv S. Mathur and Alfred Kenyon 1997

British Library Cataloguing in Publication Data
A catalogue record for this book is
available from the British Library

ISBN 0 7506 3339 5

Typeset by Florencetype Ltd, Stoodleigh, Devon
Printed in Great Britain by Biddles Ltd, Guildford and King's Lynn

Contents

Contents

Preface

Business strategy is receiving more and more attention, because competition is becoming more intense. Two questions have received most attention. First, what are the management skills and qualities that make businesses successful? Secondly, how can we best describe the competitive process, and the key to success in that process?

The present work attempts the second of these questions. The attempt began in the early 1980s with Shiv Mathur's work on competitive positioning. That work has been developed over the years and is now presented mainly in Chapter 5. From that central insight, the present framework has been constructed. Its focus is how competitive positioning builds sustained profit or financial value. That task includes the critical topic of the distinctive resources of a business.

A central thesis is that strategy must shape what customers choose to buy: offerings. In maintaining a close focus on the offering, and on how customers choose it, the framework departs from many other accounts of competitive strategy.

This view of competitive strategy leads to a new perception of corporate strategy. Corporate strategy decides what cluster of offerings, not of profit centres, factories or subsidiaries, makes a company profitable. Ultimately business strategy chooses what profitable customers we want to win.

We have had fun developing this framework, but we have had enormous support from many friends and colleagues. It is a real pleasure to acknowledge this here.

Pride of place must go to those stalwarts who have read through an entire earlier draft, and given us invaluable advice: Shelagh Heffernan, Alec Chrystal, Sudi Sudarsanam, Archie Donaldson, Charles Baden-Fuller and Peter McKiernan.

Some helpful friends have given us the benefit of their expertise on particular, more technical, parts of the text. Here again, Shelagh Heffernan has contributed Appendix 6.1. The other stalwarts are Geoffrey Barnett, Andrew Campbell, Chong Ju Choi, John Chown, Rob Grant and Robin Wensley. We are also greatly indebted to colleagues who had not met us personally, but helped us with advice in response to letters: Jay Barney, David Collis and Frederic Scherer.

Some other colleagues have helped us enormously with their moral and personal support, and especially by using and testing our framework in class. We must single out Hugh Murray and Axel Johne, but we also owe much gratitude to Humphrey Bourne, Ann Brown, Paul Raimond and Gordon Wright.

We are delighted to pay tribute to those who have attended executive seminars and to the many students who have received this framework and given us invaluable feedback. Especially helpful were first of all those who attended an elective on corporate strategy. Secondly there were some dozens of students who used this framework for their MBA projects. Lynn Carter Smith, Peter Cowap, Tim Kent-Phillips and Robert Sullebarger deserve special mention among our project students.

Finally, we have had a lot of logistic and practical help from Shobha, Rittu and Tarun Mathur. Tarun has helped particularly by verifying some facts and the realism of some illustrations.

With so much help, the mistakes are all our own!

Shiv S. Mathur
Alfred Kenyon

Outline: The framework in a nutshell

This book presents a framework of business strategy. This outline of that framework may be helpful, but a mere outline cannot do justice to the reasoning behind the framework, nor present all its elements. Figures in brackets refer to chapters, e.g. (3) = Chapter 3.

- Business strategy in this framework consists of (3):
  - (a) competitive strategy, which positions a single competitive offering in relation to customers and competing substitutes,
  - (b) corporate strategy, which manages a company's cluster of offerings, by deciding what offerings to add, retain or divest.
- Only an individual offering competes in the sense of being chosen by customers. Each competitive strategy therefore concerns one offering (3).
- Both competitive and corporate strategy have a financial goal: making the company more valuable to its owners in the long term. This is true of the smallest one-person business as well as of the giant corporation. If the business does not at least earn its cost of capital, it cannot survive independently (2).
- Competitive strategy picks profitable, or more strictly, value-building offerings (8). An offering builds value, i.e. earns more than its cost of capital, if it simultaneously exploits (12):

(a) a favourable market opportunity, by addressing a set of customers willing to pay prices (6) at which the offering can meet the financial objective,

(b) the company's own distinctive resources which give it an edge over competitors (10–12).

These two conditions are like the two blades of a pair of scissors, which can only cut together (12).

- Favourable market opportunities arise from the way an offering is positioned, which is done either:

  (a) by differentiating the offering, i.e. distancing it from competing substitutes in order to make customers willing to pay value-building prices (5–6), or

  (b) by competing on price, with a low degree (if any) of differentiation, and a very competitive unit cost (5–6, 8).

- Differentiation is a matter of how customers see the offering. What customers see of an offering are its outputs, those features that customers take into account when choosing (4–6).

- Differentiation is a matter of degree. The more differentiated an offering appears to be to customers, the less do their choices depend on price (6).

- Differentiation can be in several dimensions and sub-dimensions, which represent a number of generic competitive strategies. Chapter 5 describes and classifies a rich variety of them. They represent different ways in which offerings can be positioned in customers' eyes (5).

- What customers compare and choose are competing offerings. They do not choose 'firms' (3), nor are their choices bounded by 'industries' or by discrete markets, with publicly visible boundaries. The real world of the advanced economies is one in which most offerings are differentiated to some degree. That means that each offering has a unique set of competitors, not wholly and exactly shared with any one of those competitors. Each offering thus has its own 'private' market (4).

- Businesses normally have to be organized into profit or cost centres with separate accountability. Hence they cannot normally be organized into individual offerings, which may even cut across such centres. Each offering therefore needs an internal sponsor, who sponsors not only its planning and selection, but also monitors its implementation. Sponsors will often be shared by a number of offerings (21).

- Markets are not equally competitive. Differentiation makes a market less competitive. So can oligopoly, a market condition in which there are only a few competitors, or at any rate only a few dominant competitors. In such markets it is harder to predict the outcome of the competitive process (7).
- A competitive strategy builds value over time. The offering must be robust enough to sustain its value-building over whatever time it takes to beat the cost of capital. It must therefore be armoured against competitive attempts to erode its value-building capacity before the goal is attained (10–12).
- The need for sustained value-building can be met in two different ways (10–12):

  (a) in competitive strategy, by deploying distinctive resources which are specific to the competitor and armoured against imitators to the necessary extent,
  (b) in corporate strategy, by a flair for successfully picking winners and by skill and judgement in timing additions and divestments of offerings.

- Corporate strategy manages the cluster of offerings owned by any one company. There is evidence that in the period 1960–1980 company managers had an excessive urge to make their companies bigger, by adding offerings to their clusters: a diversification spree. Since 1980 managements have become more self-critical. There has been much divestment, which has made many companies more valuable. Companies should expand, provided that the nature of their business and skills requires expansion to build value. There is much scope for such growth, but none for the dash for size that characterized earlier decades (13–17).

3

- Strong safeguards are needed against over-expansion. These consist of the better-off test and some filters, applied to every decision to add or retain an offering. The test measures whether the company is more valuable with or without the offering. The filters guard against uncompetitive feather-bedding, against over-optimism, inertia and the reluctance to change course. Together these requirements and the next apply a stringent value-centred discipline (14).
- The better-off test cannot be passed by an unrelated diversification. The offering needs to be related to the rest of the cluster by one of six specified links. The most important of them is 'synergy': the sharing of resources and other efforts with other members of the cluster. Relatedness does not consist of belonging to the same 'industry' as other parts of the cluster (16).
- Corporate strategy's task of managing the cluster includes the management and strategic allocation of the company's resources, which tend to be shared among offerings (10, 16, 17, 21).
- The framework applies equally to domestic and international business. In international business it is helpful not to over-estimate the significance of political states, For example, it is often wrong to regard one state like Singapore or Venezuela as one separate 'market' (18–20).

1 Purpose, scope and basics

Introduction: The purpose of this book

This book is about business strategy, meaning strategy in business. The task of business strategy is to make the business more valuable by a specific route: that of targeting profitable customers. If this book helps managers to see how they can best do that, it will have achieved its purpose.

The book therefore makes two fundamental assumptions. The first is that business exists to satisfy its financial funding markets. This assumption is discussed in Chapter 2. The second is that a business can only achieve this financial aim in its customer markets, by successfully targeting profitable customers. Customers are profitable if the business can sell to them at margins which yield returns at least equal to the cost of capital.

The focus of this book is on the strategic issues of competitive business. Its distinctive feature is its concentration on how customers choose what they buy. In normal conditions it is the customer who decides whether and what to buy.

The objective: financial results from customer markets

The primary focus of this framework is therefore on financial results and customer markets. This emphasis is not of course unique. Many have said that the purpose of business is to produce financial results, and very few writers would deny that financial results are mainly achieved by success in customer markets. However, that central insight is not always

followed through. Much writing and much managerial practice gives one of two extreme impressions. One is that
financial results depend entirely on operating efficiencies. At
the other extreme the object of business strategy is seen as
maximum sales volume and market share, meeting customer
preferences as if that alone were enough to produce acceptable levels of performance. The first focuses exclusively on
costs, the second ignores them.

Demand and supply issues

A focus on customers and their choices does not imply that
strategy is just a matter of taking care of the demand side.
A central message is that if a competitive offering is to be
successful, i.e. sustain the building of financial value for its
company, it is likely that it must simultaneously:

- occupy a favourable market position in relation to
  customers and competitors, discussed in Part Two, but also
- exploit the company's distinctive key resources, which are
  defined and discussed in Part Four.

An offering adds value if these two features, like blades of
a pair of scissors, find a simultaneous advantage.

In economic terms, the first of these two requirements
covers the demand, and the last the supply side of the
task. In the context of strategy, the demand and supply
sides confront managers with very different challenges.
Consequently strategy must deal with each of these issues
separately before bringing them together. This book will
therefore not get properly to grips with supply side issues
until Part Three and especially Part Four. Chapter 12 will
finally bring the two sides together.

Non-profit-making enterprises

Business strategy is concerned with the challenges of creating
financial value in competitive markets. Some departments
of state and some public agencies and corporations, as well

as private charities, handle similar tasks. In fact, governments have recently tried to simulate market conditions[1] in their business or near-business operations. The aim is to become more responsive to the varying needs of their customers or clients. The framework outlined in this book may be of some value to those who manage such enterprises. On the other hand there will also be fundamental differences. A state health service will seek to look after the needs of those most in need, such as the poor and the old, who may be the least profitable customers in financial terms. A private healthcare business on the other hand may not be able to afford to serve them. The ultimate goal of the activity must affect its strategy.

Development of business strategy as a discipline

As a distinctive topic business strategy dates from around 1960. Some important ideas are older than that, but had developed as part of some other discipline like economics. Strategy has made great strides, especially in the hands of economists like Rumelt and Porter, since the 1970s. There is nevertheless little agreement about its meaning, its purpose and its structure.[2]

In the 1960s strategy was first thought of as a formal, largely financial, planning process. The unquestioned goal of strategy was growth. Companies had learned the art of preparing budgets for the current year. Planning often just extended the process into years 2–5.

By the mid-1970s the Boston Consulting Group's portfolio management concept, founded on the growth/share matrix, became very influential with managers.[3] This came in response to the problems faced by companies which had by then become larger and more diversified, in a more hostile economic climate.

Already before strategy (as distinct from business policy)[4] became a separate discipline, marketing had treated the offering, rather than price, as the principal variable. Strategy did not from the outset focus on the choice of what was to be sold, but Porter's *Competitive Strategy* (1980) put the seal on this reorientation with its dichotomy between

7

differentiation and cost leadership. It gave prominence to the competitive positioning within its industry of each offering,[5] which Porter called 'product' or 'service'.

Since then academics have mainly focused on three areas. One is to explain why some companies are persistently more profitable than others, and the corporate resources which confer this persistent 'competitive advantage' on them. The second area is whether industries and strategic groups[6] within industries are in practice appropriate units for analysing performance.[7] A third one, stimulated by a major contribution from Porter[8] himself, is the distinction between competitive and corporate strategy. Whereas competitive strategy is in this book seen as positioning a single product or service, corporate strategy manages the company's cluster ('portfolio') of such competitive offerings. Kay[9] has synthesized this set of ideas and also made much more explicit the objective of adding financial value.

Modern business strategy has therefore moved towards studying the competitive process, towards asking what offering or offerings will make this company more profitable.[10] The effect of that move is to make the offering, rather than price/volume the principal variable. This reverses the priorities of traditional microeconomics, which took the offering as given, and set out to find the offering's optimum price and volume,[11] in specified market conditions. Whereas the main concern of microeconomics is the efficiency of the economy, that of business strategy is the prosperity of the business itself.

The role of this book

This book puts forward an integrated framework which builds on all these more recent ideas. Its dual focus is on the customer who chooses between competing offerings and on the special endowments which help a business to excel at serving specific groups of customers. The intense focus on customers yields the insight that the unit of competitive strategy has to be the individual competitive offering and its positioning in relation to customers and competing substitutes.

Corporate strategy is seen as managing the company's cluster of offerings. It too therefore concerns what the company should sell. In developing these concepts, the book probes deeply into the nature of differentiation and into the kind of markets in which differentiated offerings compete.

What is thus presented, is a coherent framework of:

- what business strategy is, what it helps managers to achieve, and its subdivision into competitive and corporate strategy, and
- how these two categories illuminate all the other dimensions of strategy like time-frames and geographical span, the demand and supply sides, formulation and implementation.

One disclaimer is needed. Although this is an attempt at a comprehensive treatment of the topics just listed, there is no systematic coverage here of the important behavioural and organizational aspects of business strategy. Behavioural issues are given their due priority where they arise, but are not covered systematically, or as a sub-topic in their own right.

As mentioned at the beginning, it is hoped that managers will find this framework both insightful and useful.

Care with words

A theme which will run through this book is the need to take care in the use of words. Business strategy uses terms like industry, firm, competition, differentiation, resource, competitive advantage, and conglomerate. They all trip off the tongue quite easily, but they mean very different things to different people. Unfortunately their meanings matter. Misunderstandings about them can cause mischief of any degree, from trivial to catastrophic.

If key words cause ambiguity between managers, they can cause even more of it between them and business academics. Up to a point the two sides have learned to understand each other better. A rising proportion of managers have MBA or similar degrees, and therefore know what academics are writing and saying. Many others are exposed to articles, seminars or in-house exchanges with those who use academic concepts, frameworks and models. Nevertheless, there is a gulf between the two worlds. If academics rigorously define 'industry' as a group of competing substitutes, how many managers in the real world are conscious that the model does not apply to say the steel industry, with its combination of 'products' like castings, pipes, sheet metal, guns and cutlery which are not particularly close substitutes? Its common feature is that it makes, processes or uses a single material.

Academics can use such models without getting confused about their meaning, but is it fair to expect managers to have or to keep them in mind whenever they use an academic framework for thinking through their problems? The steel manager who attended a meeting of the trade association yesterday, may be forgiven for not automatically associating an 'industry' with just competing substitutes.

Language is not a glamorous topic. This is because well used words are inconspicuous. The trouble is that bad, ambiguous language can wreak so much havoc, as we shall see.

Views of 'business strategy'

The first object lesson of the need to take care with words is the expression 'business strategy' and its exact meaning. A managing director known to the authors, when asked what the company's strategy was, said 'to move the factory' some miles from where it then was. Another company might say its strategy is to restructure its European operations to come under a single headquarters instead of separate headquarters in each European country. A third company in the UK might say its strategy is to make an acquisition in the United States. Others might answer 'to become a world class manufacturing company', or 'to become the industry leader', or 'to double earnings per share over five years' or 'to reduce the company's debt equity ratio to 80 per cent'.

All these examples are taken from real life, and their variety illustrates how little uniformity there is in people's ideas of what is meant by 'business strategy'.

Mintzberg's 'emerging' business strategies

The need to take care with this expression has been greatly reinforced by the very influential Henry Mintzberg and his school. Mintzberg's most controversial contribution is his acceptance that the term 'strategy' can mean any of 'plan, ploy, pattern, position and perspective', and that a strategy 'may appear without preconception'.[12] This formulation includes in the term 'strategy' ploys or even patterns which can 'emerge' from the managers' actual past conduct. The formulation is therefore not confined to deliberate and conscious decisions.[13]

Mintzberg is reacting against the formal planning school which treated a plan and a strategy as interchangeable terms, and treated both as an extension of the financial budget into years 2–5. In rejecting this, Mintzberg must surely be supported. Formal plans of that type have little chance of helping businesses to become more profitable, because there was a great deal wrong with the concept:

* Plans did not focus on the competitive markets and offerings of the business.
* They centred on accounting numbers, not on earning or beating the cost of capital of each of the offerings, adjusted for their different risks. Consequently they did not even make financial sense.
* Numbers produced by formal plans were not usable as control figures; consequently, there was little link with subsequent actual performance. They were neither a forecast, nor a management commitment. They were not a useful management tool.

Mintzberg rejected formal plans mainly for their rigidity, their lack of an implementation stage, and their tendency to favour a top-down procedure.

Mintzberg's case against formal planning systems is persuasive and widely supported.[14] Where he fails to convince, is in his extension of the concept of 'strategy' to,

- tactical and trivial meanings like 'ploy',
- undeliberate, 'emergent' processes.

It is self-evident that ploys are a necessary and healthy part of the manager's armoury. It is equally self-evident that a business frequently finds that it has drifted into a beneficial change of direction, by a series of instinctive reactions to changing circumstances or information. These are all part of good management, but that does not justify the label 'strategies'. Managers need a word that signifies *a conscious decision to adopt a major direction-setting objective together with its implementation path.* Only that can usefully be called a strategy. Such a strategy can and should be flexible and responsive to changes in the news or in manager's understanding of the environment. If these adaptations and responses are conscious and deliberate, they are within a useful meaning of 'strategy'. If they are a process of drift, they are not.[15]

'Deliberate' adoption need not mean formal or written adoption. Again, a decision process is better when it includes contributions from the coal face, but the word 'strategy' does not lose its practical usefulness when it describes a decision taken just in the chief executive's mind. It does however lose that usefulness if it covers too wide a range of meanings. That happens if it can also refer to something,

- minor or trivial, or
- never consciously articulated even in thought, or
- discovered not by thinking forward, but by merely contemplating and rationalizing past conduct.

These meanings need to be excluded not from the concept of good management, only from the word 'strategy', if it is to remain a useful word. The list of 'plan, ploy, pattern, position and perspective' is too wide-ranging, not just too alliterative, to describe a serious concept. When the single label 'strategy' is stretched to include opposites like 'plans' and non-plans, it must snap.

Mintzberg[16] also rightly stresses that opportunistic action must often override plans or strategies, and that opportunistic actions may be more rewarding than rigid plans. That is very persuasive, but it does not make a case for calling such actions strategic.

Special scrutiny is needed for one of the many arguments used by the 'emergent' school: the appeal to how managers actually use the word 'strategy'. Managers are usually under pressure to cut corners and to stop short of perfection. Under pressure it is not always easy or even possible to maintain the prudence or the discipline to think ahead. Not unnaturally however in such conditions managers would still like to dignify all their decisions or unplanned actions, however trivial, with the status symbol of a 'strategy'. They may in other words be tempted to use what they see as the language of perfection to describe imperfect practice. We might caricature them as saying: "If we do not have time to think long-term, let us call our expedients 'strategies': the in-word may make up for our omissions. Better still, let 'strategy' describe not what we set out to do, but what we have found our actual practice to be". The process is a comforting one. If any managerial conduct qualifies for the grand word 'strategy', no one is left out in the cold. Sadly, such debased use of the word serves to disguise, not to inform. Worse still, the deception is often self-deception.

To summarize, Mintzberg, like other writers, seems to be on firm ground in doubting whether formal planning systems serve much strategic purpose. Reservations about his own views are purely linguistic. To include in the word 'strategy' unplanned, undeliberate and unconscious processes, or intentions which can only be articulated with hindsight, is to empty that word of much of its usefulness. Managers should not be deflected from thinking forward.

'Strategy' and 'plan'

A strategy could be accurately described as one kind of 'plan' in the dictionary sense of 'project', consisting of a goal and an explicit method of attaining it. In that sense every strategy must be a 'plan'. We nevertheless avoid this usage of 'plan', so as to avoid the ambiguities or associations to which the Mintzberg school has rightly drawn attention.

Business strategy: a working definition

The full meaning of 'business strategy' will unfold in Chapters 2 and 3, with the distinction between its two subdivisions, competitive and corporate strategy. However, a brief preview may be useful at this point. **Business strategy** in this book concerns major decisions deliberately taken to establish what sets of customers a business aims to serve in the future and against what competition, in order to meet its financial objectives. Very broadly again, it could also at this stage be described as the sum total of competitive and corporate strategy, of the profitable positioning of individual competitive offerings and of the profitable management of the cluster of offerings by the company. 'Profitable' is here used as shorthand for value-building.

These broad formulations beg many questions, not least what is meant by a 'company' or 'a business' and its financial objectives, but they will be answered as we progress through Chapters 2 and 3.

The macroeconomic environment

Managers should of course conduct the usual financial analysis before deciding to adopt or retain a competitive offering. This means estimating the net present value of its future cash flows, discounted at its cost of capital. The process is briefly touched upon in several places in this book, such as Chapters 12, 17 and 21. The projections used in that financial analysis must naturally take account of expected macroeconomic trends, i.e. cyclical swings in demand.

Offerings are not equally sensitive to cyclical swings. Most affected are:

- offerings with a short life-span, too short for results to average out over the business cycles, and
- offerings in cyclical trades like civil construction.

This essential task of reconnoitring the macroeconomic background will not be specifically pursued in this book, which focuses on the competitive, i.e. microeconomic environment.

Addressing the manager

This book is written for the manager. It seeks to refocus business strategy on markets in which customers choose what they buy. It aims to give the manager a more systematic and more sharply defined account of how to map out future objectives and paths towards attaining them. It owes a huge debt to what others have written, but it draws above all on observation of particular businesses and their strategic problems. It does not seek to present any fresh empirical research. Instead it draws on a number of disciplines, especially marketing, microeconomics and financial theory, all of which enrich our understanding of business strategy.

Strategy (as here defined) is practised by senior people in business, many of whom have heard, read or picked up ideas and concepts developed in business schools and elsewhere. They are not strangers to expressions like differentiation, strategic groups, corporate competences, demand elasticity, transnational corporations, or even emergent strategies. This book will therefore seek to set out the meaning and inter-relatedness of some of these academic ideas wherever that may help the manager to understand the issues of strategy a little better.

Some of the ideas and frameworks – like the one in this book – come from economics, and focus on the nature of the competitive process. Many others come from disciplines like human resources and psychology, and focus on the qualities that make good strategists, i.e. top managers. The two sets of ideas obviously cover overlapping issues.

Managers, like academics, have different mental backgrounds, are trained in different disciplines, experienced in different specialisms. Some will be familiar with the language of economics, some unfamiliar. The same applies no doubt to the languages of marketing, accounting, finance, and many others. The book should be helpful to all who have an interest in strategy, but it may well be that some parts of it will make more sense to some readers than to others. This is inevitable in such a multidisciplinary topic. A recurrent theme is that customers vary in their preferences and predispositions; this is no doubt also true of readers.

The main task of this study is to set out just what a business strategy is and how it should be formulated. The framework which it presents, is designed with a sharp eye on the practicalities of implementation. Implementation itself is dealt with[17] to the extent that the implementation of strategies modifies the way a business needs to be run day by day.

Top management and its skills taken as given, not as a variable

There is now an influential school of writers on business strategy[18] who examine those top management skills which will enable a company to manage a much wider spread of businesses successfully. The wider spread may concern businesses at the frontiers of technology, or complex global businesses, or conglomerates of unrelated businesses.

In this book it is assumed that a given top management team's directing skills can change only within limits. Any more radical change would call for substantial changes in the composition of the top team itself. A given team can for example update its command of the technologies in which the company is specialized. On the other hand it probably cannot extend its skills to radically different areas.

The influential writers present some most valuable insights into what strategies require what kind of top management skills. However, as much of the radical change in skills would require significant changes in the top team, this book will treat these issues as peripheral, not central to its own purpose. This book is addressed to managers who want to improve their grasp of how they themselves, not their successors, can formulate and implement strategies better in their present companies. It is assumed that they do not wish to be replaced.

Should managers be thinkers?

Managers sometimes approach the topic of business strategy as an opportunity to show dynamic vigour. A caricature might portray an apocryphal manager almost determined to resist any temptation to think and reflect. It is as if such managers must above all avoid being caught in the act of thinking: it smacks of indecision.

'Mission statement'

1 We are in the business of leisure services.
2 Double EU market share from 22.5 per cent to 45 per cent in five years.
3 Earnings per share to grow 15 per cent p.a.
4 Debt equity ratio to fall from 80 per cent to 60 per cent.
5 Turnover per employee to rise from £180 to £200 at this month's level of prices.

The upshot is a series of defensive strategy-substitutes, like a 57-page annual form-filling exercise, or bold, prophetic lists of targets (sometimes called 'missions') such as those in the box.

There is of course a place for such a set of objectives. It motivates. It gives the company's managers and workforce some uniformity of purpose, perhaps some shared values. However, can such a list be helpfully called a 'business strategy'? First, the list is little more than a wish list of possible objectives. They are not systematically derived from what financial markets require of the business. Even less are they integrated into a coherent pattern of action in commercial markets.

The book sets out to show that reflection helps strategy. Moreover, thoughtful strategy explicitly seeks to create positive value in the eyes of the financial markets, and more if possible. Without reflection the manager cannot form very clear ideas about the purpose of the business, about the criteria of success, how success can be achieved in various possible future environments, what changes are needed from the present commercial position and resources of the business, and how those changes might be attained.

What decisions are strategic?

Rumelt, Schendel and Teece[19] take as their starting-point the fact that businesses have choices to make. *Strategic* choices (they say) include:

- goals,
- products and services to offer,
- policies for positioning themselves in product markets,
- the level of scope and diversity,
- organization structure,
- administrative systems used to define and coordinate work.

The approach via choices is a very practical one, but there is also a case for first defining business strategies themselves. It is generally hazardous to adopt particular strategies before forming a clear view of what business strategy is. If we launch directly into the task of finding a strategy to adopt and pursue, before we know what we mean by a strategy, the risk is that we might embark on a half-baked project which turns out not to be a proper business strategy. The two tasks are quite distinct. We may for example decide, like the managing director quoted earlier, that our strategy is to move the factory. It may be a few years down the road before it dawns on us that the factory move, however sound, was not in fact a business strategy, and that we are going bankrupt because we did not formulate a proper strategy, aimed at finding profitable customers.

Business strategy, culture, mission statements

Business strategy is sometimes assumed to encompass topics like corporate culture,[20] mission statements, or statements about values adopted by the company. All these are matters which a business strategy must take account of, accommodate or comply with, not something which it creates or changes.[21]

Hofstede[22] helpfully calls culture 'the software of the mind'. Corporate culture is something more fundamental than what this book calls a strategy. On the other hand, lower level cultures like attitudes to customers are closely associated with the company's key and other resources[23] which should be largely, but not invariably, taken as given. These lower level cultures can be ancillary to a strategy.

Values, objectives and mission statements stop well short of action plans. This can be illustrated from the corporate philosophy of the Bank of Credit and Commerce International (BCCI). It interestingly consisted of the following four pillars:[24]

- submission to God
- service to humanity
- giving
- success.

These kind of statements set broad objectives and contexts for a business strategy. They can also impose constraints on it. The strategist must take these as given; a competitive or corporate strategy can hardly be allowed or expected to change them. Yet they are not themselves strategies. A strategy targets a much more specific, though major objective: producing offerings to win profitable customers.

Outline of the book

Chapter 1 has introduced the book, outlined its purpose, and given a first indication of what is and what is not here meant by 'business strategy'.

Part One (Chapters 2–3) sets out the hierarchy of corporate objectives and the ethical foundations of business objectives. It classifies business strategy into competitive and corporate strategy, and describes how they interact.

Part Two (Chapters 4–7) aims to give the reader a thorough understanding of competitive markets and competitive strategy in those markets. It describes how a competitive offering is positioned in relation to its competing substitutes and customers. It defines, describes and classifies competitive strategies. It shows how the prices that sellers can charge depend on the key features of differentiation and the degree of oligopoly.

Part Three (Chapters 8–9) relates the nature of competitive positioning to the financial raison d'être of the business. It examines the elements that build financial value in a competitive strategy. It sets out how concepts like differentiation, time-frames, duration of profitable margins, volume and market share interact in competitive strategy. It goes on to look at the dynamics of competitive positioning, and how a business can either exploit its markets as it finds them or destabilize and transform them to its own advantage.

Part Four (Chapters 10–12) discusses the vital contribution of a company's idiosyncratic resources or capabilities to profitability, and what enables some companies to be persistently successful in building financial value. It also puts forward excellence in corporate strategy as an alternative route to sustained value-building. Chapter 12 then outlines a practical framework, derived from the earlier argument, for selecting profitable competitive strategies and thus targeting profitable customers.

Part Five (Chapters 13–17) moves from competitive to corporate strategy, i.e. from the single value-adding offering to the company's cluster of offerings. It discusses the criteria of success, and how they can be passed only by *related* clusters of offerings. It presents a specific list of links which relate offerings in the required sense.

Part Six (Chapters 18–20) discusses the place of geographical distance and political frontiers in business strategy, and to what extent and how this geographical dimension fits into the frameworks of competitive and corporate strategy.

Part Seven (Chapter 21) deals with the framework's organizational and management implications for the task of formulating and implementing business strategies.

The Endpiece concludes with some reflections on where business strategy might be heading.

How to read the book

This book is intended to present a coherent and reasonably comprehensive framework of the issues of business strategy. It is intended as a seamless garment. It should therefore be read as a whole. Nevertheless a busy reader could omit the appendices and Parts Six and Seven (Chapters 18–21) without missing the main structure of the framework. Chapter 15 is also outside the main structure, but should be of interest all the same.

Notes

1. For instance, the 'internal market' in the UK National Health Service, and proposals in various countries to issue education vouchers to parents.
2. Whittington (1993).
3. Abell and Hammond (1979).
4. Rumelt, Schendel and Teece (1991) p. 7.
5. Porter and subsequent writers do not strictly restrict their language to the individual offering. Much is said that gives the impression that the 'firm' is being positioned in its industry or market. We believe this is an ambiguity between the business which does the positioning, and the object being positioned, i.e. the offering. This point will be developed in Chapter 3.
6. See Chapter 4.
7. Rumelt (1991). The 1996 Annual Conference of the Strategic Management Society identified "the changing boundaries of 'industry'" as a theme for study.

8. Porter (1987).
9. Kay (1993).
10. Resource-based theory (Chapter 10) is not in effect a departure from this search for profitable offerings. It merely directs that search towards offerings for which the company has distinctive resources.

    Business strategy is of course here taken to look for where the company is going rather than for the qualities and structures required for successful direction.
11. Rumelt (1984) puts it: 'The central concerns of business policy are the observed heterogeneity of firms and firms' choice of product-market commitments. By contrast, the basic phenomena of interest in neoclassical theory is the functioning of the price system. . .'. 'Business policy' is now widely called 'strategy', and neoclassical theory is a development of industrial economics.
12. Mintzberg (1987b) p. 13.
13. Mintzberg (1987a). For another critique of these issues see Kay (1993) Chapter 21.
14. Andrews (1981).
15. Mintzberg and Waters (1985). Kenyon and Mathur (1993) point out how the qualifying word 'emergent' has added to the difficulties by spanning both deliberate and undeliberate processes.
16. Mintzberg (1990).
17. Chapter 21.
18. Prahalad and Bettis (1986).
19. Rumelt, Schendel and Teece (1991). This important paper takes stock of what the discipline of business strategy has been trying to achieve, and where it might need to go. The authors regret (p. 7) the lack of an agreed definition of 'strategy'.
20. *Corporate* culture is here used to describe the collective mental climate in which a business arrives at its decisions, rather than how it implements them, e.g. by smiling and paying attention to customers.
21. Once again, the assumption is that any real change in corporate culture would require substantial changes in the composition of the top team. If so, the incumbent top team will only undertake strategies which require such minor incremental changes in culture as are within that existing team's scope.
22. Hofstede (1991).
23. Chapter 10.
24. Lessem (1989) quotes some of these.

Part One Fundamentals: The Framework and its Main Building Blocks

Chapter 2 looks at what business strategy aims to achieve, and sets it in its financial and ethical environment. Chapter 3 sets out and defines the main building blocks: competitive and corporate strategy, offering, competitive positioning, inputs and outputs, and how some of these concepts relate to management structures. It completes the definition of business strategy.

2 Objectives: what is business strategy for?

Corporate success and the financial and commercial markets

The box in Chapter 1 illustrates certain approaches to corporate objectives. Not the least of its shortcomings is how the list jumbles commercial and financial objectives.

This chapter explores the ultimate goals of business and therefore of business strategy. It seeks to sort out to what extent ultimate goals are financial, commercial or ethical. Some would personalize that and ask whether a business exists for its investors, its stakeholders, or society at large.

The chapter thus explores *why* strategies are needed. There are a number of answers, but they are not equally fundamental. The ultimate objective of a business has to be financial: to earn returns at least equal to the cost of capital. Capital is scarce, and financial markets determine its equilibrium price, which will vary with the risk of each venture.

That rather formal statement about earning at least the cost of capital is probably the best way to define the purpose of a proposed *new* business. Most managers however work in an existing business, and experience the ultimate supremacy of the financial markets in a different and threatening way. Satisfying those markets is also a condition of survival. If we do not earn the returns expected by the financial markets, the independent survival of our business is in jeopardy.

The fundamental goal is financial: to earn more than the cost of capital

A **business** is brought into being by the investment of funds in a risky commercial venture, in order to earn returns greater than the cost of those funds (next section below): this basic objective is *financial*. It is not for example worth investing money in a corner store, if its expected returns are no better than the risk-free return on treasury bills, or on a savings account. More formally, the fundamental purpose of a business is to build financial value. That means that its expected future cash flows, discounted at its cost of capital, result in a positive net present value.

In that calculation the investment has to be quantified at the opportunity cost of the resources employed. The opportunity cost of resources is either their acquisition cost (if new) or their value in their best alternative employment inside the company or their net disposal value. The resources here include not just the net assets covered by balance sheets, but also any intangibles excluded from that list, such as the skills of the management and workforce. Practical measurement steps are listed in Chapter 17 under the two headings 'Analysing proposals for additions' and 'Analysing whether to retain or divest offering F'.

The cash flows must for this purpose of course be calculated after deducting as a cost the market value of for example the owner's own services to the shop. That value might be the best salary which the owner could alternatively earn, say by managing someone else's shop or by managing a football team.

The cost of capital

The fundamental purpose of a business therefore is to earn returns which will at least amortize its *risk-adjusted* cost of capital. The cost of capital is a central concept of financial theory, derived from how the financial markets work. Whether a business is funded in the financial markets or not, those markets determine its cost of capital. I may invest my own inherited capital in my business. However, whether that investment makes sense for me, depends on the opportunity cost of that capital – on what returns I might obtain from the best alternative investment open to me. That opportunity cost is what my business must beat. If I can earn better (risk-adjusted) returns in some other venture, then I should put it into that other venture, not into my own business. The best yardstick is ratios derived from published financial reports and share price information. Those ratios must for that purpose of course be adjusted for the lesser marketability and probably higher risk of my own business.

The **cost of capital** of any investment is in this book defined as that investment's weighted average cost of equity and debt, the latter after tax. A company can here be regarded as the sum of its investment projects.

Each project or offering has its own degree of risk, and the greater the risk, the higher the cost of capital. The returns required from a given business must therefore cover the cost of its particular degree of risk. Risks are of many kinds, but the most fundamental category is competitive risk: the risk that another, more attractive shop will open close to our shop, or that consumer tastes move away from the type of retail service that we are equipped to provide.

Threats to independent survival

The primacy of financial returns holds for a continuing as well as a new business. The independent survival of an established business is threatened if it fails to earn its cost of capital. This threat can take two forms: bankruptcy or hostile takeover. Those who are funding the business now, may either withdraw their support or decline to finance any necessary growth or development, leaving the business un-financeable. The threat of hostile takeover is at present a serious problem only for listed companies in certain countries: the US, the UK, and others where hostile takeover is a common occurrence. If such a listed company fails to convince the stockmarket that its future cash flows will meet its cost of capital, it will see its share price drop, making a

27

hostile takeover both feasible and tempting for any predator able to make better use of the assets. Whatever the threat, the yardstick of the independent survival of a business of any size is set by its financial markets.

Expected returns are the yardstick of value

Financial markets assess an investment in a business at the net present value of the *expected future* cash flows from that investment. If the market expects future returns to diverge from past returns, then the past level is irrelevant to financial value. Expectations are what matters. In practice expectations are of course powerfully shaped by the past track record; if only because the past is known and the future is uncertain. The distinction is nevertheless important. Stockmarkets and other financial markets are very sensitive to expected changes of trend, and will value companies accordingly.

Reported price earnings ratios, like those listed in the *Financial Times* and *Wall Street Journal*, show wide dispersions. This is largely because the reported ratios relate today's share price to the last reported *historical* earnings per share. These are always significantly out of date. Share prices on the other hand incorporate the market's current view of *prospective* earnings. If the financial press could reliably ascertain and list prospective earnings multiples, these would no doubt be less widely dispersed.

Financial value and shareholder, owner or investor value

The objective of business strategy, we have said, is to boost the net present value, but of precisely what? The answer is **shareholder value** which Rappaport[1] defines as corporate value less debt.[2] In other words, he defines the combined value of the company to its shareholders and lenders as 'corporate' value. This book is concerned simply with shareholder value. The leverage of debt to equity is a matter of financial policy, which is outside the scope of this book.

28

It will be tacitly assumed that this leverage will be optimized from the point of view of the owners of the equity.

In fact of course a company may have a capital structure with more than one class of shares, such as preference shares and ordinary or common shares. To simplify, it will be assumed that there is only one class of shares, which fully carries the risk of fluctuating results.

With these simplifying assumptions, we can use the expressions 'financial value', 'shareholder value', 'investor value', or 'owner value' as if they were interchangeable terms. It is helpful to have available some terms which do not presuppose a formal company or ownership structure.

Managers' guiding principle should be to create shareholder value, i.e. to manage the company in such a way as to improve its long-term value to shareholders. Shareholder value is measured in terms of a given investor's or owner's interest in the business.[3]

Financial value is close to, but not identical with, **profitability**. In most contexts the two are closely correlated. In other words, actions which boost the company's accounting profitability, more often than not improve its financial value. The difference between them is due to the accounting definition of 'profit', a difference discussed in Chapter 8.

Shareholder value must be sharply distinguished from financial size. A listed company's financial size is its market capitalization. This can be increased not only by boosting its share price, but also by increasing the number of shares issued, perhaps to new shareholders. If so, the company's financial value and its financial size do not necessarily rise or fall together. This will now be illustrated.

The **market capitalization** of a company is the number of issued shares multiplied by the share price. If Holdings plc has issued ten million shares, which have a market price of £2.00 each, the market capitalization is £20 million. This will rise to £24 million, if Holdings plc acquires Sellout plc by issuing a further two million Holdings shares to the owners of Sellout, and if Holdings' share price remains at £2.00 per share. There are now 12 million Holdings shares at £2.00, giving £24 million. This however will not make any individual shareholder better off. His or her 300 shares are worth £600 before and after the acquisition of Sellout. The company's financial size has gone up, but no change has occurred in its financial or shareholder value.

The returns to any such shareholder or investor is what managers should maximize. It is the sum for which the shareholder can sell the holding in the market, plus any cash paid to the shareholder by the company. For example, if the company were to buy back 10 per cent of its own shares for £2.00 per share, our shareholder would receive 30 × £2 = £60 cash. In addition, if the share price has remained steady at £2.00, the shareholder would retain 270 shares worth £2 each = £540. The shareholder's total wealth would be £540 + £60 cash = £600: again no change.

However, if as a result of either the acquisition of Sellout or the buy-back of shares the share price were to rise to £2.10, the shareholder would have gained: 10p × 300 = £30 in the first case and 10p × 270 = £27 in the second.[4]

What needs to be boosted is the value of what investors hold, together with any cash receipts brought about by the actions or decisions of the managers.

The source of financial returns is commercial success

However, though this financial objective of the business is fundamental, its attainment is primarily a matter of competitive success in winning profitable customers in commercial markets. The arbiter of whether a business survives is its financial market, but the *means* of survival, its returns, are decided by customers in its commercial markets.

This is not just a good model of a business, illustrated in Figure 2.1. It is also echoed in financial theory. For example, the β parameter in the capital asset pricing model for practical purposes measures the degree of cyclicality of the principal *commercial* market or markets[5] in which the company is seen to be operating.

Thus the ultimate reality of business is the need to satisfy financial markets by success in winning profitable customers

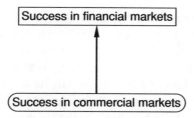

Figure 2.1 *The fundamental business objective and its source*

in *commercial* markets. This is mirrored in the basic framework of business strategy. In the next chapter we shall classify business strategy into the two classes of:

- competitive strategy and
- corporate strategy.

Competitive strategy operates in commercial markets only, corporate strategy is more closely concerned with financial markets, but again by selecting profitable customer markets.

Pure dealing

A classification of business strategy into competitive and corporate strategy excludes one type of business activity which has no customers. Nor of course does it have competitors anxious to win the same customers' buying preferences. We call this pure or 'proprietary' dealing. What are sometimes called market makers, are one example of pure dealing. Market makers make profits in financial and commodity markets by buying and selling financial instruments, commodities, or derivatives like options or futures. In the traditional pre-1986 London stockmarket the smaller[6] jobbers were pure dealers. Other pure dealers are more properly called 'speculators'. Dealers' sole source of profit is a nose for a price at which they can deal profitably. They deal impersonally, their profits depend on price, not on customers. Their dealing price is all they offer. They are described in more detail in Chapter 15.

We exclude pure dealing from our definition of business strategy, not because that activity is not a business, but because this book is focused on selecting and successfully competing in customer markets. Pure dealer strategies require a very different kind of book. We do however in Chapter 15 discuss a particular form of pure dealing, that of the corporate 'raider' or catalyst, which happens to play an important part in discussions of corporate strategy.

Short termism and the importance of time-frames

One further fundamental concept must be introduced at this point: the time perspective. Objectives can be short- or long-term. Managers may have in mind value and performance for just the current financial year, or they may focus on a period ahead of (say) seven years. In many businesses important investment decisions look forward to returns which cannot come in less than three to seven years from now. When Eurotunnel first decided to go ahead with the construction of the Channel Tunnel, it knew it would earn no returns for at least seven or eight years. Years are also needed to implement investment projects like process plants, power stations, theme parks, mass transit systems, or the development of a new aircraft or aero engine. It can also take years to design, make and bring to the market a new mass-produced consumer durable.

Managers of companies in some countries are nowadays widely thought to be 'short termist'. This expression is not always sharply defined, but it usually implies an over-preoccupation with short-term financial results and liquidity, and inadequate attention to building the business up for a prosperous future. In many cases such neglect positively destroys long-term value. For example, a company fearing a takeover bid may dismantle its entire information technology overhead. Over the next few months the cash saved may improve reported results, but in the medium term it may impair the company's ability to control its business and serve its customers. Short termist managers appear to be fire-fighting, reacting to pressures, not creating opportunities.

Appendix 13.1 will suggest that short termism may have a financial cause. Here we simply look at it as a managerial phenomenon. Where managers are said to be short termist, they are invariably believed to pay excessive attention to the financial markets, for example by giving undue priority to dividends, and not enough to their commercial markets. Generally short termism is induced by a belief that the company's current financial performance is so poor as to expose it to hostile takeover or bankruptcy.

It is in the commercial markets that a longer view is needed; for we cannot successfully compete for customer preferences today unless we planned and invested in a winning strategy some years ago. Strategy is by definition concerned with a longer term. Obviously not all major business decisions take as long to earn their first returns as the Channel Tunnel. In some fast-moving businesses a new competitive posture can be introduced in a matter of months. This might for example be because the critical new capital asset can be purchased off the shelf. In such a case the 'longer term' is relatively short. A new strategy means some major change of direction, and will take whatever time-span is dictated by the characteristics of the offering.

Short termist action is usually self-defeating. It may buy time, but probably very little time. If it averts immediate loss of independent survival, its consumption of the seed-corn tends to ensure recurrent threats. Once that consumption becomes apparent, the company's credibility in the financial markets will be fatally impaired.

To sum up, the fundamental objective of business, and therefore of business strategy, is to enhance *long-term* owner value.[7]

Is a business an ethical agent?

At this point it is worth questioning some of the fundamental assumptions about the purpose of business activity. The contention that the fundamental purpose of a business is to create long-term financial value, may appear to conflict with an influential contemporary view which regards a business as having social responsibilities to a wider range of 'stake-holders', not just its investors. The other stakeholders include its employees, its customers and suppliers, the community or society affected by the operations of the business, and the environment. This view assigns to a business some non-financial objectives such as social welfare and conservation. It thus disputes the monopoly of the financial objective.

Strictly therefore the term 'stakeholder' includes the company's investors as well as the other groups. Like many other writers, we shall however here and there adopt the convenient shorthand which restricts the term to non-investor groups, such as employees, customers and suppliers, and the community.

The case for this stakeholder view can be stated as follows: Business is no different from other human activities. Human beings can have no single, exclusive loyalty which releases them from all other loyalties. Business managers' special duties to the owners of the business do not entitle them to injure or ignore the interests of others. A long-serving employee may well have 'invested' a greater proportion of his or her economic worth in the company than many a share-holder. We all have conflicting loyalties and duties, and business managers must manage their dilemmas just like the rest of us.[8]

Put like that, the stakeholder view sounds very persuasive. Its weakness however is that it mistakes the essential nature of a business. A business is not a moral agent at all: it is an inanimate object. It is an investment project, brought into existence to earn in excess of its cost of capital. Its raison d'être is financial.

The long-standing employee may well have a strong moral claim to a reciprocal commitment by those running the business, but any such commitment can only be honoured as long as the business continues to exist. Once it fails to meet its financial survival condition, the business is likely to cease, and with it any commitment to the employee.

The stakeholder view misses the point when it debates only how the cake should be divided up between the owners and other stakeholder groups. That debate becomes pointless when there is no cake to divide: when the business has failed to survive. The fact that the condition of survival happens to favour the investors, is at this fundamental level beside the point.

It will now be clear that the stakeholder view in its extreme form fails to make four vital distinctions:[9]

- Between the inanimate business and its human managers as the bearers of loyalty to anyone.
- Between the investors as people and the financial value of the business in which they have invested. The anti-stakeholder view, properly expressed, sees the financial success of the business, not that of its investors, as the object of an overriding loyalty.
- Between the legal and moral responsibilities of a business. The law rightly entitles those who were killed or injured by Union Carbide in Bhopal to legal redress against the company as a legal person: that does not make the company a moral person.[10]
- Between the company's financial interest in its stakeholders and any moral commitment to them that might go beyond that interest. The company operates more profitably if it keeps its stakeholders happy. Moreover, social and other pressures may work against the company if it is not seen to treat them well.[11] Over this large area, the company's long-term profitability and its claimed duty to stakeholders are in harmony. Outside that area, the financial interests of the business and its alleged duty to stakeholders are in conflict, and the survival condition suggests that the financial interests must prevail.

None of this gets away from the fact that the raison d'être of the business is financial. Its managers are human beings with different personal value systems and loyalties, some to the business, some to others, including stakeholders. The value systems of managers may well clash with the financial interests of the company which employs them. We shall return to that issue later.

Ethical dilemmas and short and long time-frames

An inanimate business must therefore take account of the values of society which may impact on its long-term prosperity, even though they cannot be its own values. Nevertheless, the gulf which is often observed between those values and the goal of adding financial value would shrink if financial value was universally recognized as being a longer- rather than shorter-term objective. The objective of earning the cost of capital is defined by the financial markets, and Appendix 13.1 will argue that a flaw in the financial markets may be one of the causes of the short- versus long-term conflict.[12]

Over a longer time-frame a business has a *financial* interest in respecting social values. In the long term it cannot prosper by damaging the interests of its stakeholders. If it treats workers badly, it will need to pay over the odds to attract labour. If it damages the local environment, it will alienate local interests and incur extra costs or a reduction in sales as a consequence of that hostility. Consumer boycotts[13] are one of many mechanisms through which this can occur. Conflicts of interest between financial and social objectives are therefore much less acute in the long than in the short run. Many of the examples which are usually cited to support the stakeholder view, like unhealthy working conditions, assume a short termist financial objective.

At a more fundamental level, business cannot function without markets (in goods and services, in labour, in capital and debt and the like) and markets need a background of accepted rules of behaviour if they are to work.[14] In other words, businesses have a collective long-term interest in observing those rules without which they cannot function effectively. Sternberg[15] summarizes these as ordinary decency and distributive justice. Ordinary decency consists of 'fairness, honesty and refraining from coercion and physical violence'. Distributive justice is a principle both of allocation and selection. It governs remuneration, but also who should be hired and fired, which products and plants should be financed. The criterion is always what value various claimants contribute to the long-term owner value of the business.

In fact, many of the reasons that prompt well informed critics to call for ethical constraints on business, stem from abuses of power by those who manage businesses. 'Bad' businesses rig markets, exploit employees, defraud suppliers, bribe customers and authorities. All of them amount to abuses, distortions and malfunctions of markets. There is of course a contradiction in the concept of ethical constraints: compliance under pressure is not ethically motivated. Two responses are needed. Society must by political or social means regulate markets so that they serve social ends. Business managers for their part must accept the logic that business cannot do its job without well functioning markets: the conduct of business therefore has to observe Sternberg's ordinary decency and distributive justice for its own long-term well-being.

Ethical conflicts of managers

This whole discussion has concerned the ethical responsibilities, if any, of the business itself, not those of the managers. The distinction between the business and its managers is fundamental. A manager has chosen to work for a business, and that choice gives the manager stringent responsibilities towards the business and its long-term owner value.

However, no human being is just a worker, employee or manager. Managers have divided loyalties, because they are not just managers; they are also spouses, parents, children of parents, neighbours, citizens, adherents of religious faiths, members of the human race. They also have close working relationships with colleagues, superiors and subordinates. These forge very strong loyalties, duties and responsibilities. The closer of these ties can bring managers into conflict with the financial raison d'être of the business. The wider ties are also there, but may be less prominent in the managers' minds. By becoming a manager, a person does not cease to have normal secular or religious value systems, or responsibilities towards all those with whom she or he is in non-business relationships.

The manager will therefore, even on the longer view, be caught between conflicting,

- social and financial objectives,
- value systems and
- loyalties to various individuals and groups of people.

A manager may for example have philosophical, political or religious values, offended by (say) the production of weapons, tobacco, or contraceptive products, or by exports to an apartheid regime. Any of these are in potential conflict with managers' duty to promote the owner value of the business. Conflict could for example occur if trading with an apartheid regime failed to trigger extra pressures from the community or other customers or pressure groups,[16] and thus extra costs.

Again, in some societies bribery might in practice be tolerated or part of the way of life, and still be morally unacceptable to managers. Managers as human beings also have clear moral duties to employees and other stakeholders. In all these ways they will at times experience conflict with the financial objectives of the business. It would clearly be misleading to see such conflicts as being between the business and the stakeholders.

It is also wrong to identify the financial raison d'être of the business with the interests of owners as people. Loyalty is owed to the owner value of the business, not to the owners. If a major shareholder had committed a tax fraud and had some interest in reducing the owner value of the business, the managers would still have the duty to enhance that value. In fact, the shareholders are probably furthest from managers' minds when they are straining to keep the business afloat. If the business fails, the managers' own jobs and therefore their families may suffer; and so may their colleagues and subordinates and *their* families. These closely related stakeholders are much the strongest reason why managers want the business to succeed; stronger by far than the often

unknown and transient shareholders. The financial imperative is the impersonal reason why the business exists: it
commands human loyalties for the sake of groups of people
other than the shareholders.

As a human being therefore the manager has loyalties to
the business, to some personally known stakeholders and
investors, and to all the other stakeholders and investors:
other fellow-employees who may lose their jobs, the neighbours who may suffer from dangerous products or dangerous
processes, and the environment which may deteriorate with
polluting waste discharge or global warming.

All this is a comment on the stakeholder view, which
requires the manager to balance duties to the owners with
supposed duties to other stakeholders. It concerns the
manager's duties in his or her capacity as a manager. A very
different case is that of the manager or of any other employee
who defrauds his employing business for his or her own
personal gain. The fraud can consist of appropriating cash
that belongs to the business, or other property, or taking time
off without good cause. That is theft, and theft is always an
offence against the owners of the stolen property, in this case
the owners of the business. In that sense all employees, not
just managers, have duties to the owners as people, but this
has nothing to do with the duties of managers in their
capacity as managers.

Collective and individual ethical values

One more distinction must be made. A company is often said
to have an explicit or implicit system of values, which is part
of its 'culture'. What is meant, is that the management team
has a *collective* set of values, so that 'the company' is used as
a shorthand expression for the collectivity of the managers.
An example might be a dedication to the quality of what is
offered to customers.

Such a collective value system is rather different from the
political, philosophical and religious value systems noted
earlier. These clearly belong to *individual* managers, although
some of them could also become part of a company's culture.

It is evident therefore that a manager needs to manage moral dilemmas and conflicts of many kinds. Examples are conflicts of loyalty between various groups with claims on the manager, conflicts between their own personal value systems and those of stakeholders, and also between their own private value systems and the collective corporate culture.

The owner-manager

Most businesses start up with the owner as manager. The self-employed consultant, or the dentist or shoe repairer who practises on his or her own, runs an owner-managed business. Many such people are content to run their business at a loss, especially after at least notionally charging for the value of their own time. If they do, then they are clearly not investing to earn the cost of capital. They may have a variety of motives. Mary may run her flower shop as a hobby: she finds it interesting work, and is willing to sacrifice the amount of her loss in order to occupy her time in this way. William on the other hand may run his veterinary surgery as a charity. His motive is to be of service to animals and animal-loving people. He is willing to donate his loss to that charitable purpose.

Such an owner-manager cannot be accused of theft from the owners. I cannot steal from myself.

Summary of ethical issues

We are now ready to pull together what conflicts managers may experience between their own affiliations and their duty to create financial value. First, only managers are ethical agents with conflicting responsibilities. The business merely has an ethically neutral, financial reason for existing. Secondly, that conflict is rather less acute for a manager who seeks longer- rather than short-term financial value. Society might achieve much if it managed to cure short termist incentives in business.

Thirdly, some social value is actually wasted and destroyed if a business is forced to take its eye off the ball of financial value. Even a small business is complex and risky. Without a clear line of accountability and a clear-cut financial raison d'être it becomes hard, if not impossible to manage.[17] In a perfect world, a company pursuing long-term financial value is by that very fact creating social value. In the real world, markets are distorted and imperfect, yet profitability is still a fair approximation to how a business can best contribute to social well-being. Financial value may not be the perfect social goal, but the alternatives have all failed because they centralize instead of decentralizing economic decisions. They take power away from ordinary people like customers.

Finally, if the long-term financial interests of business do clash with the values and rights of the wider community, is the remedy not at least partly with society itself, and with its elected local and national politicians? The injured parties are ultimately human persons. They are consumers as well as employees, neighbours and voters. Office holders, legislators and regulators, or even pressure groups who operate consumer boycotts have the opportunity to ensure that the legal system and the structure and rules of markets serve the best interests of the community. This will go a long step further to harmonize the social and financial responsibilities of business managers. As human beings they still have conflicts to manage, but the conflicts will then be much less acute. Consequently they will be that much freer to concentrate on the complex tasks of creating long-term financial value in volatile and shifting markets. To sum this up, society will be better served if it takes responsibility for minimizing conflicts between its own objectives and the financial objectives of business.

Conclusion

This chapter has stressed the financial raison d'être and survival condition of the business. It has gone on to define financial value as the fundamental corporate objective.

41

Financial performance must be the ultimate yardstick of business strategy. 'Stakeholder' objections to the primacy of financial performance affect the moral duties of managers, not those of the business.

The principal means to improved financial performance is success in competitive commercial markets. That success today depends on strategies adopted some time ago. How long ago, depends on the logistics of each competitive market, i.e. on how much time is needed in each case to change the competitive positioning of the business. We have yet to refine that concept so as to distinguish between competitive and corporate strategies. This will be done in the next chapter.

Notes

1. Rappaport (1986).
2. Rappaport defines debt as the *market* value of (a) borrowings and (b) of capital such as preference capital. We are here, for the sake of simplicity, ignoring non-equity share capital (which is certainly not debt).

   Rappaport emphasizes the market value of debt, arguing that its book value was likely to overstate its burden – thus understating shareholder value. The debt would sell for less in the market if interest rates had risen since the debt was first incurred. Whenever the debt is marketable, and the debtor company can reduce its burden by market or hedging action, Rappaport is clearly correct in valuing debt at market. However, much debt, especially bank loans and trade debt, is not marketable, and even when it is marketable, loan covenants may entitle the creditor to enforce payment of the contractual amount. Moreover, market values can decline as a result of changes in perceived credit risk, which the debtor may not be able to hedge by market instruments. To sum up, there are situations in which shareholder value must account for debt at the present value of its contractual amount.
3. It would of course be much simpler if we could substitute the share price for the value of the shareholding, and say that the objective is to maximize the share price. Unfortunately the share price can change as a result of a number of transactions which leave the shareholder value unaffected. For example a merger or acquisition can involve complex changes in shareholding, A shareholder who held 10 shares worth $1,000 each, a total value of $10,000, may after the merger hold 20 shares worth $500 each in the same company, or 40 shares worth $250 each in some other

company. In both cases the value of the shareholder's investment is unchanged by the event, but in the first case (20 shares in the same company at a price of $500), the share price has halved.

4. Throughout this illustration taxes have for the sake of simplicity been ignored.
5. What it directly measures, is of course the cyclicality of a given company's share price relative to the index of the entire stock-market; in other words, what is measured is strictly a financial market phenomenon which serves as a proxy for a phenomenon in the market for what a business sells.
6. *Leading* jobbers may not have been pure dealers, if their leading positions, i.e. their high 'market shares', were a source of extra volumes of profitable deals. In that limited sense therefore they may have had reason to treat their counterparties as though they were customers. See Chapter 15.
7. Sternberg (1994).
8. A variant of this view attributes this duty not to the managers, but to the shareholders. Thus one authority argues that share-holders have moral responsibilities: 'Within such a modern realisation that ownership brings certain moral responsibilities it would not be surprising to suggest that this certainly includes the ownership of business companies, which are so much more than their material assets and which form a focal point of a whole inter-locking network of human beings: employees, dependents, suppliers, communities' (Mahoney, 1993).
9. Kenyon (1996).
10. Velasquez (1988) sets out how the legal fiction which treats a company as a *legal* person, has led to the linguistic ambiguity which seeks to extend its legal responsibility into the moral field.
11. Sternberg (1994).
12. Theoretically there is no conflict in an efficient financial market, because the discount factor applied by that market will resolve the tradeoff between near-term and longer-term returns. The question has been raised whether financial markets are in fact efficient enough to do this. Chapter 13 and Appendix 13.1 argue that market efficiency is not the real financial issue. In any case there is also the question whether managers and others perceive finan-cial markets as overvaluing the short term. For a discussion of the 'short termist' controversy see Marsh (1990).
13. Craig Smith (1990).
14. Brittan (1995) Chapter 1.
15. Sternberg (1994).
16. An important type of pressure group is the ethical investment movement which seeks to boycott morally undesirable businesses and encourage morally desirable ones (Sparkes, 1995).
17. Brittan (1995).

3 Competitive and corporate strategy: firmlets and companies

Introduction

This chapter sets out the separate tasks of competitive and corporate strategy. In order to do this, it clarifies what part of the business it is that has either of these strategies and where in the business its strategic decisions are located.

The individual offering

In 1990 Rover Group marketed two models of the Land Rover. These were aimed at two entirely different markets; the first for superior family cars, the second for industrial workhorses. In the market for quality cars it *positioned* a well trimmed version, called Discovery, for a limited set of potential customers and against a known set of competitors: other quality cars. It produced a tailored product for a narrowly defined market, was able to charge a high price and earn high margins. This **competitive positioning** was an excellent example of a *competitive strategy*.

In the other market, that for industrial workhorses, Rover offered the Defender. This was a basic version of the same marque, positioned against a different set of competitors for a different set of customers. The Defender represented a separate offering and a separate competitive strategy from the Discovery.

A **competitive strategy** is the triangular positioning of a single offering vis-à-vis a unique set of potential customers and competitors.[1] We call an **offering** what customers select or reject. This concept is central to the framework of this book, and needs to be clarified.

First, the term 'offering' covers both tangible 'goods' and intangible 'services'. In the modern world the borderline between tangibles and intangibles is getting fuzzier, not that it was ever of major, if any, strategic significance.

Secondly, the offering is the unit of customer choice. What customers choose, is an individual offering. They do not choose the multioffering 'firm'. In the sense of being chosen by customers, such a 'firm' cannot possibly be said to 'compete'. We return to this point below.

Identifying the single offering

The final clarification of what is meant by an offering, concerns the complex matter of what exactly constitutes an individual offering, just what separates it from its closest neighbour. A company sometimes markets what might at first sight look like either two offerings or one. Appendix 3.1 lists and analyses a number of apparent borderline examples.

By a single offering this book means an offering which has a single competitive position: a single three-cornered relationship with customers and competitors.

Borderline cases are of two kinds:

- where customers see two offerings as either complete or very close substitutes;
- where customers see them as so complementary as to make it uncertain whether they are separate, or parts of the same offering.

The cases in Appendix 3.1 at first appear very complex. In fact however, the test of whether they are separate or one is a simple one: is it a single and inseparable process in which their prices are determined? If yes, then they are one offering. Moreover, in real life there is rarely much doubt about the answer to that question.

Inputs and outputs

An offering has two types of attributes:

- **outputs**: benefits and drawbacks which consciously or subconsciously influence customers' choices, and
- **inputs**: all other attributes, efforts and resources that do not enter the customer's selection process.

It is outputs, not inputs, that position an offering in customers' eyes. This is therefore a critical distinction. An example or two will help. First, a home-delivery pizza service may aim at being faster than its rivals. If competitors' delivery times influence customers' choices, then speed is an output. The internal communication system which achieves the speedier delivery, is almost bound to be an input. Secondly, if customers take picture quality into account when choosing television sets, then picture quality is an output. On the other hand the R&D, the precision plant, the highly skilled workforce and the quality assurance programme that produce a higher resolution picture, are all inputs. Thirdly, free range eggs command a higher price than battery eggs because customers value the humane conditions in which the hens are believed to have laid these eggs. The 'free range' label therefore is an output, not an input. None of this questions the competitive importance of inputs: only they can deliver the outputs.[2]

Perhaps still closer to the borderline is the case, very realistic in microelectronics, where customers' choices are influenced by how clean the factory or the clean-air environment in the factory is. If that cleanliness matters to customers' choices, then what in most circumtances would be an input becomes also an output. The special circumstance here is that customers are influenced by an aspect of the production process. Another example of an output is the couturier's presence in all the fashion capitals of the world – London, Tokyo, New York and Paris – if its appeal to customers is substantially enhanced by that presence.

46

It is not the company that is chosen by customers

It was noted earlier that the offering is the unit of customer choice. Customers choose between offerings, not between multioffering 'firms'.

Most companies have several offerings. Electrolux sells refrigerators, washing machines and other domestic appliances. These are all separate offerings, their prices are determined by separate competitive forces, and customers do not choose between the Electrolux and Bosch companies as such, but between whatever refrigerators both companies and their other competitors are selling. Electrolux may not face exactly the same set and configuration of competitors in its washing machine and refrigerator businesses.

Electrolux may well attempt to win customers over to equipping their entire kitchens with Electrolux appliances, by brand advertising or by specially discounted service terms. That will win some customers to all-Electrolux deals, but that does not amount to the company becoming the unit of customer choice. Even if most customers came to choose between competing inclusive deals, the inclusive deal would become just another offering. They would still be choosing the offering, not the company.

The point that it is not the company that customers choose, is reinforced by the fact that the same company may market two or more offerings in mutual competition. An example are the Rolls-Royce and Bentley marques. Such competition for customers between sister offerings can in fact sometimes be more intense than between unrelated competitors. Similar examples are Yves Saint-Laurent's Paris and Opium perfumes, or some models of Electrolux and Zanussi refrigerators.

What competes for customers is therefore the offering, not the company. It makes no sense to speak of the company as being the subject of a competitive strategy. The *collectivity* of its offerings cannot have a single competitive position. Nor does it make sense to speak of customers choosing a company, of price being determined for a company, of competitively positioning or differentiating a company. None of these can apply to more than a single offering.

Some dissenters rest their argument on the phenomenon of brands. Indeed some of them see customers' choices to be not between the Electrolux and Bosch *companies*, but between their *brands*, rather than between individual offerings. Car buyers with a brand loyalty to Toyota, Rover or Volkswagen are interpreted as thereby choosing the company. However, as just noted, these customers are still choosing between offerings. In their minds the reputation or attributes of the preferred marque are simply an important part of the output profile presented by the offering. Moreover it is no more than a part of that profile: however enthusiastic Giuseppina may be about Fiat, she will not be buying Fiat next time if she needs an estate car or a people carrier to seat two adults and five children with all their luggage, and if no Fiat model meets those needs.

Procter & Gamble and Unilever provide another example. They are commonly called competitors because each sells washing powders and a few other *offerings* which are close substitutes to those sold by the other. To call the two companies competitors is just a shorthand way of indicating that in a number of their markets customers choose between their respective offerings. The shorthand can however mislead. It can obscure first the fact that over a wide range of offerings they fail to compete for customer preferences: Procter & Gamble does not contest the markets for sausages or ice cream. Unilever does not sell nappies.

Secondly, even if Unilever and Procter & Gamble each had only three offerings, all in competition for customers with those of the other, the two *companies* would still not be competing for customer choices. This is because the competitive positions of their offerings in each of the three markets are bound to be different. They will for example face different customer preferences and different third party competitors such as Colgate Palmolive, in each of the three markets. If the competitive positions had been uniform, with a single price-determining process, they would by definition not be separate offerings!

The company

Every separate offering thus operates in a separate market. Each offering also has a unique competitive positioning, distinct from that of any other offering that may be marketed by the same company. In this book a **company** is defined as an independent business entity, not owned by another business. This is not the legal definition of a company. It does not matter here whether a company happens to take the form of a legal company or is a partnership like a firm of accountants practising in partnership, or even a self-employed person running a business.

Tasks of competitive and corporate strategy

This is a very simple structural model of the business world. That world consists of companies, each with one, several or many offerings. For each offering the company needs a competitive strategy. We can now define **corporate strategy** as the management by a company of the composition of its **cluster** of offerings. Its task is to make decisions to add, retain or divest offerings.

Land Rover has served as an example of a competitive strategy. Courtaulds and TI Group in the UK and Morgan Guaranty in the United States present good illustrations of corporate strategies executed over the decade up to 1991. Morgan Guaranty, Courtaulds and TI have all changed their clusters of offerings substantially, divesting what did not fit the new corporate strategy, and acquiring the types of businesses that did fit. In Courtaulds' case the culmination was a demerger which split the company into two independent parent companies, one for bulk textiles and the other for the speciality businesses. The Courtaulds case illustrates how such a split can substantially improve the financial value to shareholders: the sum of the parts was worth more than the previous whole.

Offerings are not management units

Corporate strategy is therefore the management by a company's head office of the composition of its cluster of offerings.

Managers will not find it easy to see their companies in that light, because their model of the company tends to consist of a head office and accountable profit centres. That is a financial model. It contrasts with the *competitive* model consisting of a company and its competitive offerings. Moreover, there are a number of valid reasons steering them away from such a competitive model:

- Managers have to manage people and physical assets. They must therefore manage organizational units.
- Organizational units tend to be profit centres, such as subsidiaries, divisions, 'businesses', or strategic business units (SBUs). All these are defined not as competitive units chosen by customers, but as discrete profit centres. Other companies may be subdivided into cost centres like factories, sites, or distribution units.
- An offering is hardly ever a single profit centre, let alone a single cost centre, or under a line manager of its own. It seldom has its own discrete collection of costs. A single offering can also straddle several profit centres.[3] More usually, one profit centre, like a toiletry or a small domestic appliance division, contains a number of offerings.

The head-office-and-offerings model therefore cuts across well established organization structures. It cannot easily or naturally become part of the language in which managers think. Yet competitive strategy has to be formulated for what competes for customers.

The need to formulate competitive strategy individually for each offering, does not however make that task impossibly onerous. It sounds much more onerous than it is. We have defined a company as any independent business. An independent corner shop or window cleaner is a company. The vast majority of companies have so few offerings that the chief executive can decide the competitive strategy of each and every offering. Where companies like IBM are too complex for that, the task can be devolved as described in Chapter 21.

The offering as firmlet

It follows that if managers are to think strategically, i.e. in terms of customer choices, they need to be steered away from the conventional model. Instead they need a term which represents that part of a business which corresponds with a single offering. They need this because that part of the business needs a separate competitive strategy. As this is an unfamiliar organizational concept, it needs an unfamiliar label. We use the word **firmlet** to stand for that notional part of a company which has a single offering. If organization charts could show offerings, they would be firmlets.[4]

It is very easy to misunderstand what the term 'firmlet' means and why it is introduced. Firmlets and offerings are very nearly interchangeable terms: so why will the word 'offering' not suffice? There are two reasons:

- The primary reason is the need to change the managerial language away from all the things that do not compete for customers to what does compete for them: the offering. What does not compete for customers, is organizational units like companies, SBUs, or profit centres. The habit of thinking of competition in terms of units that customers do not choose is deeply embedded. The introduction of the 'firmlet' concept therefore has a negative and defensive purpose. Its positive flip side is its focus on customer choices.[5]
- A secondary benefit concerns corporate rather than competitive strategy. Here too the organizational overtones of the word 'firmlet' are helpful.[6]

Corporate strategy discusses what offerings should be in one and the same company, and thus under its 'head office'.

Practising managers naturally tend to see those issues in terms of chains of command between organizational units. Offerings are not normally such units. 'What offerings should be under my head office?' may hit communication blockages. 'What *firmlets* should be under my head office?' on the other hand may cause less blockage, because a firmlet sounds more like an organizational unit. Moreover, Chapter 21 will show that chains of command can be set up for offerings or firmlets, even though they are not separate units.

In other words, the discussion is about offerings. Offerings are not normally organization units, but we need here a language that treats them as quasi-organization units. It is needed in this limited strategic context. Firmlets are not part of the management structure, but the strategic thinking advocated in this book needs to treat them as building blocks that can be fitted into chains of command.

Not only are firmlets not organizational units, they also do not normally hold separate resources like key people or physical assets. Resources are precisely what profit centres like SBUs hold, usually for numbers of firmlets or offerings. Land Rover's luxury and workhorse models are two firmlets, but would naturally form a single profit centre or business unit.

It will no doubt be objected that the firmlet concept drives a wedge between responsibility for business strategy on the one hand and day-to-day management on the other: it complicates the world of the manager. The answer is that this untidy complexity is inherent in the competitive facts of business. This framework has not invented the untidiness of the real world; it merely acknowledges it. Without this more complex language managers have again and again slipped into an illusory world in which *they* can by their own decisions bring about results which will in fact depend on decisions taken by people outside the company: customers and competitors.

The 'firm'

This chapter has argued that the company and its profit centres (which include subsidiaries, divisions, business units, strategic business units and the like) do not compete to be chosen by customers.

At this point it is also worth summing up why the word 'firm' is even less useful as a unit of a customer-centred business strategy. It is used in a wide variety of senses. Very often it is used vaguely, as if a sharp definition were not helpful. That alone should serve as a danger signal.

Only very rarely nowadays[7] is 'firm' used of a single offering, to mean a 'firmlet'. Much more often it is used to describe an entity like General Electric, with its thousands of offerings. More often still, it refers to a business like a garage which sells petrol on the forecourt, new cars in its showroom, car servicing in its workshop, and groceries in its shop. Each of the offerings has its own distinct set of competitors, and therefore its own competitive strategy. The term 'firm' does not aid clear strategic thinking.

How business strategy is structured

At this point it is useful to bring together the various parts of business strategy and to present a preview of how they fit together.

Competitive strategy concerns the future positioning of an individual offering for customers and against competitors. Corporate strategy is the management by a company of the composition of its cluster of firmlets or offerings. Its objective is to maximize *financial* value. Its task is to manage the composition of the cluster so as to enhance the company's value in its financial markets. As the cluster is a collection of offerings, i.e. of competitive strategies, we come back to the hierarchy discovered in Chapter 2. The ultimate *yardstick* of success lies in the financial markets, but the *source* of success must be performance in chosen commercial markets. It follows that corporate and competitive strategy both serve to generate financial value, corporate strategy directly, competitive strategy indirectly via success in commercial markets.

This is evidently only a preview. The whole story will unfold in later chapters. Customers are won by the outputs of a single offering or firmlet. That single firmlet however can only deliver winning outputs by mobilizing winning inputs. Yet inputs, due to economies of scale,[8] normally need to shared by *a number* of firmlets: a winning combination of inputs is likely therefore to be the fruit of a successful corporate strategy.

One of the aims of corporate strategy is to assemble clusters in which inputs deliver the most profitable competitive outputs. In this way corporate strategy makes a positive contribution to successful competitive strategies; it does not merely collect them. It puts together under one roof offerings which together have a competitive set of inputs at competitive unit costs.

Redefining 'business strategy'

This simple company-and-firmlets model reorients business strategy, shifting its focus to the individual offering and how customers choose it. It classifies the field of business strategy as consisting of competitive strategy and corporate strategy. In this framework there is no business strategy that does not fit into one or the other of these two categories. We have in Chapter 1 restricted our definition of business strategy to a significant intention about one or all of the future offerings of the business in its commercial markets. There is room in this language, for example, for a 'turnaround' or 'international' strategy,[9] but that will normally consist of corporate strategy plus possibly some competitive strategies. However, there is not room in this vocabulary for an 'information systems strategy'. Sub-strategies of that kind should be called functional policies. The word 'strategy' in its original Greek sense means leading an army, not just its supply corps or its administrative staff. Appendix 3.2 discusses examples of financial strategies, and why they are not here included in the term 'business strategy'.

Any particular competitive or corporate strategy begins with its formulation, and goes on to its selection, adoption and finally implementation. Deliberate adoption does not however cast a strategy in stone: it can and should be modified if fresh news or experience suggests that.

However, what identifies one strategy and distinguishes it from another, is:

- in a competitive strategy, the offering's triangular positioning in relation to customers and competitors, which is shaped by its outputs;
- in a corporate strategy, a decision about the cluster, i.e. to add, retain or divest an individual offering or firmlet.

Summary

This chapter has described the central part played in business strategy by the single offering, and outlined the separate functions of competitive and corporate strategy. A company's corporate strategy plans the composition of its cluster of offerings or firmlets. Competitive strategies have to be made for each offering or firmlet. A competitive strategy has to succeed in its commercial market. A corporate strategy is more directly concerned with the company's financial market. However, corporate strategy too owes its success to a judicious choice of commercial markets.

* * *

Appendix 3.1

Identifying a single offering

This appendix discusses in detail and with illustrations how to determine a separate single offering.

Are the following pairs of items marketed by the same company one offering or more than one?

1 Nescafé Gold Blend freeze dried instant coffee jars of (a) 100 and (b) 200 grams.
2 An Electrolux washing machine model sold in (a) Germany and (b) Switzerland.
3 (a) White and (b) pink Kleenex tissues.

4 A presentation pack combining a silk shirt and tie.
5 A newspaper with two classes of customers: (a) readers, (b) advertisers.
6 A supermarket selling food, but also alcoholic drinks, flowers, cosmetics and healthcare products.
7 (a) Kenwood drinking water filters and (b) Kenwood cartridges which will only fit Kenwood filters.
8 (a) Electrical appliances and (b) their repair and service (provided they were bought from the store), offered by the same electrical retailer.
9 (a) The preparation of accounts and (b) the submission of computations derived from those accounts to the tax authority, both offered by the same firm of accountants.

The principles which must guide the answers are the following:

- In hardly any of the cases can the question be answered without more detailed information.
- What can make the items a single offering in each case, is either:

  (a) closeness of substitutes: they must be so close that their prices are effectively determined together, or
  (b) a degree of complementarity[10] so high that customers predominantly regard them as effectively one offering, comparing their *combined* price with the combined prices of competing combinations.

- Customers may not be unanimous or homogeneous in their attitudes. What matters, is whether sufficient proportions of customers regard the collection as a single offering, to ensure that prices are in each such case effectively determined as a single package.
- The test is always the extent to which prices are jointly determined. There are sub-tests which can provide clues. Closeness of substitutes can be investigated by comparing output features, and the degree of complementarity by looking at how necessary or attractive it is to customers to obtain the items from a single supplier. However, the

decisive test is price determination, and fortunately sellers seldom have any difficulty in applying that test.

These principles enable us to group the nine examples:

- In Examples 1–4 closeness of substitutes is the issue.
- In Example 5 (newspaper) the two offerings are neither close substitutes nor complementary in customers' eyes: this is not a borderline case at all, but simply two separate offerings.
- In Examples 6–9 complementarity is the issue.

We can now review the individual examples.

Example 1: Instant coffee jars

The question here can be restated as follows. The predominant determinant of customer choice, price apart, is either the label or the size of the pack. If it is the label, then the closest substitute for the Nescafé 100g jar is the Nescafé 200g jar. If the label alone is decisive, then the prices of these two packs will be jointly determined: they are a single offering. If on the other hand the jar size is the decisive choice criterion, then customers will compare the Nescafé 100g jar with whatever group of offerings enters into its price-determining process. The prices of Nescafé's two jars are in that case not both determined in the same process. That makes them separate offerings.

Example 2: Washing machines across a political border

Chapter 18 deals with the significance of political borders. The German and Swiss Electrolux washers are very close substitutes if customers can easily cross the frontier to shop for the better bargain. However, with such a heavy and bulky item this is not easy. There may also be other differences. Electrolux may have different terms of sale and service in the two countries, or the two countries may have different electrical safety standards, or different voltages, sockets or wiring colour codes. As always, the test is the degree of inter-dependence of the prices in the two countries. In this case complete or near-complete interdependence is unlikely, but not impossible. They are probably not a single offering.

Example 3: Kleenex tissues

Here the different shades represent customer preferences, and moves by competitors to increase their volume. A competitor will offer any extra shade only of it expects enough extra sales to compensate for the extra costs. As in Example 1, whether prices of white and pink tissues are co-determined, depends on the weight carried by the colour in customer choices. If loyalty to the label carries practically all the weight, and price sensitivity between the two colours is very high, they are one offering.

Example 4: The presentation pack

Here the pack is clearly a different offering from the shirt and the tie bought as separate transactions. The combination is more convenient for those customers who want to buy both items together. The seller has some latitude in pricing the pack. If the price is set too high, however, customers will arbitrage by buying the items separately. The presentation pack is a separate single offering.

Example 5: A newspaper's editorial content and advertising pull

This is a trick example. The two items have completely separate customers, and cannot possibly be a single offering. Prices are determined in two separate markets.

Example 6: A supermarket selling four or more groups of lines

This is the hardest of the nine examples. In a sense a super-market no doubt competes with more specialized food, drink, flower and chemist retailers. However, it is likely that the predominant group of customers regard a rival supermarket as its closest substitute. This majority see it as a one-stop weekly family shopping facility. They want to shop in one shop, not four or more. To these customers, the food, flower, chemist, etc. lines are complementary. To the minority they are not. Whether it is one offering or more, depends not on whether the one-stop shoppers are a majority, but whether the minority is important enough to cause prices to be determined separately. However, which prices? The price which is here being determined is the set of mark-up margins which the supermarket can charge. It may well be that these margins depend much more on customers' preferences between different supermarkets than on their preferences between a supermarket and its specialist competitors. If so, it is a single offering.

Example 7: Water filter and replacement cartridges

Kenwood supplies both the filter and its cartridges. No other cartridges fit the Kenwood filter; so complementarity is complete. Kenwood's intention may well be to make its profits out of cartridges, and to get as many filters out into the field as possible so as to maximize its profits on cartridges. Clearly up to a point it must pay to reduce filter prices so as to be able to gain either volume or margins in the sale of cartridges. It is difficult here to see how the pricing of the two items can be separate or independent. This is a fairly clear case of a single offering.

Example 8: Sale and service of electrical appliances

The electrical retailer in Example 8 may think of itself as selling a single retail-plus-service offering. However, the degree of complementarity is here much less than in the Kenwood case. Some customers may prefer to shop around separately for retail and repair services. They might for example wish to buy appliances in one shop which offers a wide choice, and to patronize a specialist repairer in the vicinity. That repairer may offer quicker or cheaper repairs, or hire out apparatus to use while the customer's own is in repair. Whether it is one offering or two, depends on how many actual and potential customers look for a combined service and how many want to make separate choices. That degree of complementarity must be tested by investigating whether the determination of prices is a single process, or separate for the two items.

Example 9: Professional accounting and taxation services

This case is similar to Example 8. The difference here is that the accounting firm which has prepared the accounts, has an advantage of familiarity with the figures, compared with any alternative tax accountant who will have a learning cost. The client too may save some cost by not having to explain the figures to a new expert. Nevertheless, a client may prefer a cheaper local firm for the accounting, and perhaps a more specialized tax consultant if tax savings are both important and dependent on specialized expertise. Again the test is whether the prices of the two items are determined separately or together. If a sufficient proportion of customers compare the combined cost with the combined cost from rival accounting firms, then the two prices will be determined together, and they are a single offering. What has no bearing on the question, is whether the accounting firm quotes and invoices a single price for the two items, or separate prices for each.

Summary

To sum up, borderline cases arise when two or more items are either close substitutes or highly complementary, and in both cases the test is whether their prices are determined separately, or together.

As suggested in the text of Chapter 3, the principle is more complex than the practice. In practice it is rarely hard to sort out whether the pricing of two items is a single process, or can be separate and independent.

60

Appendix 3.2

Financial 'strategies' outside the framework

Introduction

Part One has for the purpose of this book defined both the term 'business strategy' and its scope. We can oversimplify this by saying that in this book business strategy is either competitive strategy, the targeting of a particular set of profitable customers, or corporate strategy, the targeting of a cluster of such sets for the company. The common theme is offerings which target profitable customers.

Chapter 2 argued that the central task of all business management is the creation of financial value. Financial goals are therefore paramount. However, the essence of competitive business is to create that financial value in customer markets.[11]

This appendix discusses some financial 'strategies' which are excluded from the term 'business strategy' in this book, and the reasons for their exclusion.[12] Some of these exclusions may cause consternation and a sense of *Hamlet* without the Prince of Denmark. They could be legitimately included in some different definition of business strategy. However, this appendix will set out why they are deliberately excluded here.

This appendix will in any case ignore the acquisition or disposal of what are effectively company shells, like tax haven vehicle companies, pure tax loss companies and the like. The reason for not dealing with such transactions in this appendix is that they concern mere fiscal or legal devices. Not only are they not business strategies: they do not even look like business strategies, as they do not add or subtract groups of customers. The assumption in this book is that only the addition or abandonment of potential customers constitutes a business strategy.

On the other hand where a fiscal or financial benefit is an element in a diversification strategy which enters new customer markets, or in a divestment strategy, this book treats it as subsidiary to a diversification issue. The effect which these financial elements can have on corporate strategies is covered in Chapter 17.

We shall particularly look at the following types of exclusion:

1 Addressing new customers at home or abroad not because the customers are profitable, but in order to save tax.
2 Reorganizing a group's internal ownership and control structure in order to save tax.
3 Improving the capital structure or leverage of the company, by acquiring another company or by changing the company's own external ownership structure, e.g. by a management buyout.
4 Adding offerings or firmlets in order to enlarge the company's financial size, in order to make the company more powerful in its financial markets.

Exclusion 1: Tax-based changes in the operating profile of a group of companies

There are a number of tax motives for enlarging a company[13] by acquiring one or more other companies. One suggestion was that profitable US companies with positive cash flow find it more tax efficient to invest in acquisitions than to use the cash to pay dividends, especially when capital gains are taxed at lower rates than distributions to shareholders.

It has been pointed out[14] that there are better ways of achieving those tax benefits, for example portfolio investments in non-controlling shareholdings. Alternatively, it might at times be more tax effective to give shareholders the option of stock dividends. It is in any case likely that any tax benefits of retaining the cash are outweighed by the motivational disadvantages. Managers of a highly leveraged company are more likely to run a tight ship than managers with ample access to cash.[15] Anyway, Part Five will argue that an unrelated diversification can be a highly damaging use of surplus cash.

62

A better example is that of tax losses. In some tax regimes it is possible for accumulated tax losses in Company A to be offset against the taxable profits of another Company B in the same group, even if A and B were not in the same group when the losses were incurred. In that case it is beneficial for A to acquire B or vice versa. B's profits become more valuable as a result of the acquisition because at least part of them then cease to be taxable.[16] The assumption here is that the company with the tax losses is not a mere shell, but enters into the merger lock, stock and barrel with its commercial operation.

In these and other examples the acquisition aims at a once-for-all tax benefit. In the next example the tax benefit is more strategic in the sense that the acquisition is in principle intended to yield a continuing benefit. It seeks to relieve the company of a continuing fiscal handicap. It arose[17] where a UK parent company had overseas subsidiaries earning substantial profits, and not enough domestic earnings to service its dividends to its own UK shareholders. This need for access to the overseas subsidiaries' earnings was increased and sharpened by the advent of the UK's imputation system of corporation tax, and in particular its advance instalment: advance corporation tax (ACT). The only way the UK parent could obtain that access was to get some or all of the overseas subsidiaries to pay dividends to the UK parent. Such a dividend was likely however to incur a burdensome extra 'withholding tax' levied by a subsidiary's government on its dividend remittance to the UK. The problem was therefore a technical financial one.

Two UK companies, BAT Industries (BAT) and Standard Chartered (SC) Bank illustrate this trap. During the 1970s and 1980s both companies lacked profits in the United Kingdom. Historically both had explicit policies of operating and targeting customers exclusively outside the UK. BAT's reason was its long-standing deal with Imperial Tobacco to refrain from competing in the UK. When BAT and SC later tried to reverse that policy and enter the UK, they ran into commercial difficulties, at least in their respective core offerings of tobacco and commercial banking.

The pattern of profits earned outside the UK, and a UK overhead not covered by profits earned in the UK, left these companies short in the UK in three separate dimensions:

- taxable UK profits,
- accounting profits, legally available for dividends to shareholders, and
- cash to pay dividends to shareholders.

In the absence of sufficient internal dividends from their profitable non-UK subsidiaries, BAT's and SC's UK operations thus had accounting and tax losses and cash deficits in the UK, broadly equal to their central overhead. To fund the overhead and the dividend to their UK shareholders, they therefore needed to draw internal dividends from overseas subsidiaries despite the heavy withholding taxes.

This set of problems caused by the deficit in the UK became dramatically more onerous when the UK changed, in around 1970, to the imputation system of corporation tax.

Imputation and ACT

The imputation system of corporation tax as it was before the 1994 Finance Act is here described in the present tense. It splits the corporation tax charged on a company's annual taxable profit into two elements or instalments: advance (ACT) and mainstream. The ACT instalment is a charge on the dividend distributed by the company. ACT is levied at the standard rate of *income tax* (the tax on the income of individuals) on the equivalent gross amount. So if the standard rate is 30 per cent and the dividend £70,000, then the ACT is 30% of £70,000 × 100/(100 − 30) = 30% of £100,000 = £30,000. An individual shareholder who receives a personal dividend of (say) £70, is then treated for tax purposes as if he or she had already paid £30 income-tax on a gross dividend of £100. The company's ACT payment is 'imputed' to the shareholders.

The effect is best explained with an illustration. The Transoceanic plc group in the 1970s had a total worldwide

Table 3.1 *Entire profit made in UK (£ millions)*

	UK	Utopia	Group
Pre-tax earned locally	10	–	10
Advance corporation tax	–1.5[a]	–	–1.5
Mainstream corporation tax	–2.5[b]	–	–2.5
	6.0	–	6.0
Parent's dividend	–3.5	–	–3.5
Retained	2.5	–	2.5

Table 3.2 *Entire profit made in Utopia (£ millions)*

	UK	Utopia	Group
Gross earned locally	–	10.0	10.0
Utopian corporation tax	–	–4.0[c]	–4.0
		6.0	6.0
Dividend to parent	3.0	–3.0	–
Withholding tax	–0.45[d]		–0.45
	2.55	3.0	5.55
Parent's dividend	–3.5		–3.5
Advance corporation tax	–1.5[a]		–1.5
Mainstream corporation tax	0[e]		–
Retained	–2.45	3.0	0.55

Notes to Tables 3.1 and 3.2:
a 30% of 100/(100 – 30) × £3.5 million dividend
b 40% of £10m – ACT £1.5m
c 40% of £10m
d 15% of £3.0m intragroup dividend remitted by Utopian subsidiary
e Theoretical UK liability 40% of £3m × 100/(100 – 40), but the dividend is treated as having suffered Utopian taxes (including withholding tax) in excess of 40%; hence no UK liability, but the ACT is not relieved unless and until used up against future UK mainstream liabilities.

pre-tax profit of £10 million and its UK parent paid a dividend to its shareholders of £3.5 million. The group operated in (a) the UK and (b) Utopia. The UK corporation tax rate was 40%, and the UK standard rate of income tax for individuals 30%. In Utopia the corporation tax rate was also 40% and the withholding tax rate on dividends to the UK parent 15%. The example in Tables 3.1 and 3.2 shows the effect of taxes on two alternative assumptions:

Tables 3.1 and 3.2 show how the place where profits are made affects the incidence of taxation. In Table 3.1 the entire £10m pre-tax profit is made in the UK, none in Utopia. In Table 3.2 it is all made in Utopia and none in the UK, but Utopia has paid a dividend to the UK of £3m, from which a 15% withholding tax of £450,000 was paid in Utopia.

The tables show that the retained profits after tax of the Group are £1.95m worse if the profits are all made in Utopia and distributed to the UK parent to the extent of £3.0 million. The ACT causes £1.5m of the damage and the withholding tax, £0.45m. However, the ACT played a major part in forcing the Group to draw the dividend from Utopia and thus incur the withholding tax. Without that Utopian dividend Transoceanic probably could not legally have paid its own dividend. Moreover, the entire dividend would have been a drain on its net cash position as well as on its reserves of undistributed profits.

Companies like BAT and SC therefore faced severe problems in servicing their UK stockmarket's expectations of cash dividends and funding their central overhead. This forced both to seek UK acquisitions. BAT entered unrelated fields like cosmetics, financial services, and multiple retailing, a diversification policy which was not entirely successful. SC made unsuccessful efforts to acquire existing UK commercial banks.

So much for the problem and its causes. Our question is, was this quest for UK sources of profits a business strategy? There are three points to be made.

First, the usage. There is nothing perverse or unusual about defining a tax-motivated restructuring as strategic. For BAT to enter the fields of financial services and cosmetics was certainly a major change of direction. It also brings the company into new customer markets.

Secondly however, these customers were chosen not for their inherent profitability, but for their tax status, and that motivation is outside our definition of business strategy. The scope of this book is restricted to the targeting of profitable groups of customers. That makes it necessary to exclude a fiscal motivation from our use of that term.

Lastly, there is also a point of logic. Business objectives form a hierarchical pattern. Managers do not serve their investors well if they incur more tax than is necessary. Yet tax minimization must always be secondary to competitive success. After all, the ultimate form of tax avoidance is to make no profit!

The primary test of a company's goals is whether they make business sense. They must also make tax sense, but that is secondary. It may be a good idea for a tobacco company to go into cosmetics, but tax cannot be a sufficient reason. Unless there are profitable customers in cosmetics who add value to BAT's particular cluster, tax benefits do not justify a move into that field. In any case it is easy to lose more in the costs of a poor fit than is gained in tax savings.

SC has made some less than spectacularly successful attempts to generate UK profits. Each of the attempted acquisitions was within the field of financial services, so that relatedness[18] was at least a strong possibility. On the other hand BAT's diversification efforts appear to have had rather less business logic,[19] apart from the intended tax effect.

Business strategy in this book means a set of proposals to target collections of profitable customers. With this focus on profitable customers, the term excludes purely financial restructuring. The targeting of profitable customers is of course financially motivated, but mere objectives are not strategies.

Exclusion 2: Remodelling ownership chain to reduce tax burden

Tax burdens are sometimes reduced by legal restructuring. Good examples are dividend 'mixer' or 'routeing' vehicles interposed between a parent company and its operating subsidiaries in other countries. If the vehicle company is advantageously placed in a low-tax country with suitable networks of double taxation conventions, a dividend can flow from operating subsidiary to parent with a reduced cost in withholding taxes.

In the above cases of BAT and SC, the tax-driven 'strategy' did have the effect of adding new offerings, new sets of customers to the group's commercial operations. The interposition of the mixer vehicle does not even do this. It merely changes the legal ownership structure of the group. This case would not even in normal parlance be counted as 'strategic'. It is simply good tax planning and therefore good management. It is in any case outside our definition of 'business strategy'.

Exclusion 3: Diversification or restructuring to improve financial leverage (gearing)

A corporate acquisition can be used as one way to change the leverage (or gearing) of a company's capital structure. Other things being equal, a rise in the ratio of debt to equity cheapens the weighted average cost of capital because interest on debt is a tax-deductible expense. At the same time the interest burden also leverages the earnings: a given dollar reduction in profits comes closer to throwing the result into loss, and ultimately throwing the company into insolvency. Leverage makes the company more vulnerable. Consequently very low-leveraged companies may need more leverage, and very highly leveraged companies may need less.

A reduction in Company A's leverage can be achieved by acquiring a very low-leveraged Company B. Perhaps B is cash-rich and therefore negatively leveraged. The most efficacious method is for A to pay out the previous shareholders with equity shares in A. A's equity is increased, and A's debt can be reduced by repayments funded with B's surplus cash.

An increase in leverage can of course be achieved in a number of ways. One is a leveraged buyout (LBO). A common form of this is the management buyout (MBO). The effect of an MBO is that much of the equity will be owned and controlled by the company's managers, whose financial resources tend to be stretched by the transaction. An MBO must therefore be structured with very little equity and much debt. The motivation for LBOs may be that the company would otherwise become insolvent, and that its performance will be improved by the intensified motivation of managers turned part owners. As LBOs invariably result in heroic degrees of leverage, the tax benefit of the higher interest leverage is necessarily outweighed by the very high risk of this arrangement. Otherwise MBOs would be the norm rather than the exception.

An MBO is not an acquisition; it is essentially a change of ownership with no change of management and not necessarily any change in the commercial activities. On the other hand, buying a cash-rich company may well entail the acquisition of other businesses. However, as entry into new customer markets is not the strategic objective or motive of either of them, they are once again not business strategies within the scope of this book.

Exclusion 4: Diversification to enhance financial clout

Our last exclusion concerns diversifications undertaken in order to give a company with its offerings the benefit of greater financial 'clout'. Firmlets are added to the cluster in order to create a financially larger company. Those who advocate such moves may well have in mind a reduction in the company's cost of capital.

This line of thought is one part of the wider belief that size is a worthwhile goal in its own right. That wider aim is discussed in Chapter 14, which lists a number of different meanings of 'size'. Here however we are concerned only with one of these, financial size. In the case of a listed company this is market capitalization.

An increase in the financial size of the company may conceivably improve its ability to fund itself in the following ways:

- There is a step function at the point where the company can be listed on a stock exchange and raise equity in the market.[20]
- There is a similar step function at the point where the company can raise debt by way of quoted or otherwise marketable securities, e.g. in the bond market.
- The above two step functions concern access to wider sources of funds. That access is likely in its own right to reduce the cost of debt still further. Lenders' liquidity is doubly improved. They are contractually free to sell their securities in the market, and the borrowing company can, if need be, raise equity in the market to repay its debt. However, the borrower incurs an appreciable extra cost in complying with listing requirements.
- There is a belief among some managers that financial size itself reduces risk and therefore the cost of equity. The suggestion here is that the market's risk premium is inversely related to market capitalization, other things being equal. In other words, that the variability of expected returns is inversely related to financial size. This in turn could only be true if the law of large numbers was applicable to financial size. That would only be the case if growth in size had the effect of stepping up the diversification of risks in a portfolio. That however, would need to be a function of a larger number of economically separate activities, not of the greater size of a given set of activities. Size on its own cannot diversify portfolio risk. In that form this belief is therefore fallacious.[21]
- Lastly, it is possible that bank and similar lenders of unmarketable debt might reduce the rate of interest, or rather the margin above the lender's cost of funds, to a larger borrower. This benefit is borne out by empirical research,[22]

but the causality here is quite complex. Banks may find a larger company a better lending risk in the following circumstances:

(a) If size improves the company's access to alternative sources of funds from which to repay, especially to equity or long-term debt raised on a stockmarket. In that case the lower cost of bank debt is indirectly due to the company's better access to the securities markets, which is size-related.

(b) If it has larger, more valuable assets as security. This would apply even if the debt was not specifically secured on the assets concerned, as long as they are not pledged to other, higher ranking lenders. Typical assets here might be real estate. This has undoubtedly been a lending principle in the past, but has been increasingly called into question in recent decades.[23] The main weakness is that many asset values are correlated with the prosperity of the companies which own them. This is particularly true of real estate. Only in rare cases does the land or buildings have a remotely comparable value in any alternative use. Moreover the alternative use must not be vulnerable to the same economic cycles, and the cost of converting from one use to the other must be low. These conditions are seldom met, as lenders found to their cost in the real estate slump of the late 1980s and early 1990s. In short, asset security is largely a fallacy. Banks are gradually absorbing that lesson.

To sum this up, the belief that the cost of capital falls as financial size increases, is true only to the extent that size gives better access to securities markets. In any case, the benefit is likely to be outweighed by the extra costs of any diversification which is motivated merely by size.[24]

Finally, as the quest of mere size is not a quest for profitable customers, a strategy with this aim is outside the scope of business strategy as defined in this book.

Summary

This Appendix has reviewed some commonly discussed financial 'strategies' which this book has not treated as 'business strategies'. They could all be legitimately included in that term, but have nevertheless been deliberately excluded here. This book is only about competitive and corporate strategies framed to target profitable customers.

Tax-based diversifications do not amount to business strategies as defined in this book. Justifications founded on the company's financial size are of limited value, and again fall outside the scope of business strategy as defined in this book.

Notes

1. Mathur (1992).
2. See Part Four.
3. Chapter 21.
4. The implementation and organization structure aspects of competitive strategy are discussed in Chapter 21.
5. The term 'firmlet' is therefore not introduced as an *academic* innovation. Its function is to help *managers* to avoid semantic traps.
6. See Part Five.
7. Originally the word 'firm' implied a single-offering unit. That is how traditional microeconomists like Marshall (1890) used it. Since the advent of the multioffering business, the word 'firm' has continued to be used despite the big change in what the word had come to convey. After all, a given 'multiproduct firm' had probably been founded as a single-offering enterprise many years earlier. The significance of the change may not always have been heeded.
8. Microeconomics lays great stress on the distinction between economies of scale and economies of scope. Scale economies are those achieved by expanding the production and sale of one 'product'. Scope economies are achieved by sharing costs across two or more 'products' (Baumol, Panzar and Willig, 1982).

    That distinction is hardly relevant in the framework put forward by this book, which uses offerings rather than products as the competitive unit. It is unusual for an offering to have non-variable costs which are not shared with other offerings (variable costs are those directly proportional to sales, e.g. direct labour and materials).
9. See Part Six.

10. This case is relevant to the concept of relatedness in corporate strategy, and is referred to under 'Link Three' in Chapter 16.
11. Chapters 2 and 15 refer to one exception to this, the pure dealing business, which is at least not primarily concerned with customers.
12. A not wholly dissimilar series of potentially value-creating financial benefits is discussed in Rappaport (1986), pp 210–214. Rappaport's discussion is restricted to possible benefits from mergers.
13. In the present context, the expression 'company' in this book is the equivalent of what is technically a group of companies consisting of a parent company and subsidiaries.
14. Ravenscraft and Scherer (1987).
15. Jensen (1988).
16. Ravenscraft and Scherer (1987).
17. The 1994 UK Finance Act has mitigated this problem.
18. See Chapter 16.
19. This refers to the initial act of diversifying out of tobacco and into financial services. After the initial entry into that field, subsequent acquisitions of financial businesses were no longer clearly unrelated.
20. We ignore the intermediate stages of unlisted securities markets.
21. Chapter 14 will in any case argue that this risk is better diversified by investors in their portfolios than within the company.
22. Ravenscraft and Scherer (1987).
23. BIS (1986).
24. See Chapter 14.

Part Two   Understanding Competitive Strategy and the Nature of Competition

Part Two develops many of the most important concepts. It stresses the triangular positioning of an offering in relation to customers and competitors. Chapter 4 redefines the market in which competition takes place in a modern world of differentiated offerings. Above all Chapter 5 describes how a business differentiates its offerings. The interrelation between differentiation, price and oligopoly is then discussed in Chapters 6 and 7. All this is intended to sharpen the understanding of the nature of competitive positioning and strategy, before relating it specifically to financial value and profit in Parts Three and Four.

4   Competitive strategy: (a) The map of differentiated competitive markets

Introduction

This chapter begins our exploration of competitive strategy. It briefly introduces the key concept of differentiation, and then explores where competition takes place. The convention is to say in an 'industry' or 'market'. In other words, competition is taken to occur within either an industry or a market. Alternatively an industry is itself taken to be a kind of market. These two terms are explored in some depth. One conclusion is that the concept of the 'industry' is none too helpful in thinking about the competitive process. The other conclusion is that competition does take place in markets, but that in a world of differentiated offerings the boundaries of those markets are rather different from the conventional view of them. This has important practical implications.

Differentiation: the key concept

Chapter 3 defined competitive strategy as the positioning of a single offering in relation to a unique set of potential customers and competitors.

Whose point of view determines how an offering is positioned? The answer to this must be the customers' point of view. The objective of a competitive strategy is to win the preferences of its target customers. It follows that the customers' views determine how the offering is in fact positioned, how it compares with competing substitutes. I may think my café is preferable to yours in the next street, but if the customers prefer yours, they prove me wrong.

Customers see two competing offerings, A and B, as being either indistinguishable – price apart – or different in some degree. This is the critical feature of positioning an offering, and brings us to the concept of differentiation of its offering by a seller.

Differentiation is the central concept of competitive strategy. It is complex, and will need to be explored in three stages. In Chapters 4 and 5 (Stage 1) we make two simplifying assumptions:

- That the positioning chosen for the offering will turn out to be profitable. In Chapter 6 (Stage 2) we shall remove this assumption, and discuss how the purpose of differentiating an offering, of distancing it from its competing substitutes, is to boost the seller's freedom to set prices. Distancing is the means, pricing freedom the end.
- That our offering and its competing substitutes are sufficiently numerous and fragmented to deny to any one of them, or to any group of them, a dominant power to set prices. This assumption will be removed in Chapter 7 (Stage 3), which considers the cases of monopoly and oligopoly or circularity.

Defining differentiation

A definition of **differentiation** needs to look at the concept from two angles. One is its purpose – its 'why' face. The other is how it sets about achieving that purpose – its 'how' face.

- The *purpose* of differentiation is to make the offering less price-sensitive, to make customers give less weight to the price in their buying decisions. This face will be developed in Chapter 6.
- The *means* of achieving that aim is to distance the offering's non-price outputs from those of substitutes, i.e. to make those outputs distinctive and valuable to customers. Differentiation is the principal[1] means of positioning an

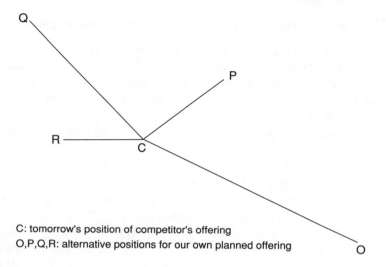

C: tomorrow's position of competitor's offering
O,P,Q,R: alternative positions for our own planned offering

Figure 4.1 *Qualitative and quantitative distancing of planned new offering*

offering in relation to customers and competitors. This 'how' face is developed in this chapter and especially in Chapter 5.

This second face of differentiation is the process of positioning the offering's non-price outputs at a chosen distance from those substitutes, in the eyes of choosing customers. A **competing substitute** is simply one which customers regard as competing. Differentiation results in a **differentiated** offering. An offering is **undifferentiated** from its substitutes when customers are unaware of any difference, and choose only on price.

The word 'differentiation' is used to describe both (a) the seller's choice of the direction and distance and (b) the resulting differentiated position of the offering.

The distancing of an offering from substitutes

The distancing of an offering from competing substitutes can be viewed as having a qualitative and a quantitative aspect. In Figure 4.1 the qualitative aspect is represented by the *direction* in which positions O, P, Q and R diverge from what is here assumed to be a single competing substitute C. The quantitative aspect takes the form of the *distance* of each position from C.

In Figure 4.1 the four alternative positions of the new offering are distanced from C in different non-price directions. Supposing C to be a small cordless vacuum cleaner, then O might have more powerful suction, P a better shape for cleaning in a confined space, Q might be lighter, and R might be sold with a more helpful set of instructions. Chapter 5 presents and analyses some of the most important dimensions in which an offering can be distanced, and thus differentiated.

The purpose of differentiating an offering is – as noted earlier – to make the offering less price-sensitive: this is principally accomplished by choosing (a) the specific outputs which are to distance the offering from its substitutes, and (b) its distance from them.

Competition for customers takes place in markets

As indicated in the introduction, the two key terms here are 'market' and 'industry'. We now tackle these.

Where *does* competition for customer preferences take place? The arena of competition we call a 'market'. A **market** is a communication system for determining the price of competing offerings. Its area contains those competitors whose offerings have a significant actual or potential influence on one another's prices. It contains all actual and potential competitors with that much influence, and no others. All competitors in a market are substitutes competing for the same customer group's dollars. A market and its boundaries can therefore be identified only by the list of significant competing substitutes.

Why 'significant' competing substitutes? Because ultimately all offerings in the entire economy are substitutes to some degree. People may for example decide to cut their urban housing costs and spend more on commuter travel, or to spend less on food and more on leisure pursuits. There is thus a sense in which pastimes compete with pasta dishes: both compete for the same customer's dollar. This important model of the world was originally framed by Robert Triffin.[2] However, the distance between two offerings will in most cases be too great for them to influence each other's prices. It saves time to think of a market as including just those offerings which significantly compete in practice.[3]

A market includes potential as well as actual competitors. Competitors who do not at present, but might in the future try to capture our customers, can significantly influence prices long before that attempt actually occurs. For example in the English Channel the ferry companies took the threatened entry of Eurotunnel into account for some years in anticipation of the event. Potential competitors' influence on prices derives from the mere threat of competition. The market is said to be 'contestable'[4] by them.

The key assumption

It is well-nigh universally[5] assumed that competition takes place in markets which have three features. They are assumed to be:

- *publicly visible*, in the sense that all participants know exactly who the competing suppliers and the interested customer groups are, e.g. we all know who sells and buys bar soaps,

- *inclusive*, in the sense that every single supplier in the group competes with all the others, so that all bar soaps, irrespective of whether they are carbolic or presentation tablets, are in mutual competition, and
- *exclusive*, in the sense that there is no competition across the boundaries of the group: none of the bar soaps compete with shampoos or perfumes.

Industry analysis

Competition is also widely said to take place in 'industries', as well as markets. An industry too is taken to be publicly visible, inclusive and exclusive. This view therefore treats 'industry' as a type of 'market'.

It is worth subjecting this concept of the 'industry' to some intensive and extensive scrutiny. There is a very influential belief that competitive strategy should use as a central tool a process known as 'industry analysis', which is widely associated with Porter's famous five-forces model.[6]

There might broadly be two grounds for advocating an analysis of the industry as an aid to the formulation of competitive strategy. One is that members of the same 'industry' may have similar skills, assets, capabilities, competences or other resources, and may need watching for that reason. The topic of resources is explored in Part Four. The other ground is the assumption that the industry is the market in which a new offering will compete. That is being scrutinized in this chapter. To the extent that the 'industry' is found to be a poor representation or even proxy of the market in which an offering competes for customers, the case for industry analysis is weakened.

Industries as markets

The concept of competition occurring in industries runs into two major difficulties:

- the ambiguities caused by the multiple meanings of 'industry', and

- the wider difficulty in seeing competition occurring within an 'industry' or market common to the entire set of competitors.

The first difficulty then is that the terminology breeds ambiguity. The word 'industry' is widely used in a variety of meanings, of which 'market' is only one. Common examples are:

- a group of suppliers of competing substitutes[7] – in other words, a market,
- a group of suppliers of whatever is bought by a class of customers irrespective of whether the items are competing substitutes, e.g. the defence industry in the sense of whatever typically has the armed forces as customers,
- a group of suppliers of offerings using a common discipline, such as the engineering or chemical industries,
- a group of suppliers using a common raw material, like the plastics industry.

It is clear that only the first meaning, that of 'market', is relevant to competitive positioning. The difficulties of that first category will presently be examined.

The defence industry cannot be of competitive significance, as aircraft carriers do not compete for customer choices with grenades. Nor can the chemical industry: explosives do not compete with pesticides or acrylic fibres. Nor can the plastics industry: cable insulation is no substitute for drainpipes, shopping bags, or telephone receiver casings.

These examples may look extreme, but these usages of 'industry' and 'market' do blunt the way people think about competition. Companies have been known to spend money to find out their 'market share' of the European electronics or chemical industry.

The public market

We therefore proceed to the second difficulty, that of thinking of competition as occurring in industries. This second one is more deep-seated, and it concerns not just industries, but any market. This second difficulty applies wherever the word 'industry' is used in the sense of 'market', as a group of suppliers of competing substitutes.

This concept can be briefly called the model of the **public market**, i.e. a market with the previously mentioned three features of public visibility, exclusivity and inclusivity, as if it had a ditch around it. All can see what buyers and sellers of bar soaps are within the area, all sellers compete with each other, none with sellers on the other side of the ditch.

The difficulty is quite simply that this neat model bears little resemblance to reality in developed, free economies; to a world of differentiated offerings.

Illustrations of public markets

The public model of markets and industries is so firmly entrenched that its shortcomings are worth illustrating first with some short examples and then with a more fully worked out example from tourist accommodation in central London. Some of these illustrations refer to so-called 'industries', some just to 'markets': that distinction does not matter for this purpose.

- *The aircraft industry*: Superficially this is a compact, homogeneous group. However, do customers regard freight-carrying transport planes as close substitutes for the Airbus or the small private passenger jet? This casts doubt on inclusivity. Yet the transport planes compete with freight-carriers by land or sea. This questions exclusivity.
- *Courier services*: The courier service competes with the fax machine, and both compete with electronic mail, but how many people would regard that bundle of offerings as part of the same market or industry?
- *Automobiles*: It is common to describe the market in automobiles as buoyant or flat. Yet inclusivity is negated by the evident fact that a Rolls-Royce is no substitute for a Lada. Nor does the automobile market meet the condition of exclusivity. For Rolls-Royce cars compete for consumers'

dollars against yachts and holiday villas in Spain, whereas the Lada may compete against motor-cycles.
- *Apparel*: The raincoat, a garment, does not compete with cravats, but it does compete with the umbrella, a non-garment. Again, there is neither inclusivity nor exclusivity.

Whether we use an industry model or any other public market model, inclusivity and exclusivity take us away from, not towards, real-life customer choices.

An illustration from the tourist trade

So much for caricatures. The yacht may compete with the villa, even if the differentiation between them is not one of great subtlety. It must not however be thought that these glaring examples are some kind of exception to the rule. The next example is more detailed, and will point to the need for a modified concept, that of the private market.

The Dorchester Hotel in London's Park Lane illustrates the difficulty of thinking in terms of conventional industries or markets in a mature economy. In what 'industry' or 'market' does it compete for tourists? In the 'hotel industry', or the 'British hotel industry', or even the 'London hotel industry'? It surely does not compete with *all* hotels in London, nor are *all* its competitors hotels. Luxury service flats close by in Mayfair are probably much closer substitutes than a two-star hotel a few miles away in Earl's Court. What competes is what customers might choose instead.

Their criteria might in the Dorchester's case include first the quality of the amenities offered and secondly location; a five-star hotel in Edinburgh may offer equivalent amenities, but for the tourist it is not a serious substitute.

Customers may well regard the Savoy, a couple of miles away in the Strand, as a far closer substitute than the Dorchester's less elegant neighbour, which we will call the Chain Palace. In fact, customers may see the Chain Palace as only a distant competitor to the Dorchester.

In Figure 4.2 the Dorchester (D) competes closely with the service flats (S) and less closely with the Chain Palace (C).

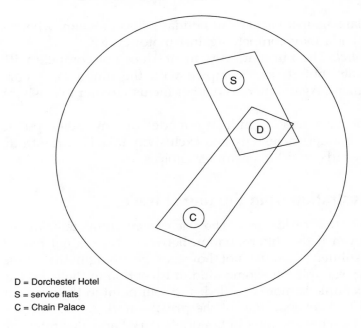

D = Dorchester Hotel
S = service flats
C = Chain Palace

Figure 4.2 *Alternative 'industries'*

D competes with both S and C, but they do not compete with each other. If we were determined to define an industry or market here, it could conceivably be one of three possible combinations.

- D and S, the two closest competitors. This omits C's competition with D.[8]
- D and C, the two 'hotels': this omits the closest competition, between D and S.
- All three: that includes C and S, which are not in mutual competition.

None of these three combinations make a realistic public market. What the example of the Dorchester sheds doubt on, is the public market. Each of the possible applications of that model requires that the group is publicly visible, and that competition for customers within the group is both,

- exclusive, with no competing substitutes outside it, and
- all-inclusive, with every member a close enough substitute for every other member.

The Dorchester example illustrates the difficulties of meeting those conditions in real life.

Public and private markets

As the example of the Dorchester illustrates, that concept of the group with a ditch around it fails as a model of competitive relationships in the real, differentiated modern world.

Earlier in this chapter the boundaries of a market were conventionally defined as containing all those actual and potential offerings which effectively compete for customers. This means that they have a significant influence on one another's prices. What must be rejected as unrealistic, is the public market with its three features of public visibility, exclusivity and inclusivity. However, that kind of a public market is what people have in mind when they talk about 'the' steel, banking or computer industry. They tacitly assume that any such market or industry has those three features. The Dorchester's case illustrates that the model of the public market does not portray real markets, not even if they are narrowly defined as containing only fairly close substitutes.

Superficially this picture of a ditch around a defined set of suppliers might of course appear a reasonable description of the market in hotel rooms, or perhaps central London hotel rooms, but we have seen that it does not stand up to closer inspection. The Dorchester Hotel is not a member of such a group surrounded by a ditch. By no means all its significant substitutes compete with each other, let alone exclusively with each other.

There is evidently not one single market in which central London hotel rooms compete for the preferences of tourists, but possibly even as many as there are hotels. By no means all potential clients see hotels of different qualities, facilities and locations as close substitutes.

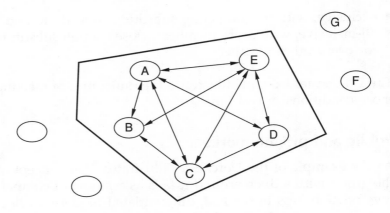

Figure 4.3   *Public market of offerings A, B, C, D, E*

Their prices may vary with a number of features: location, size of rooms, quality of furnishings and decoration, facilities like en suite bathrooms, TV, telephone, the level of service, lifts, porterage. Effective competition occurs within relatively small numbers of close substitutes. These vary from case to case, and can include non-hotels like service flats.

The model of the public market is illustrated in Figure 4.3. For the sake of simplicity it is assumed that there are only five hotels in central London. The composition of the set of competitors is commonly and publicly known. The market consists of a discrete group of competitors A, B, C, D and E. Each of them is in competition with all the other four, and none have competitors outside that group. Offerings A, B, C, D and E all share the same market, surrounded by a ditch or gap.

The private market

In fact, however, each offering is likely to be differentiated, and therefore to have a unique *private* market, as in Figure 4.4. A **private market** is 'personal' to a single competitor. Its list of competitors is not wholly shared with any of the other competing offerings. Their respective lists will partly overlap, but no two of them will be identical. This is another way of saying that each offering is differentiated.

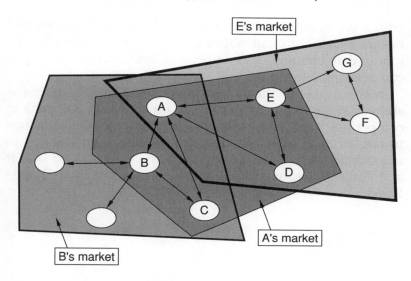

Figure 4.4 *Private markets of offerings A, B and E*

Figure 4.4 illustrates this concept of a private market. Offering A's market overlaps with those of B, C, D and E. On the other hand offering E is close enough to A, D, F and G to compete with them, but not to B or C. In this pattern it is not possible to draw the boundary of 'the' (publicly defined) market common to all the parties. It is on the other hand perfectly possible to draw a boundary for the private market of A, or of any other single offering.

We return here to the illustration from automobiles. The passenger car 'industry' or market is widely defined as including everything from the Rolls-Royce to the Lada. However, we have already noted that those two cars are not mutual substitutes. Some customers might regard the Mercedes 600 or the Bentley or the Jaguar as a substitute for the Rolls-Royce, but not the Toyota Camry. Some customers may choose between the Camry and the Jaguar, others between the Camry and the Range Rover, but not the Ford Escort. The Escort may or may not be seen as a serious substitute for the Lada, but it certainly is for the Volkswagen Golf. And of course, the Rolls-Royce – unlike the Jaguar – competes with a yacht, and the Lada with a motor-cycle. Each offering has its *private* list of substitutes: there is no common list, no group that includes all competitors and excludes all non-competitors.

In the model of the private market, when an offering is shifted, so usually is its market. In other words, a change in competitive positioning almost invariably entails a change in the set of competitors. If a car manufacturer decides to upgrade its offering, tomorrow's competitors may be Jaguar and Rolls-Royce, whereas today's were Jaguar and Range Rover.

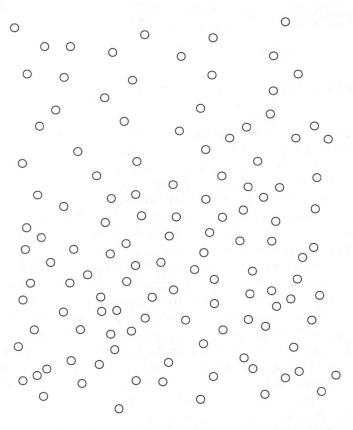

Figure 4.5 The galaxy of offerings: Triffin's world of general equilibrium

The galaxy

The wider economy of private markets can be depicted as the galaxy with a continuum of offerings, pictured in Figure 4.5. Any one offering has competing neighbours, but each such neighbour has a partly different competing group. There is no particular stopping point in this pattern: it is in that sense that it forms a continuum. By contrast the world of public markets forms a discontinuous pattern like Figure 4.6,

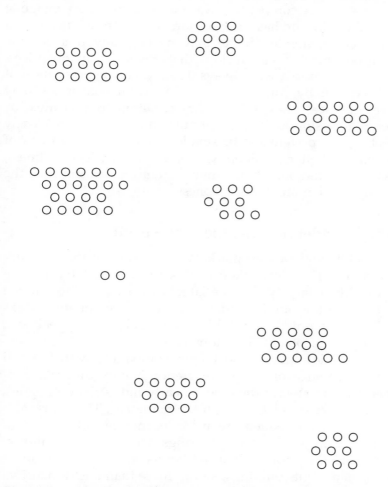

Figure 4.6 *Clumps of offerings. Public markets, e.g. industries*

with clumps of offerings and ditches or gaps between the clumps. Within each clump all offerings are substitutes: it is inclusive. At the same time its members have no substitutes in other clumps: it is also exclusive. These are two of the three features that make up the conventional image of an 'industry' or 'market'.

Perhaps we should pause here for reflection. The differentiated galaxy of Figure 4.5 departs of course from the model of pure competition. That model too could be represented by Figure 4.6. Pure competition was never[9] a very close image of the real world, and has become more remote from it in modern advanced economies. Some may nostalgically pine for the 'disappearance' of that world with its theoretically low prices. In fact, that utopia was always illusory. However, suppose it had existed. By comparison with it, what consumers may 'lose' in prices, they gain in choice. Differentiation must be seen in terms of outputs, not inputs, in terms of more closely meeting the preferences of smaller, more diverse groups of customers, better availability, greater variety, less drabness, less regimentation. Choice may in many cases improve the quality of life more than cheapness.

Which model best fits the real world?

The public and private markets are models of the competitive arena. The view taken in this book is that the private model fits a largely differentiated world of business much better than the public model. After all, differentiation seeks a degree of uniqueness which is intended to appeal to a specific set of potential customers.

The public model is no longer compatible with the real world, in which offerings are predominantly differentiated. This was not always the case. In early industrial economies, offerings were relatively undifferentiated. This was also the case in subsequent retarded economies like those of Eastern Europe in 1989: offerings were drably uniform. However, the more advanced an economy is, the more variegated are its offerings, and in more than one dimension, as Chapter 5 will show. The greater variety that results from differentiation could in fact serve as a measure of how advanced an economy is.

The galaxy of private markets therefore represents the modern advanced economy as a complex overlapping and interlocking continuum. Participants and offerings in one market are also to be found in neighbouring markets, but in varying combinations and interrelationships. The public market is seen as only a limiting case. In some rare cases[10] it may fit reality. It might for example be found in a pure commodity market like the market for copper. However, away from a formal metal exchange, even copper trading may be influenced by differentiation between the services performed for customers by particular sellers. The publicly defined market is thus of limited usefulness to the *concept* of competitive strategy.

Implications for the 'industry' and 'industry analysis'

Intermediate solutions: strategic groups

In our present context the industry is little more than a commonly used version of the public market. It is not therefore surprising that both practitioners and researchers have come up against difficulties in using the industry concept. Managers found that the boundaries of the industry were not those of the market in which they were competing, and researchers found that industries did not show uniform competitive features or performance. The first reaction was to look for smaller groups of competitors, on the hypothesis that the industry was not an accurate enough proxy for a market. An early device of this kind was the 'segment' discussed below and in Appendix 4.1. By the mid-1970s writers turned to the **strategic group** as a subset of the 'industry', consisting of industry members with similar competitive strategies.[11] Strategic groups were said to be protected by 'mobility barriers' instead of 'entry barriers'.[12] However, Rumelt[13] had by 1984 made a case for dispensing with groups at least in principle.

In reality it was not the definition or size of the group that was wrong, but the group concept, the public market itself. In the majority of cases, neither the industry nor industry analysis will assist the formulation of competitive strategies.

It is worth listing four of the fallacies which have dogged industry analysis.

First, a single industry often contains so much diversity of offerings that it cannot possibly be even a public market. For example, investment banking is recognized as an industry. However, in this 'industry' there are separate types of offerings like fund management, corporate advice, broking in stocks and bonds and venture capital which cannot possibly be in competition with each other. They address different groups of customers and to some extent different competitors.

Secondly, even in a less diverse 'industry' the concept of a public market founders on the hard rock of its already observed contradictions. The automobile industry's various actual private markets shade into each other, all the way from the Lada to the Bentley: inclusivity and exclusivity are not found for the 'industry' as a whole, or any of its parts.

Thirdly, the contradictions of this usage are compounded when analysts focus on multioffering 'firms' in such an amorphous 'industry'. For example if they take Coca-Cola and PepsiCo to compete as companies, and not just with their cola offerings. PepsiCo, the company, among other things offers fast food.

Finally, the very process of industry analysis invites a static approach which takes even a competitively defined market as given. Some of the best competitive strategies set out to reconfigure markets. This dynamic concept is more fully described in Chapter 9, but an example is the personal computer 'industry', which may appear mature and static. Yet a particular voice-operated offering might well split off from it a profitable and growing private market.

Using the model of the private market

The thrust of this chapter has been to argue that the private market is a much better competitive model than the public market, and therefore better than the industry or the strategic or any other similar group. The private market is a powerful tool for the strategist. The first step is to construct a picture of tomorrow's offerings in the chosen part of the galaxy on the lines of Figure 4.4. The strategist will take great care to exclude from the list of competitors those members of the 'industry' which will not be significant substitutes for the offering being planned. More important, the strategist will include all those substitutes which may in fact compete, but do not count as part of the industry. They may well be a majority.

Then in Step 2 the really important decisions can be made, about how the new offering is to be differentiated from this configuration of substitutes, in what dimensions, and by what distance. These matters are analysed in Chapters 5 to 7. This is the heart of the competitive strategy task.

Segmentation

Appendix 4.1 deals with the difficult term 'segmentation'. It too can be seen as one of several terms introduced to overcome the difficulties inherent in the public market. The appendix attempts to clarify what the term means, and to what extent it is worth retaining in the framework put forward in this book. In other words, to what extent it improves our understanding of *private* markets. Its conclusion is that what the appendix calls 'customer segments' are best thought of as subsets[14] of private markets with more specialized sets of customer preferences.

Where the industry and public market models remain useful

Chapter 3 defined competitive strategy as positioning the individual offering in relation to its customers and competitors.

95

It also rejected the multioffering firm as what competes for customer preferences.

The central theme of the present chapter is the need to think in terms of private rather than public markets. In the process the private market has replaced the industry as the competitive arena, because the industry is a public market. An offering can only be positioned where it competes, and that is almost invariably a private market. It remains to discuss to what extent the industry and the public market remain useful concepts.

First, it should not be thought that there are no more useful applications for the model of the public market. There are in fact cases where that model fits reality. The market in uranium might be an example, and so might the market in 3½-inch high-density computer disks. In each such case there is a group with public visibility, exclusivity and inclusivity, and a ditch round it.

Secondly, it is worth looking closely at some groups of offerings, for example TV receivers or breakfast cereals. Within these the individual offerings are differentiated, and have substitutes outside the group. In that sense their markets are private. Nevertheless in these cases the distance between the group as a whole and all substitutes outside it is substantially greater than those internal distances. There is some degree of discontinuity which may or may not amount to a ditch. In such cases the group might be seen as a quasi-public market.

The significance of the quasi-public market is quite limited. Every offering in a quasi-public market has its own private market, and it is in this private market that the seller must position it. The principal significance of the wider quasi-public market concerns the company's combined share of that market in which it has more than one offering, and its ability to use that share to achieve economies of scale and influence prices. These implications will become apparent in Chapters 8 and 16.

Thirdly, even where markets are in fact private, there may be a public market which is a useful *approximation* to a private market. If so, there may be useful published statistics which managers can use as proxy data for their private market.

That benefit particularly applies to a proxy market which happens to be a statistical industry. Earlier in this chapter we noted that an 'industry' may be defined not just as a group of competing substitutes, but also as a group of suppliers to certain customer groups like the armed forces, or of users of a specific discipline like chemistry or of a material like plastics. In addition to these there is the statistically recognized 'industry'. For official statistics, businesses have been grouped everywhere, for example in the US Standard Industrial Classification, into industries defined in some practically convenient way. They are often a mixture of the alternative definitions already discussed. These official statistics are in some cases of great practical value to business managers. A good example is the ratio of R&D spending to sales in the pharmaceutical industry.

In any case it is most useful in non-strategic contexts to have words like 'industry' or 'market', conveying some broad and useful commonality. It is helpful even to users of the framework advocated by this book to be able to talk about 'safety in the British nuclear industry' or 'the effect of the peace dividend on the defence industry' or 'credit control in the market for domestic appliances'. Great care is however needed when such a vague concept is used to refer to a group of offerings that compete for customers' choices.

Summary and conclusion

This chapter has set the scene in which competitive strategy operates. The key concept of differentiation has been introduced and defined. Advanced modern economies consist predominantly of differentiated offerings. In a differentiated world each offering competes for customer preferences in its own private market: it has a set of customers and competitors which is not wholly shared by any other offering.

Consequently, a market of differentiated offerings cannot be equated with any grouping of offerings like an industry or any other public market. The public market is characterized by its three distinguishing marks of public visibility, inclusivity and exclusivity. Where differentiation is the norm, the competitive arena is both wider and narrower than that concept. Many of the difficulties which have puzzled writers and practitioners alike, are resolved by removing the strait-jacket of the public market. This insight does not merely liberate and improve managers' understanding of their markets, it opens up a richer and wider set of practical opportunities.

There are still many practical ways in which the model of the public market and the term 'industry' continue to serve business managers. It must be rejected, however, for the formulation of most competitive strategies. Most competitive strategies need to treat the world as dominated by differentiated offerings, and therefore by private markets. Differentiation aims at some degree of uniqueness. Differentiation is what causes markets to be private, definable for only one offering at a time. The strategist who takes a short cut and goes for a publicly defined market or industry may well suffer the fate of those who positioned typewriters or British motor-cycles in what turned out to be mis-specified public markets. Threats from Honda or word processors were not considered.

The private market represents an important step in the re-orientation[15] of business strategy to focus on the individual offering and on how customers choose it.

* * *

Appendix 4.1

Segments and segmentation

Customer and market segments

The basic term **'segment'** originally meant a group – narrow enough to be a subset of a larger group – of customers with more closely matched preferences.

It is proposed here to distinguish two kinds of segment, a *customer* segment and a *market* segment. A **customer segment** is quite simply a group of customers with similar preferences. It may,

- be co-extensive with a private market, although it will normally be smaller,
- be more densely populated than surrounding parts of the galaxy, in which case it is of much greater strategic interest,
- come into existence with or without deliberate action by suppliers, or more probably by a mixture of causes, some initiated by suppliers, some not.

A **market segment** on the other hand is a subset of a public market, with a narrower, more specialized range of customer preferences. To the extent that this book rejects the concept of the public market, it must therefore also reject the market segment.

Limitations of market segments as an analytical tool

The market segment was one of several devices[16] designed to reconcile the model of public markets like industries, with the evident diversity of markets found in the real, differentiated world. Its usefulness is confined to that minority of markets which are either still public, or close enough approximations to public markets.

It is, however, worth illustrating just exactly what was meant by that market or industry segment. It was that part of a public market which could be identified by some specific output-features. For example let us assume, contrary to our earlier conclusions,[17] that the Dorchester Hotel was a member of a public market consisting of all hotels,

- located within the London area
- offering a certain list of de luxe amenities.

That imaginary public market might contain a market segment or subset served by all five-star hotels within a one-mile radius of Piccadilly Circus, i.e. substantially all those in London's West End.

As the example of the Dorchester in the body of Chapter 4 showed, a device like this does no kind of justice to the complexities of real competitive conditions. The market segment does not therefore remedy the failure of public markets to portray the true competitive process.

Using customer segments

It might be thought that the introduction of the concept of the private market has made that of the segment redundant. That is not the case, because private markets too can have subsets with more specialized customer preferences. These are here called customer segments.

In a very simple example, offering A has a private market shared with offerings B, C, D and E. A *customer segment* might refer to all those customers who regard B and C, but not D and E as close substitutes for A. We shall presently see how useful this insight can be.

'Segmentation'

The word **'segmentation'** too is used in several rather different senses. It can mean,

- 'segmentedness', which is a state of affairs which exists out there, in customer preferences, but also
- one of two things done by a competing business:

  (a) the process of analysing a market so as to identify its segments, if any,[18] or
  (b) the creation of a segment on the initiative of sellers.

We can illustrate the *analytical* process with Figure 4.7. It pictures a market in which offerings compete mainly with two output features, represented by the vertical and horizontal dimensions. To lend itself to strategic segmentation, a public or private market must contain two or more

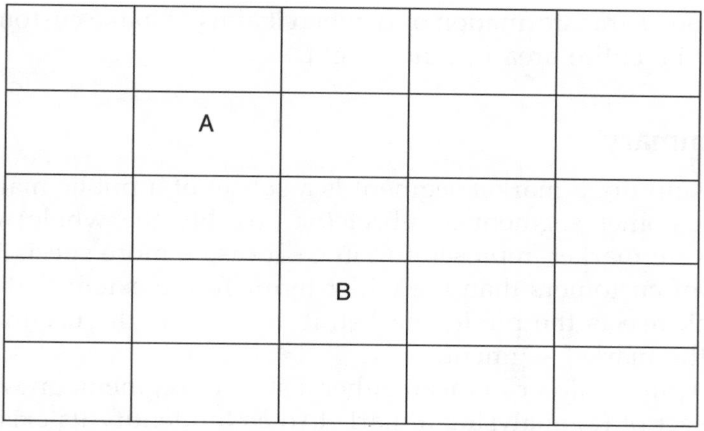

	A			
		B		

Figure 4.7 Segmentation as analysis

bunched areas of customer preferences, two magnets, say at A and B. It will pay at least some sellers to target magnet B rather than the strongest magnet A. If there were just one at A, then there would be no segments and all competitors would be attracted towards A. On the other hand if preferences were evenly distributed, with no magnets and no bunching at A or B, then sellers have no incentive to get close to any special position within the total area. The analytical process thus investigates the market – public or private[19] – and takes it as given, but uses the analysis to position an offering to address a market containing that customer segment.

The other process, that of proactively *creating* segments, is part of what will in Chapter 9 be called market transformation.[20] It occurs when a seller sets about changing preferences in a part of the galaxy, not just perceptions of its own offering. An example would be the first introduction in the late 1980s of CFC-free refrigeration equipment on the grounds that it was prudent to prevent global warming. Any promotion aimed exclusively at preferences for the seller's own offering is part of the process of differentiation, which may of course be the result of the analytical process of segmentation. It becomes transformation only when it aims to make customers see the entire area in a new light.

Summary

To sum up, a market segment is a subset of a public market, a customer segment a subset (or possibly the whole) of a private market, representing in each case a more specialized set of customers than the wider term. To the extent that this book rejects the public market, it also rejects the usefulness of the market segment.

Segmentation can mean either a state of segmentedness, or the act of (a) analysing a market so as to identify its existing segments, or (b) creating segments by initiating action which will change customer preferences in a part of the galaxy.

Notes

1. The role of price in positioning an offering is discussed in Chapter 6.
2. Triffin (1940).
3. Scherer and Ross (1990).
4. Subject to the costs of entry: Baumol (1982). Baumol's model assumes these to be zero, but the concept of contestability is most valuable even when they are not.
5. The important exception here is Porter (1980), and those who have followed him. Porter recognizes that the industry as a market is neither exclusive nor inclusive, as here defined, although it is still seen as publicly known. Consequently Porter has (a) allowed for competition from substitutes outside the industry and (b) found 'strategic groups' within industries. Various scholars have researched strategic groups, notably McGee and Thomas (1986, 1992), Rumelt (1984), Barney and Hoskisson (1990), and Hatten and Hatten (1987). Strategic groups are discussed later in this chapter.
6. Porter (1980). The model is discussed in Appendix 8.1.
7. Porter (1980) p. 5, (1985) p. 233.
8. Porter's (1980) refinement of extending the competitive market and treating C as a substitute from *outside* the industry, is no solution as that model also requires C to compete with S, i.e. it requires inclusivity as well as exclusivity. In any case this device does not sit easily with the definition of the industry as the group of substitutes within which competition takes place.

9. Nor indeed was it ever intended to be!
10. Brooks (1995).
11. Caves and Porter (1977).
12. These barriers are discussed in Chapter 11.
13. Rumelt (1984) 'The group concept is frequently all that is needed, but there is no theoretical reason to limit mobility barriers to groups of firms. I shall therefore use the term *'isolating mechanism'* to refer to phenomena that limit the ex post equilibration of rents among individual firms.'
14. In special cases a customer segment may constitute an entire private market.
15. See Chapter 3.
16. One of the most influential of the academic solutions has been the concept of the strategic group discussed earlier in this chapter.
17. See pp. 86–87.
18. The term 'segmentation' has puzzled students of competitive markets for a long time. It has been definitively discussed by Dickson and Ginter (1987).
19. Figure 4.7 is of course, like all such models, an oversimplification of reality; this applies all the more to private markets that shade kaleidoscopically into each other. However, the underlying principle that segmentation is worth while only where there is multipoint bunching, applies equally to private markets.
20. Dickson and Ginter (1987) describe a similar process as 'demand function modification'.

5 Competitive strategy: (b) Classification of competitive strategies

Introduction

How can an offering be differentiated? How will customers see it as differentiated? This chapter identifies and classifies the various possible types of competitive positioning for an offering in its triangular relationship with customers and competitors.[1]

Classifying competitive strategies

There are a number of types of differentiation. Effectively[2] these amount to types of competitive strategy. They constitute different ways of positioning a competitive offering.

It is in practice helpful to distinguish two dimensions along which the outputs of an offering can be differentiated. We call these the merchandise and support dimensions. Those differentiating features which customers perceive in the way the seller helps them in choosing, obtaining, and then using the offering, constitute its **support** dimension. All other differentiating features belong to what is here called its **merchandise** dimension.

An automobile's merchandise features would include its colour, shape, size, performance characteristics, facia board, and in-car entertainment; its support features would include the test-drive, instruction book, promptness of delivery, servicing arrangements and service agent network.

A restaurant's merchandise features would include the waiter service and the quality and presentation of the food, drink and accommodation, whereas its support dimension might cover the ease of booking a table, the car park, help with interpreting the menu, and credit and debit card facilities.

The distinction is mainly practical. What matters is not the precise borderline between merchandise and support. It does not matter much whether we think of help with understanding the menu as merchandise or support. What matters is that in deciding how to position our offering, we do not neglect either dimension. Maybe we are the unsuccessful competitor who has not spotted that customers might be attracted by helpful explanations of the menu. The next chapter shows how even the most common, even the most 'commoditized' offerings like paper clips can be differentiated in the support dimension, and command a price premium[3] in a smaller, less competitive market area.

Support features may in some cases be technical; if so, they might consist of process and application know-how, help with design, procurement and subsequent use. Such support is as likely to be supplied in cosmetics as in engineering. It cannot be overstressed that all merchandise or support features are by definition outputs, not input features or efforts. Input features are those which cannot influence the choosing customer.

Differentiation is a matter of degree. In each of these two dimensions, merchandise and support, we can select a high or low degree of differentiation. That decision is in fact very significant. It gives us the four base cases of competitive strategies, as illustrated in Figure 5.1.

High and low differentiation and price sensitivity

As noted in Chapter 4, differentiation can be seen by customers as a distance, as a lack of closeness, to substitutes.

A more quantifiable way is to see it as the reciprocal of price sensitivity, which is more fully discussed in Chapter 6. The more differentiated an offering is, the less will its sales depend on customers' price comparisons. A highly differentiated offering may appeal to a comparatively narrow group of customers, but those customers will see no close

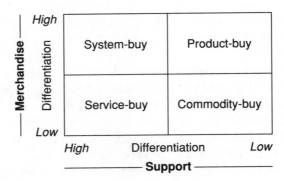

Figure 5.1 Four main competitive strategies from two main dimensions

substitute, and will not choose a substitute because it has a slightly or moderately lower price. The price difference would have to be commensurately high to affect their choice.

Price sensitivity measures how sensitive the sales volume of an offering is to marginal changes in price differentials between that offering and its substitutes. It therefore indirectly measures the price consciousness of the customers.

In a limiting case the degree of differentiation is zero or infinite. Where it is zero, i.e. in the bottom right corner of Figure 5.1, the offerings are homogeneous, and the slightest price difference would shift customer choices. Where it is infinite, i.e. in the top left corner, the offerings are not substitutes at all and no price difference would shift choices.

The four generic forms of differentiation

Figure 5.1 labels four generic forms of differentiation showing how offerings are positioned in relation to competing offerings. If an offering is bought with little awareness of differences in either dimension, it is a **commodity-buy**; if highly differentiated in both dimensions, a **system-buy**. If differentiation is low in merchandise, but high in support, it is a **service-buy**, and in the reverse case a **product-buy**. The unfamiliar suffix '-buy' serves to stress that all the labels describe how *customers* perceive offerings in comparison with their substitutes.

These four generic forms of differentiation should not be thought of as peculiar to this trade or that. Any offering can be transacted in any of four ways. For example a photo-copying facility can be offered in all four ways:

- Photocopying facility as a **system-buy**: The offering is differentiated in both the merchandise and the support dimension. The supplier, with distinctive skill, analyses a customer's requirements, recommends a configuration of equipment and environment most appropriate to those requirements, then designs, supplies, installs and main-tains the specified configuration as part of a unique package.
- Photocopying facility as a **product-buy**: Here the offering is differentiated in the merchandise dimension, but not in the support dimension. The photocopying installation offered is a 'Rolls-Royce' installation with special features and robust quality. To the customer it is differentiated by way of merchandise, but undifferentiated as regards any individual support from the supplier.
- Photocopying facility as a **service-buy**: Here the offering is differentiated as regards support, but not merchandise. The supplier acts as adviser, analysing the customer's requirements and specifying the installation from a range of standard equipment. The supplier specifies, installs and maintains the recommended configuration.
- Photocopying facility as a **commodity-buy**: The offering is indistinguishable from that of many competitors. Help given by the supplier may well be significant, but is no different from help given by competitors. The customer chooses whatever is cheapest to buy and use. Cost alone governs the buyer's choice.

Sub-dimensions of differentiation

The four-cell matrix of Figure 5.1 shows the classification of differentiation in the support and merchandise dimensions. We shall now show how each of these two dimensions can in its turn be subclassified. When we have thus shown the different types of both support and merchandise differentiation, we shall then go on to show how they can be combined into a single more detailed 16-cell version of the four-cell matrix.

Types of support differentiation

There are two dimensions in which a competitor can differentiate the *support* component of its offering: personalization and expertise.

Personalization

Personalization is a measure[4] of the care and attention given to each individual customer, perhaps with a special welcoming smile, a cordial handshake, with extra care to ascertain personal circumstances, needs or preferences, or perhaps with the use of the customer's name. Like expertise below, personalization is predominantly a matter of degree. Its differentiation is from the competitors' types and degrees of personalization.

Greater personalization is often a painstaking process. In order to achieve it, a business may make distinctive efforts to learn about the individual customer's problems, needs and operating logistics. The benefits of this effort can reach far beyond the present offering. The business obtains an insight into a customer's needs and preferences which it can use to design successful offerings in the future.

The personalized form of differentiation can win high degrees of customer loyalty. It can also impose switching costs. Both discourage a transfer of custom to competitors.[5]

Expertise

The other subdimension is expertise. **Expertise** measures customers' perceptions predominantly of the degree[6] of superiority displayed by the seller in the brain-power, talent, skills or experience in delivering and implementing the

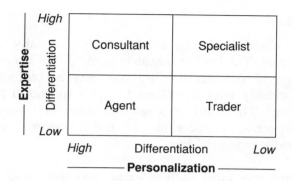

Figure 5.2   Support differentiation: the four modes

offering. Personalization conveys distinctive familiarity with the individual customer, expertise with the nature and use of the offering.

The combinations

Figure 5.2 displays a simplified model of the possible modes of support differentiation. Each axis represents the degree of differentiation, i.e. distance from substitutes. It shows the four modes of support which can characterize an offering. They are here called 'consultant', 'specialist', 'agent' and 'trader'. We must again stress that these modes can be selected for *any* offering, no matter whether the offering is a helicopter blade, an interest-bearing current account or milk chocolate.

Leading insurance brokers can serve as our illustration. They bring together those who wish to transfer risks and those who wish to accept and carry or redistribute them. The former are buyers of cover, the latter underwriters. We assume that our broker competes with other brokers by helping that buyer to identify, contain and manage risks. Of course the broker could also differentiate its merchandise, say by providing access to particular types of underwriters. The broker can position its support in any of the modes in Figure 5.2.

1 Consultant

Here the client might be a large technologically complex manufacturer. The broker might in some detail investigate a novel type of product liability risk, say in biotechnology, working closely with the client to get a thorough grasp of the problem. The result is a set of recommendations about what respective proportions of the exposure are most economically managed by,

- operating measures such as extra laboratory tests,
- insurance cover, or
- retention, i.e. self-insurance.

The broker then selects the most appropriate underwriters and places with them the percentage of loss to be covered.

This is a customized, comprehensive and unique service. In an extreme case the broker might identify a novel form of risk and its unique impact on the client's business.

2 Specialist

In this mode the broker's ability to work closely with any one client is not exceptional. The specialist is seen to have special skills to pinpoint whatever policy is most appropriate to the client's clearly identified, but not unique, type of problem. The chosen policy would also suit other similar clients needing similar solutions. The offering is especially attractive to clients who do not need tailor-made solutions.

3 Agent

Where the broker transacts as 'agent', what stands out is not the broker's grasp of the nature of the individual client's risks, but his or her attentiveness to, and intimate understanding of the client's operating procedures. The process by which the broker identifies the cover needed, places the risks and handles claims, thus becomes relatively painless to the client.

4 Trader

The broker who competes as trader, offers whatever level of expertise and personalization is normal in the market. One broker's support is indistinguishable from that of others.

Insurance broking has simply served as an illustration – practically any kind of business has the opportunity to select one of these four modes of support differentiation.

Types of merchandise differentiation

There are also two dimensions in which a business can differentiate the *merchandise* component of its offering, by content or by aura.

Content

An offering differentiated by its **content** would be seen by its customers to have unique performance capabilities, or to be preferable for its technical, physical or aesthetic output-features. Even the company's size may add to the attraction of its offerings, if it makes customers feel safer – as in bank deposits – or better able to rely on its reputation, as with Microsoft or Toyota.[7] In a nutshell, content concerns what the offering will *do* for the customer.

Aura

Aura on the other hand concerns what the offering 'says' about the customer. It reassures customers that they have made the right choice of offering as it will speak well of them, both to themselves and to others. 'It will say the right things about you' is the message conveyed by aura, without specifying any content output-features. Offerings differentiated by aura are often symbols of status and good taste. Both aura and content may rely on intrinsic qualities, but they are quite distinct in their function. For example a cashmere pullover may be both comfortable and chic. Brand names like Pringle can convey not just better content, but also better aura. The Rolex President is not bought solely as a means of ascertaining the time.

In a nutshell, content concerns what the offering will *do for*, aura what it will *say about*, the customer.

If a razor blade were known to be made in the same plant, but sold under the brand names of Gillette on the one hand and Boots or 7-o'clock on the other; or if a man's tie were known to be of identical design and manufacture, but marketed under the respective names of Hardy Amies and that of a well-known chain store, then there is no doubt that there are customers who will pay a higher price for the Gillette and Hardy Amies names. That preference is hard to explain in terms of any intrinsic difference between the higher and lower priced offerings, for it is known that there is none. No, the explanation has to be in terms of the extra value placed on the prestige or status conferred on the customer by the name. It would be an oversimplification to characterize the higher price itself as creating lasting extra attraction: what the higher price is intended to do, is to reinforce an aura created by the higher ranking brand. Razor blades are perhaps more likely to have this lifestyle attribute in developing countries. Again, volume cars are now often marketed with the stress not on their performance, but on the statements they make about their owners. This form of 'lifestyle' differentiation is particularly attempted by manufacturers of perfumes who advertise their goods largely by stressing what they say about the wearer. Some perfumes signify independence; others femininity and romance.

An interesting aspect of aura is that of ethical or socially responsible purchase behaviour.[8] There is no doubt that socially responsible and politically correct attitudes have progressively set customers against the fur trade, against animal experiments in cosmetics and against the offerings of companies with an exploitive record as employers in South Africa under apartheid. The damage to such businesses was often due to initiatives from pressure groups. Examples of business responses are:

- telecommunications companies differentiating their offerings by advertising that they are 'equal opportunities employers',
- tins of tuna advertised as humanely caught by methods safe for dolphins,
- Indian carpets promoted as made without the use of child labour.

The degree of success of these pressure groups is not free from doubt. For example, lead-free petrol did not take off in the UK until it received preferential fiscal treatment, i.e. until it was offered at a discount. There is evidence that socially responsible purchase behaviour is heavily centred on small middle-class groups of consumers.[9]

In any case, differentiation of this kind tends to be defensive rather than aggressive. Nevertheless in some cases it can no doubt serve to alienate customers, for a while at least, away from unreformed suppliers. What is not in doubt is that this type of differentiation is classifiable as aura. Its intended benefit is to the buyer's self-respect.

Aura can sometimes come about without any major advertising or promotion. When a novel offering first reaches the market, it is not just its practical benefit that attracts buyers, but also the way it raises the owner's esteem in both his or her own and the wider community's eyes. Examples might

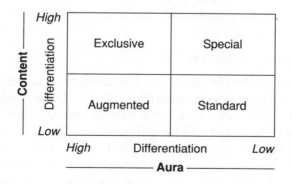

Figure 5.3 *Merchandise differentiation: the four modes*

be those who bought the first lap-top computers, the first camcorders and the first Filofaxes. Advertising and promotion can of course help to create an aura, but they have other functions too; for example to draw customers' attention to better content.

The aura of an innovator's offering can persist for some time even after competitors have introduced otherwise similar offerings. In the 1970s Harley Davidson and BSA motor-cycles retained their social status long after they been technologically overtaken by Japanese rivals. One explanation of such lasting advantage is that early customers have formed a commitment to it through playing a part in the offering's original development.

The combinations

A simplified model of merchandise differentiation is shown in Figure 5.3. Training shoes will serve to illustrate the four types of merchandise differentiation.

1 Exclusive merchandise

In this case the content is significantly differentiated through qualities like softness and durability. Aura may also gain from these distinctive qualities up to a point, but a much more significant gain could be achieved by associating the shoe with a star athlete. The wearer in that case obtains not only better performing shoes but also a higher status.

2 Augmented merchandise

In this case only the aura, not the content is differentiated. There is nothing special about the shoes. Their construction is known to be very similar to that of many other trainers. However they might still be differentiated by aura, provided that customers are convinced that they confer a special status on the wearer. That special status would serve to reassure not only themselves, but also others, of their good taste. Branding and advertising is a common, though not the only way to establish a superior aura. Naturally, brand labels are prominently located where they attract instant attention. To the uninitiated there may seem to be little difference between the ordinary training shoe and some of its heavily branded versions. Yet those who know about these things would not regard the two as substitutes at all. Their similarity as footwear is irrelevant to those in the market for 'street-cred'.

3 Special merchandise

Special merchandise offerings are differentiated in content, but not in aura. The shoes are known to have distinctive performance characteristics. They might for example be specially suitable for running on difficult terrain or of particularly light weight.

4 Standard merchandise

Standard merchandise shoes are no different from many substitutes. They are not distinctive from competing trainers in either content or aura.

Fuller classification of differentiation

We have now refined the support and merchandise dimensions of differentiation into two subdimensions each. We can present this more detailed pattern of permutations as a comprehensive 16-cell matrix in Figure 5.4. This is a more detailed version of the four-cell matrix of Figure 5.1.

This 16-cell matrix merely illustrates how any of the four modes of merchandise differentiation can be combined with any of the four modes of support differentiation.

In Figure 5.4 the horizontal and vertical dimensions do not represent a continuity of greater or lesser differentiation. The top row and left-hand column are the most differentiated, the bottom row and right-hand column the least differentiated, but the intermediate rows and columns do not continue that pattern. Their relative positions show only qualitative

Merchandise	System-buy			Product-buy
Exclusive	Exclusive/ consultant	Exclusive/ specialist	Exclusive/ agent	Exclusive/ trader
Special	Special/ consultant	Special/ specialist	Special/ agent	Special/ trader
Augmented	Augmented/ consultant	Augmented/ specialist	Augmented/ agent	Augmented/ trader
Standard	Standard/ consultant **Service-buy**	Standard/ specialist	Standard/ agent	Standard/ trader **Commodity-buy**
	Consultant	Specialist	Agent	Trader

Support

Figure 5.4   Fuller classification of competitive strategies

differences, not degrees of differentiation. There is no inherent logic making *'special'* more differentiated than *'augmented'*; or *'specialist'* more differentiated than *'agent'*.

At one extreme however is the limiting case of full differentiation in the system-buy mode of differentiation: this means fully differentiated support and merchandise; it combines exclusive merchandise with consultant support. Conversely, the extreme commodity-buy case, where competition is entirely in terms of price, combines standard merchandise with trader support. Between these two extremes, there are infinite shades of differentiation in both the main and the subsidiary dimensions; only the diagram cannot show them. What the diagram does however illustrate, is that all 16 combinations are possible.

The 16 permutations

Some of the sixteen combinations may at first sight seem odd, but all are usually worth considering. A strategist should not exclude any of them in principle. The only thing that matters is whether customers exist who at a given set of relative prices would prefer any given cell to all the others. In fact some of the less obvious combinations may be the most rewarding. Unusual offerings are often the most profitable. At the same time, the more unexpected a strategy is, the more will it catch the competition off balance.

This full range of competitive strategies can be illustrated in many ways. Carpets will serve as our illustration. To bring out the richness of this framework we make the simplifying assumption that the markets are close to public ones. For the same reason some of the 16 cases will carry an element of caricature.

Carpets come in a multitude of varieties. They range from cheap mass-produced goods to hand-crafted Persian and Chinese rugs, imported for Millionaire's Row. In our categories, they vary from standard to exclusive merchandise. Somewhere between these extremes are well-known brands and heavy duty carpets: augmented and special merchandise.

The same infinite variety is found in the support dimension. At one end is the no-frills barrow boy in the street market, the discount store or auction house; and at the other end there are the interior designers who will advise on the overall design, supply and fit the carpets and underlays, and then clean and restore them for years. The variety ranges from trader to consultant. Between the extremes is the willing and smiling shop assistant, the agent and the specialist fitter and adviser.

Figure 5.5 illustrates the 16 permutations of the two subclassifications, i.e. the 16 possible types of differentiation.

The odder the better?

Some of these combinations may at first sight appear improbable. One example is the fourth row: *exclusive/trader*. Yet there

Generic strategy	Merchandise		Support		Illustration
	Aura	Content	Expertise	Personalization	
Exclusive consultant	H	H	H	H	Hand-woven with full support (including aftercare).
Exclusive specialist	H	H	H	L	Hand-woven; technical help with choice, fitting.
Exclusive agent	H	H	L	H	Quality carpets; delivered, attentive staff, no other support.
Exclusive trader	H	H	L	L	Market traders selling quality carpets fallen off backs of lorries.
Special consultant	L	H	H	H	Heavy duty carpets, full contract support.
Special specialist	L	H	H	L	Heavy duty carpets; technical help with choice, fitting.
Special agent	L	H	L	H	Heavy duty carpets, delivered attentive staff, no other support.
Special trader	L	H	L	L	Heavy duty carpets only sold, not delivered.
Augmented consultant	H	L	H	H	Branded carpets, full support.
Augmented specialist	H	L	H	L	Branded carpets; technical help with choice, fitting.
Augmented agent	H	L	L	H	Branded carpets, attentive, helpful staff.
Augmented trader	H	L	L	L	Branded carpets, no delivery.
Standard consultant	L	L	H	H	Basic carpets with full support.
Standard specialist	L	L	H	L	Basic carpets; technical help with choice, fitting.
Standard agent	L	L	L	H	Basic carpets, attentive, helpful staff.
Standard trader	L	L	L	L	Basic carpets, no delivery.

H = high, L = low degree of differentiation

Figure 5.5 *Illustration of 16-cell matrix of generic competitive strategies: carpet supply and support*

are a number of auction houses that sell handwoven carpets with minimal support. Nor is it unheard of in London to find open-air markets with quality carpets 'fallen off the back of a lorry'. Any irregularity in the transaction would not preclude such differentiation.

Again the thirteenth row, *standard/consultant*, may raise eyebrows. Yet such suppliers exist. They target customers who are willing to pay for support, but are content with a basic carpet. These customers might include retired gentle-folk or seaside guesthouses.

None of this is mere theory. We may find one of these less obvious combinations highly profitable to adopt, or at least we should be prepared for others to adopt it, to the detriment of our own business. Forewarned is forearmed.

Advertising and differentiation

This may be the most convenient place to discuss the place of advertising. **Advertising** does not merely draw attention to the *existence* of an offering. It also seeks to influence the way it is perceived by potential buyers and therefore its *positioning*. It is essentially a tactical operation, because its relatively fleeting impact inevitably means that it occurs when an offering is already on the market or immediately about to be on the market. Nevertheless when a new offering is strategically designed, there needs to be a plan for noti-fying customers of its advent and for any direct attempts to influence its reception. That process is instrumental to the positioning of the offering, and is to that extent strategic.

Advertising can of course also be used in an effort to re-position an existing offering. However, in the terminology of this book, that repositioning creates a new offering. That use of advertising is essentially part of the same strategic process as the offering's 'first' positioning.

Advertising has two distinct strategic purposes. The first is to draw attention to the new offering, i.e. to how its merchandise and support are differentiated from substitutes. Its purpose is to inform the customer of the offering's distinc-tively attractive output-features. Thus insurance companies

119

may differentiate their support by advertising the quick response and helpfulness of their claims department. Suppliers of other financial offerings might stress the expertise of their trained 'advisers'. Makers of automobiles might seek to highlight their merchandise differentiation by advertising safety features or space for passengers and luggage. Pepsi may advertise that it 'tastes better'.

The second use is a direct shaping of customers' perceptions and preferences, not indirectly via the offering itself. It is an effort to influence perceptions in a way which does not necessarily involve actual experience of the offering. When advertising is directed at aura, it evidently tends to be of this kind. It might for example aim at influencing customers to think of themselves as 'green' or as having a gracious or healthy[10] life-style. Thus it may be claimed that perfume X or car Y will make a statement about a woman's independence, that a coffee brand Z will make the consumer irresistible to a neighbour, that detergent S will signify that mother cares, or that T brand of sports shoes will convey the prowess of the Olympic gold medallist who promotes it. In cold print these claims may look less than rational, but the essentially irrational psychology of aura advertising can at times be very effective. Witness the innovative Californian motorcycle campaign claiming that 'you meet the nicest people on a Honda'.

Summary

This chapter has presented the classification of differentiation in the support and merchandise dimensions. It serves to show the richness of the available competitive options. This is by no means universally appreciated.

How the strategist should select between these options, depends on the capabilities of the business and on the relative profitability of each strategy. These matters are discussed in Chapters 8 to 12.

Notes

1. The ideas presented in this chapter were developed in Mathur (1984), (1988), (1992).
2. See Chapter 6.
3. The expression 'price premium' must in this type of context mean the ability to raise the price as a consequence of differentiation. See e.g. Porter (1985) p. 130 and his definition of differentiation as aimed at reducing price sensitivity in Porter (1980) p. 38. A price premium therefore here means the amount by which a price can be raised as a result of a decision to differentiate an offering. Raised by comparison with what? The reference point must strictly be the price that could be charged in the alternative strategy with which the decision compares the strategy concerned. That alternative could for example be to leave the present offering unchanged, or it could be the seller's next best strategy. Decision criteria always compare the results of one decision with those of some alternative decision. Chapter 6 will clarify that the words 'differentiated' and 'differentiation' are in this book used as technical strategic terms which refer to the act of differentiating and the positioning which results from it. An offering can in this sense be *different* from substitutes without being 'differentiated'.
4. Chapter 6 notes that personalization is one of a number of subdimensions which may predominantly, but not invariably, be perceived by customers as differentiating an offering along a single scale: attention to individual customers' personal needs and preferences. This is in contrast to content, for example, where the predominant perceptions are likely to be multidimensional rather than single-scale. In the multidimensional case it is far more difficult ex ante to rank the price sensitivity of offerings.
5. Part Four discusses why offerings need protective armour against encroachment by competitors and how that armour is obtained.
6. Expertise too, like personalization, may be predominantly – but not invariably – seen by customers as a single-scale phenomenon.
7. That advantage of size could in some circumstances amount to a case for increased market share. That topic is critically explored in Chapter 8.
8. See N. Craig Smith (1990), especially Chapter 6 pp 175 onwards and the other texts quoted there.
9. Craig Smith (1990).
10. Dickson and Ginter (1987).

6 Competitive strategy: (c) Differentiation and price

Introduction

Chapter 5 has given us a richer and more detailed understanding of differentiation as the means of positioning an offering. This was done by classifying the various modes in which an offering can attract different groups of customers.

The present chapter seeks to clarify three topics, all of which advance our understanding of the nature of differentiation:

1 The need to think in customer-centred output, not input terms.
2 Differentiation's purpose of making the offering less price-sensitive by distancing it from its substitutes. This topic raises some related sub-topics:

   (a) The two types of distancing, single-scale (i.e. up-down) and multidimensional.
   (b) The difficulties inherent in (i) treating differentiation as occurring along just a single up-down scale and (ii) treating that scale as measuring just a single all-embracing attribute: 'quality'.
   (c) The very successful new offering.

3 A review of the various strategic roles and characteristics of prices.

Most of these issues have a tendency to cause misunderstandings, which in their turn have led to poor, and sometimes disastrous decisions.

Managers need to think in terms of customers and outputs

First the centrality of outputs. Chapter 4 defined differentiation as resulting in a distance or remoteness of an offering from its competing substitutes. As this distance is what choosing customers see, it must be a matter of the offering's outputs, i.e. of the output features which influence customers' choices.

It is not its intrinsic nature, but its external positioning that defines an offering or its competitive strategy. The four generic forms of differentiation in Figure 5.1 illustrate this. They apply no less to intangible offerings ('services') such as unit trusts, cheque accounts or laundry services than to tangible offerings ('products') like computers, light bulbs, or timber.

In other words, the most fundamental and powerful distinction that competitive strategy must make, is between inputs and outputs, first introduced in Chapter 3. Yet that distinction is by no means universally made by managers. Most people find it hard to break themselves away from a mind-set, in fact from a language, which concentrates on inputs. One even comes across managers who lay claim to differentiation on the mere grounds that they are doing something differently, either from competitors or even from what they themselves were doing before. It is so easy to ignore the viewpoint of the choosing customer. That resistance to an output language is not surprising: inputs are what managers can and therefore must control.

Even writers on marketing[1] have been known to classify the subject of marketing by input-, or even production-based categories. The categories in Table 6.1 are typical of those commonly used.

Such categories are sometimes put forward as if they each required entirely different competitive insights. However, they are input distinctions. They concern how the offering is produced and delivered. Inputs tell us something about offerings, but cannot give insights into competitive issues, because competition is for customers, and customers choose only outputs, not inputs.

Table 6.1 Classifying offerings in input terms

Category	*Common characteristics*
Services	Intangibility
Financial services	Need special resources and skills
Capital goods	Need special sales procedures

The irrelevance of these categories to competition for customers is plain to see. Business schools and credit cards both provide intangible services, but they do not compete with one another. On the other hand, the local courier faces competition not only from other sellers of intangibles, like another courier, but also from sellers of tangibles like fax machines. Categories like intangibles are not designed to illuminate the nature of markets or competitive issues.

Fallacies prompted by an input language

In order to ensure a focus on outputs, Chapter 5 attached the suffix '-buy' to the generic forms of differentiation in Figure 5.1. Without that suffix, the terms 'system', 'product', 'service', and 'commodity' in common parlance describe input features of offerings. Without '-buy' they therefore carry the limitations inherent in an input language and an input mode of thought.[2]

Input thinking has been responsible for a lot of muddled thinking. British bankers commonly call retail banking a 'service'. They mean that they are selling something non-physical. That may be helpful, but not in the context of competition. The customer does not choose an account with Chase Bank because it offers something intangible: *all* competing offerings are equally intangible. What concerns the customer is how an account with Chase varies from its available substitutes. If customers see them as uniform in both the merchandise and support dimensions, they are conducting an undifferentiated, i.e. commodity-buy transaction, comparing only charges and rates.

Financial services provide a particularly rich vein of this type of fallacy. It is easy to confuse homogeneous financial instruments with the varied ways in which they can be sold. Thus the UK trader who wishes to buy yen payables forward, can shop around for the best rate, commodity-buy fashion. On the other hand, that trader may prefer to use a bank or broker which gives advice on when to buy, for what forward date to buy (in case the goods are delayed), or whether to buy spot rather than forward, and invest the yen until they are needed. For this the bank or broker may charge a higher bid-offer spread around the same exchange rate. The broker has conducted a service-buy transaction. The differentiated offering provided by the bank or broker is quite distinct from the undifferentiated instrument, the forward yen/sterling contract.

Security companies who market a domestic burglar alarm system with its sensors, flashing lights, sirens and digital software tend to stress the word 'system'. In their input language they are trying to convey that they are selling a sophisticated package which it took a lot of skills to make. Sales staff like the sense of prestige of the word 'system'. However, if the package were undifferentiated from substitutes in both the merchandise and support dimensions, then in an output language it would be offered as a 'commodity-buy'. Customers would choose purely on price.

'Product' too is generally used in an input sense. We can illustrate this again with the four-wheel drive Land Rover. It is natural to think of this as a single 'product'. After all, it is assembled on a single production line. However, this is an extreme case of an input language. The last thing to occupy a choosing customer's mind is the single production line. As we saw in Chapter 3, the 'single product' can be offered in two very different markets with a different positioning in each. In the market for work-horses, a basic model, the Defender, could be offered as a commodity-buy, chosen mainly on the grounds of price. However, in the market for quality cars a better-trimmed version, the Discovery, is offered as a product-buy, distinguished from competing luxury cars by its spaciousness and as a more distinctive status symbol. The input term 'product' may blind managers to the fact that these are two separate offerings, with different customers and competitors, and requiring quite different competitive strategies.

Our final example is what is commonly called a 'commodity'. An input language might regard as 'commodities' all offerings which happen to result from mature or simple production processes. Input-minded people might for example contrast paper clips with photocopiers. Paperclips sound just like a commodity, and photocopying installations just like a system. Yet some customers want to buy plastic paperclips of unusual size from a seller who treats them like a personal friend: that is a system-buy. Similarly we saw that there are some who buy photocopiers – widely regarded as systems – like a commodity, making their choice purely on price: in output language those customers are conducting a 'commodity-buy' transaction. The input language has served to obliterate the competitive output features of these offerings.

These examples show the advantage of the extra precision which our output language gains by means of the suffix '-buy'. Each of the four generic forms of differentiation in Figure 5.1 represents a special type of triangular relationship between an offering and its customers and competitors. Each of them can be selected for any kind of business: paper clips can be offered and bought as system-buys and domestic burglar alarm 'systems' as commodity-buys.

Words are powerful management tools. For example, experience shows how hard it is to see our own business as customers see it. A customer-centred output language makes this a lot easier. It forces us to think of our own offerings as choosing customers see them.

The input-output distinction: conclusion

It should now be evident how vital it is to look at each offering with a clear distinction between:

- how it looks to customers, and
- the seller's concerns of costs, resources and competences.

126

The manager who fails to focus on an offering's outputs, is apt to fall into the trap of designing an offering which looks attractive to everybody except the customers.

This focus on the choosing customer is the crux. The triangular relationship between the offering, its customers and its competitors is central. The job is to *design* the offering so that it will be preferred by the targeted customers, at a price attractive to the company. That means mapping out those output features, those benefits and drawbacks of the offering which influence a customer's choice. They exclude the *inputs*, such as the materials, labour, production and distribution processes, the culture, resources and skills. Inputs make up what a seller offers, but do not directly influence the customer's choice. Inputs may play a key role in *shaping* a competitive position,[3] but outputs *define* it: define what influences the customer.

The practical benefits of the distinction to managers can be listed and illustrated as follows:

- It discourages the fallacy that a superior input must automatically be preferred; for example, having twice as many waiters hovering around customers in a restaurant: diners might prefer more privacy.
- It reminds us to value inputs for their outputs: how will a change of material, e.g. from wood to plastic, affect buying decisions, or is it our new glossy, laser-printed wrappers that sway customers' choices for or against our offering?
- It highlights that some output changes might make an offering more attractive to customers, yet require minimal inputs and costs: e.g. adding a blue colouring agent to a washing powder.

Differentiation: why and how?

The second topic of the chapter revolves around the purpose of differentiation. When the term was defined in Chapter 4, its two faces were noted. Its 'how' face distances an offering from its substitutes as described in Chapter 5. Its 'why' face explains the purpose of that distancing: to make customers less price-sensitive in their buying decisions. This 'why' face is now developed in this chapter.

To differentiate an offering is to reduce its vulnerability to price competition by distancing its non-price outputs from those of substitutes. 'Differentiated' thus has to be used in business strategy as a technical term, meaning *'made less price sensitive'*. It follows that much ambiguity is saved if 'differentiated' is not also used to mean merely 'different' from substitutes. If a planned offering is very different from its future substitutes, and our strategy is to reposition it where it is only a little less different, but cheaper, then the strategy is one of price competition. The resulting position of the offering is still very different, but not 'differentiated' in this strict language.[4]

Previous chapters have discussed differentiation largely in terms of its 'how' face, of distance from substitutes. Its 'why' face, its purpose of shifting customer decisions away from price comparisons, was largely left on one side. Price is, however, one of the two main categories of outputs, along with differentiation. Together they position the offering. Prices clearly play a part in the choices made by customers, and are therefore outputs. They are the only outputs which do not differentiate one offering from another.[5]

The relationship between differentiation and price sensitivity is discussed here in Chapter 6 on the assumption that competition takes place in a fragmented market in which no small group of dominant sellers need to anticipate and watch one another's moves. The presence of such a dominant group is known as 'oligopoly' or 'circularity': this will be discussed in Chapter 7.

Distance and price sensitivity

The 'how' face, distance from substitutes, is the effect of endowing the offering with distinctive outputs, using the subdimensions illustrated in Chapter 5. The resulting picture is best visualized in the galaxy of Figure 4.5. An offering positioned in a relatively empty part of galactic space, can be more distant from substitutes, and thus more differentiated. This should make it less price-sensitive than an offering in a more crowded part.

The 'why' face of differentiation, its purpose, gives the seller greater freedom in pricing the offering, making its sales volume less vulnerable for example to price-cutting by competitors. In stepping up the degree of differentiation of our offering, we not only make it more distant from its substitutes: we above all make it more immune to price competition. Differentiation may enable us to improve our margins for any given volume of sales. This has brought us to the central theme of this chapter, the effect of differentiation on pricing freedom.

Price sensitivity is in economic language called price elasticity, which is related to the slope of the demand curve. It can be measured as the effect of a unit price change on the volume of sales of a given offering. It is clearly governed by how distant the offering is not from individual substitutes, but from the collectivity of all its significant substitutes.[6] Appendix 6.1 presents an algebraic formula for assessing the overall price sensitivity of an offering from its price sensitivity to each significant substitute.

The more differentiated an offering is, the less will customers compare prices when choosing between it and its competitors. At the extreme ends of the spectrum, the picture is very clear. When an offering is entirely undifferentiated – the pure commodity-buy case – customers compare prices only, and there will only be one price at which the offering can be sold. Sellers have in this case no latitude in setting prices. On the other hand, if we assume an offering to be infinitely differentiated – i.e. with no substitutes: the pure monopoly case – customers cannot compare prices at all.[7] Latitude in setting prices is very wide at this end of the spectrum.

Clearly those extreme cases are rare. In most competitive situations customers pay some degree of attention to prices and some to differentiation between substitutes.

Differentiation is a distancing designed to reduce the price sensitivity of the offering. There is however a sense in which offerings can be distanced with no such intention. For example where the strategist decides to go for cost reduction and price competition, that move is a negation of differentiation, and outside its definition. If Uzbekistan Airlines undercuts its competitors on the London–Delhi route by extending its unpopular stopover in Tashkent so as to cut costs, it deliberately makes its offering cheaper and less attractive in its non-price dimensions. Its strategy is one of price competition: the opposite of differentiation. The fact that the offering has now (price apart) become even more unattractive by comparison with its competitors, is just a by-product of that strategy.

Most competitive positionings involve some tradeoff between differentiation and price competition. However, it is important for the seller to be alert to the management implications of the extent to which each of these two elements influences how customers choose. Differentiation requires attention to the distinctiveness of the outputs. Price competition on the other hand requires an emphasis on unit cost control. Distinctiveness *can* go with lower unit costs, but that is not a universal pattern. Alertness is vital in many companies where quality and costs are the responsibilities of different sets of people.

Single-scale and multidimensional differentiation

Differentiation is sometimes loosely discussed as though it occurred on a measurable scale, and was thus just a matter of degree. It is as though all we have to do to see how differentiated an offering is, is to measure its distance from some reference point.

That view makes a number of assumptions. For the moment we are concerned with just one, which is that differentiation distances an offering in a single dimension, such as how long it takes to deliver a pizza. That is one kind of differentiation, but there is also multidimensional differentiation, where the various substitutes can be distant from the offering in an infinite number of directions. The boxed illustration shows this in simplified form.

Illustration: an automobile model

A competing set of car models differs in just three distinguishing features:

A: automatic transmission,
B: side impact protection system (SIPS),
C: catalytic converter.

Different models may have ABC, AB, AC, BC, A, B, C, or none of them, a total of eight multidimensional permutations. There may be a plausible hypothesis (but no more) that Model 1 with ABC will turn out the least, and Model 8 with none of the features the most price sensitive, but there is no telling how Models 2–4 with AB, AC and BC for example will rank in price sensitiveness. The problems are:

• Price sensitiveness requires a measure along a single scale or dimension, whereas the distancing features are in this illustration multidimensional.

• Price sensitivity can be tested by test marketing an offering at various prices and noting the effect of price changes on the volume of sales. No such cold, objective test is available to measure distances from other offerings, but attitude surveys can at least rank the substitutes, and may succeed in obtaining some rough measure of distances.

• The distancing process can treat the offering and each of its substitutes as a pair, and assess the distance within each pair, whereas price sensitivity is meaningful only for the offering as such: it results from the way the offering with features AB (say) is positioned against the collectivity of all seven of its significant substitutes in this illustration. After all, the offering can only have a single price, which confronts all its competing substitutes.

Our automobile illustration is of course an example of merchandise[8] differentiation. If differentiation were entirely in the dimension of support, and more particularly personalization, it would be much easier to assess the distance between offerings and rank their likely price sensitivities. That is because personalization comes much closer than merchandise differentiation to being a matter of a single, unidirectional scale.[9]

The case where offerings lie along a single scale can be called 'rankable' distancing, and the case where there is no such single scale 'non-rankable'. The price sensitivities of the offerings cannot in those cases (as in the automobile example) easily be ranked ex ante. Rankability can serve as a shorthand way of distinguishing the two kinds of distancing. Either of them runs the risk of making the offering more price sensitive, but that outcome would by definition run counter to the purpose of differentiation.

Sometimes offerings are easily rankable. For example, the customer may perceive an offering as being either more or less well adapted to his or her personal needs or preferences, or delivered with a greater or lesser degree of expertise. Where offerings are not easily rankable, each offering simply has qualitatively different features, as when one laptop computer is lighter and the other faster.

The real world is of course too variegated to permit us to simply equate support differentiation with single-scale and merchandise with multidimensional differentiation. Personalization or expertise for example can occur along an unlimited number of dimensions, and customers may see it as a multidimensional process, whereas merchandise differentiation such as content may be along a single scale such as the reliability of cars. However, these are not the usual cases.

The interrelationship between the two kinds of distancing, differentiation and price sensitivity, is represented by Figure 6.1.

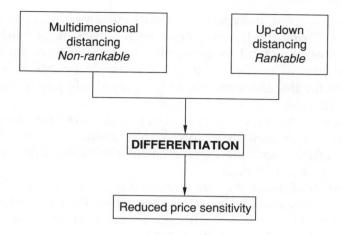

Figure 6.1 Differentiation, distancing and price sensitivity

Differentiation is indirect and uncertain

While the example of the automobile is still fresh in mind, we do well to digress briefly to reflect on the hazardous nature of the differentiation process.

First, when we plan to position a new offering in relation to its substitutes, we must of course map out *tomorrow's* substitutes and where tomorrow's customers, not today's will see them. Tomorrow is shorthand for the period during which our new offering will be available to customers. This is usually after a time-lag during which the new competitive strategy and its positioning is prepared and implemented. Today's competitors and their positions in their markets are irrelevant. It follows that the competitive positioning that we intend, may not be the one that we shall achieve. We have to do our best to anticipate possible shifts on the part of customers and competitors, but we cannot be sure that they will not nevertheless surprise us. This timing issue is developed in greater detail in Chapter 8.

The uncertainties and complexities which confront the strategist, are in fact the following:

133

- As just noted, unexpected shifts by customers and competitors during the time-lag between the decision to market a new offering, and its availability to customers. A 'shift' on the part of customers may for example be one towards care for the environment, or towards single-parent households.
- Even if the intervening shifts of customers and competitors were accurately foreseeable, there are long odds against an accurate assessment of the future price sensitivity of our offering.
- Our confidence in our expectation of customers' price sensitivity must be especially low where the differentiation is multidimensional, with no common measure of comparability between substitutes.

The causal chain between the decision to differentiate and the achievement of any specific degree of price sensitivity is therefore neither simple nor certain nor direct.

Together, these three sources of uncertainty form an important part of the risks of enterprise.

Differentiation seen as occurring along a quality scale

After this brief digression it is worth reviewing a popular variant of the single-scale view of differentiation. Managers sometimes discuss differentiation as though it simply meant distancing offerings along a *quality* scale: as if going upmarket meant more differentiation, going downmarket less. A more differentiated offering attracts greater buyer preferences and can command a higher price. Moreover, moving up or down this scale is seen as a complete description of the act of differentiating: any five-star hotel is thus by definition 'differentiated'!

We have seen earlier in this chapter that there certainly is such a thing as differentiation along a single scale. It is the up and down or rankable case. Offering A may well be seen by customers as more personalized, or as offered with greater skill and experience, than offering B. However, the language which simply characterizes differentiation as targeting better quality, has the following drawbacks:

- First, no single scale is appropriate in the large number of cases where competition is in non-rankable or multi-attribute form. That was illustrated by the automobile example. A three-star hotel may be differentiated by its lake with wildfowl.
- Secondly, the language is unhelpful even where customers see a clear and evident quality scale. This might be the percentage of real fresh lime juice in a lime squash drink. Even here it is little use to the strategist to describe the scale as just 'quality'. The strategist needs a specific description, indicating for example the proportion of fresh lime or perhaps of 'fruit'. 'Quality' is not a practical specification.
- Thirdly, even where there is a single scale, and even where this can be identified with a specific attribute like (say) the sugar content of milk chocolate, the direction in which that attribute is seen by customers as driving quality, is not always unambiguous. Some may associate more sugar, some less sugar, with better quality.[10]

The difficulty with this quality-scale language is the vagueness, and indeed the emptiness of the term 'quality'. If tax adviser A is less expert than B, but more personalized, is A 'better' or 'worse'? Differentiation needs a much sharper, less cavalier language than this.

However, worse is yet to come. Practitioners sometimes extend this language so as to call an offering either differentiated or undifferentiated,[11] as if differentiation were a 'yes/no', rather than a 'how much?' concept.

That yes/no usage, and some variants of it, implies some arbitrary fixed, perhaps notional point of origin for the quality scale. The Ford Escort might be taken as the undifferentiated 'norm', and anything 'better' than the Escort is differentiated. Among many absurdities, how would this language deal with a car of lesser quality than the Escort, such as the Lada or the infamous East German Trabant? Is the Lada *negatively* differentiated?

135

Moreover, the mentality which sees differentiation largely in relation to some fixed, but possibly distant point of reference, may well run the risk of omitting to concentrate on the offering's closest substitutes. If we are more concerned about being a five- rather than three-star hotel in London, we may forget to watch our closest rivals in the five-star category.

The view here argued is that:

- differentiation may distance offerings along a single scale, but does not do this invariably or perhaps even predominantly;
- even when differentiation is along a single up-down scale, that scale does not identify which of the many possible attributes it represents. A clear language must pinpoint the attribute, not just refer to 'quality'; and
- differentiation must always be a relative term: it uses no universally fixed point of origin, because each offering is its own point of reference.

To sum this up, customers do see offerings as being of different quality, but quality as such is not the primary scale on which they make their comparison. In any case differentiation is often or perhaps usually non-rankable. It does not invariably distance offerings on a single up-down scale. Moreover it is inherently a relative, not an absolute concept.

Very successful new offerings

All this is still part of the second topic discussed in this chapter. The last of the sub-topics raised by the interrelation between differentiation and price-sensitivity, concerns the phenomenon that some new offerings are immediately very successful. They have some mix of price advantage and differentiation which enables them to displace most previous suppliers in their part of the galaxy.

Table 6.2 illustrates this discussion with three theoretical cases. In each of the three cases a new offering – A^1, A^2 or A^3 – wins the bulk of what was offering B's market. B stands

Table 6.2 *Illustration of price sensitivity*

Percentage of B's market captured when new offering launched at:

	(1) B's price	(2) B's price less 20 per cent
A^1	5%	60%
A^2	70%	95%
A^3	99%	99%

for a number of displaced offerings, so as to simplify the discussion.

We further assume that each of the new offerings A^1, A^2 and A^3 is launched either (1) at the same price as B or (2) at a 20 per cent discount to B's price.

Table 6.2 shows that at the 80 per cent price (a 20 per cent discount to B's price) all three new offerings would largely displace B at its present price. On the other hand without any discount, at 100 per cent of B's price, only A^2 and A^3 could achieve that result: A^1 would capture only a fraction of B's market.

A^1 might be an Amstrad computer or MFI furniture. At B's price very few customers would prefer it, but at a 20 per cent lower price a majority of customers will buy it. The price sensitivity of these customers is evidently fairly high. Sixty per cent of them prefer the 20 per cent discount to B's better quality.

A^2 might be a quartz watch, the accuracy and convenience of which will be preferred by the vast majority to the watch with a mechanical movement, even at the same price. At a 20 per cent discount it will sweep the market.

A^3 would sweep the market even at B's price. Perhaps this is the pocket calculator which has displaced heavy and bulky calculating machines and comptometers.[12]

Some new offerings like A^1 evidently have a much more price-sensitive market than others like A^3, while offerings like A^2 occupy intermediate positions.

All this is only an illustration: even if we launched the new offering at either 80 per cent or 100 per cent of B's price, we should not know how many customers would in each case have bought the new offering at the other level.

In practice the strategist needs to be very clear about the intended dominant character of the strategy: is it to be differentiation or price competition? If the answer is differentiation, success depends predominantly on the offering and its attributes. If price competition, then cost control is the critical issue.

The only safe presumption is that if an offering is to be sold below the comparable prices of substitutes, the case is one of price competition. That presumption is however rebuttable in a particular case. The Honda motor-cycle in around 1970 had two huge attractions in the US market. It was lighter and cheaper than the machines it displaced. It might have been a differentiated case like A^3 or a price competition case like A^1. In the differentiated case of A^3 it would have enjoyed very low price sensitivity until competitors were able to compete with a similar machine at a similar price.

The cheaper and better offering

Customers evidently find A^3 much more attractively positioned than the old offering B. The same may conceivably even be true of A^2.

In the long run at least they cannot be offered at 20 per cent less than B unless their unit costs are correspondingly lower. Such a lower cost *and* better offering would be very profitable, but for how long? Once competitors become aware that the more popular offering can be produced at a cost way below that of their own existing offerings, they will rush to imitate the new offering and its production technology. If they succeed, they will reduce the sales of the innovator, squeeze its margins, and thus jeopardize the innovator's ability to recover the cost of capital of the pioneering innovation.[13] Even if the innovator wins, that is likely to be by means of major reductions in price and profit. First movers have an advantage with customers. Second movers may have the advantage of saving some of the first mover's learning and experimentation costs.

In other words, even with such an improbably favourable set of assumptions, this competitive strategy may fall short of being viable. It will be viable only if the innovating company can harvest high margins for long enough to amortize its investment at the appropriate cost of capital.

The strategy will be much more durable if there are impediments to imitation. These amount to market failures in the resources needed to bring the cheaper and better offering to the market.[14] Perhaps the most spectacular example is Japanese motor-cycles in the late 1960s. A competitor like Honda was able to remain a market leader for such a long time because it had a unique ability to continue innovating and differentiating its offerings.[15]

However, what matters most about the cheaper-to-produce and better offering is that the combination is inherently unstable and rare. The sustainably successful cheaper *and* better offering is not completely impossible, but neither can it be a common occurrence.

The strategic role of price

1 Differentiation and price: differentiation is more fundamental

The final topic of this chapter concerns the various strategic roles and characteristics of price. The positioning of an offering consists of deciding both its differentiation and its price. From the point of view of the manager, differentiation is the more fundamental of these two elements. As differentiation governs the price sensitivity of an offering, it is both a precondition and a source of whatever freedom the seller has in setting prices. It governs the extent to which the seller can have a pricing policy. Chapter 8 will set out how this can be used strategically.

A second practical reason for regarding differentiation as more fundamental than price lies in the time-scale.

Differentiation has to be planned some way ahead. It cannot normally be changed tactically. Prices on the other hand can be changed much faster. Retailers regularly reduce prices at the end of a season in a bargain sale so as to reduce their inventories. So whereas differentiation is always a strategic tool, i.e. always targeted at future positioning, price is a tactical as well as a strategic weapon.

This prompts two reflections:

- The lesser the degree of differentiation, the smaller is the seller's scope for a pricing policy. A strategist's freedom to set prices varies with the degree of achieved differentiation.
- The more price matters, the less control the seller has over it.

2 Perceived prices

How do customers compare prices? This may sound simple. However, it has been established that customers compare perceived, not actual, prices.[16] In any case, price is an output, and we saw earlier in this chapter that outputs consist of what influences customers' choices. Customers may be making mental comparisons which are either poorly informed or which distort available information. The obstacles to realistic price comparisons can be either lack of information about prices, or impediments in the customer's mind. Between these two ends of the spectrum, there can be a mixture of the two causes at any intermediate point.

Impediments occur in customers' minds when they have strong images of differences in quality. Thus they may believe that a nationwide plumbing business, with liveried vans that can be instantly summoned, would charge a lot more than the local handyman who responds at his leisure. Yet the nationwide business may be the cheaper of the two.

Lack of information about prices typically occurs where offerings depend strongly on technical or scientific complexity or on the human characteristics of the person or persons who make up and deliver the offering, and often on the

140

character and circumstances of each client. Price comparisons are notoriously difficult for automobile servicing and repairs, jobbing builders and business consultancy.

3 Price as an instrument of differentiation

The difficulty in comparing prices of some intangible offerings brings us to an exception to the normal relationship, in which differentiation governs pricing freedom. There is a special set of circumstances in which pricing policy can itself be used as an instrument of differentiation. In such a case price is not just an output, but also a factor which shapes another output: differentiation. This can occur where price is a significant indicator of quality to a choosing customer. It is possible only where customers are short of other, more objective criteria.

These conditions are sometimes met with tangible offerings. Too low a price for a second-hand car or perfume may – quite unfairly – signal inferior quality. However, they are much more common in intangible offerings, of which professional services are typical. A strategy consultant who charges more than others, may thereby signal a degree of differentiation to a potential client. Similarly a tax consultant, a dentist or an architect. The price charged may influence and shape the client's perception of the quality of the offering. A higher price makes it more attractive, improves its apparent content, aura, expertise or personalization. Clients do not brag that they take advice from the cheapest strategy consultant: they may not even consider one whose fees are at the lower end of the scale.

Recapitulating the characteristics of price

Price therefore has five important characteristics:

- The range within which a seller is free to set prices is normally constrained by the chosen level of differentiation, but within that constraint it gives the seller valuable strategic and tactical flexibility.

- With a given level of differentiation, the chosen price governs the volume of sales: what the seller must aim for is not just a price, but a profitable price/volume combination.[17]
- Price can in certain conditions itself be a means of differentiating.
- Price is a tactical as well as a strategic weapon.
- What affects choices, is perceived, not actual prices.

Chapter 4 defined differentiation as the 'principal' means of positioning an offering in relation to its actual and potential customers and competitors. To whatever extent the degree of differentiation gives the strategist latitude to pursue a pricing policy, price is the other means. Between them, differentiation and price define the positioning of the offering. We have seen that the pricing weapon is not wholly independent of differentiation, as the limits within which the competitor has discretion over price, are set by the degree of differentiation.[18]

Summary

Chapter 6 has delved more deeply into the nature of differentiation. Its three parts reviewed the importance of thinking in terms of outputs, differentiation's purpose of making the offering less price-sensitive by distancing it from substitutes, and the various roles and characteristics of price.

The heart of the message is the interrelation between differentiating the offering and making it less price-sensitive. This is an indirect and complex relationship. It can occur on a single rankable scale. Alternatively it can be non-rankable, where customers see the offering as different, but not along a single scale.

This is the essence of the task of differentiating an offering. A thorough understanding of its nature and complexity will help managers to see their competitive strategies in the correct competitive context.

* * *

Appendix 6.1[19]

Assessing the overall price sensitivity of an offering from its price sensitivity to each significant substitute

The objective is to relate the own-price elasticity of demand for a potential future offering to the cross-price elasticities of demand for all other offerings.

Step 1 is to define a budget constraint

$$\sum_{i}^{n} P_i D_i = Y$$

where Y = income, P_i = price of offering i, D_i = demand for offering i.

To obtain the own-price elasticity of demand for offering j, defined as a positive number, *Step 2* is to differentiate the budget constraint totally with respect to P_j, and *Step 3* is to solve for the own-price elasticity of demand for offering j. For example, the own-price elasticity of demand for offering 1 is:

$$1 + \frac{s_2 \epsilon_{21} + s_3 \epsilon_{31} + s_4 \epsilon_{41} + \ldots s_n \epsilon_{n1}}{s_1}$$

$s_j = (P_j D_j)/Y$ = share of offering j in total expenditure, ϵ_{ij} = the cross elasticity of demand for offering i to the price of offering j.

Notes

1. For example, Thomas (1978). For a review of such discussions in marketing theory see Sheth, Gardner and Garrett (1988), Chapter 1.
2. Mathur (1992).
3. Part Four will show how some inputs, called 'key resources', can play a decisive role.
4. This strict language may sound difficult, but alternative sets of strict definitions would cause even more difficulty. In practice the difficulty is confined to the fairly unusual case where a strategy

of price competition leaves an offering still very different (but a little less different than it would otherwise have been) from substitutes.

5. Because in this book differentiation is defined as concerning a non-price dimension. Later in this chapter we discuss the case where price is not of course a non-price output, but signals such an output.

6. Consequently, when an offering is in this strict usage 'differentiated', this does not merely mean that it is *different*. A differentiated offering is different:

   (a) from the collectivity of its competing substitutes, and
   (b) by being positioned at a distance from that collectivity with the object of making it less price-sensitive.

   Neither of these conditions are needed to make it merely 'different' or distant. It can be 'different' from any single offering or group of them, and without the motive of greater pricing freedom.

7. This limiting case is clearly not a possible one, because ultimately there can be no offering that has absolutely no substitute, as all offerings compete for customers' finite purchasing power.

   In any case, the proximity of substitutes is not the only influence on the price sensitivity of an offering. That ratio also varies for example with (a) income, and (b) the intensity of the buyer's need.

8. Chapter 5 discusses the dimensions of differentiation, such as merchandise differentiation.

9. This is of course not wholly true, because even personalization can pay more or less attention to different features of importance to customers. Nevertheless the overall degree of attention lends itself to some generalization: the customer can apply a scale showing how closely the offering matches his or her preferences.

10. Quality in this book simply means what customers are willing to pay more for. Some authorities have argued for more restricted usages, such as 'conformance to requirement' (Crosby, 1979) or 'fitness for intended purpose' (Price, 1990). These authors are associated with the concept of 'total quality management' and are anxious to divorce the term 'quality' from 'grade'. This is not the common usage of 'quality', nor is it the one used here.

11. 'Undifferentiated' was defined in Chapter 4 as describing offerings regarded by customers as homogeneous, so that customers choose entirely on price.

12. All these comparisons are between the new cheaper offerings A^1, A^2 and A^3 on the one hand and the old offering B. No doubt the destabilizing effect of the new offerings will bring new competitive offerings into contention. Thereafter A^1, A^2 and A^3 may be

little or greatly differentiated from their new substitutes, but nothing has been said about that.
13. In Chapter 10 this will be called a success-aping process.
14. This point anticipates our discussion of protective armour in Chapter 11.
15. The Boston Consulting Group's explanation of Honda's success rests on the experience curve, which undoubtedly played a part in the earlier stages. However, a mere lead in accumulated experience in a fairly mature field is unlikely to constitute a bar which protects against imitation for several decades. Key resources which protect a company's offerings against imitation amongst other things are discussed in Part Four. On continuous innovation see Jacobson (1992).
16. De Chernatony, Knox and Chedgey (1992).
17. As discussed in traditional microeconomics.
18. It should be remembered that in this chapter the absence of oligopoly (or circularity) is assumed, an assumption which will be removed in Chapter 7.
19. The authors are indebted to Professor Shelagh Heffernan of City University Business School for this appendix.

7 Competitive strategy: (d) The seller's view of competitive markets

Introduction

Chapters 4 to 6 have discussed competitive strategy mainly through the eyes of customers. The focus was on how *they* see competing offerings. The importance of that perspective is that no business can expect to prosper until it learns to look at itself as customers see it. This chapter begins to look at competitive strategy and differentiation from the point of view of what the seller needs to achieve: financial returns at least equal to the cost of capital of its investments; in this case of its offerings.

The reader is reminded that here and there profit is loosely taken as a proxy for financial value.[1]

Market 'entry' or 'encroachment'?

At this point a widely used concept of competitive markets needs to be examined, that of *market entry*.[2] At first it was equated with entry into an industry, and later[3] into strategic groups.[4] **Entry** means new competitors coming in with new similar offerings, giving customers increased opportunities to shop around. This should reduce profit margins.

The language of 'entry' implies a public market, like an industry or strategic group. In a world of private markets[5] **'encroachment'** is a more appropriate word than 'entry'. From here on, 'encroachment' will replace 'entry' whenever private markets are referred to. 'Entry' is of course retained for references to public markets.

Industrial economics developed the concept of **barriers to entry.**[6] This was an early attempt to explain how super-normal profits might persist in what were assumed to be industries operating as public markets. Part Four will show that the persistence of super-normal profits earned by differentiated individual offerings is best explained by distinctive key resources owned by companies marketing those offerings.

Markets and profit margins: Differentiation and circularity

We now come to a fundamental pattern of how businesses relate to competitive markets.[7] Competitive markets vary in two principal ways, i.e.:

- The *number* of competitors: the extent to which the *number* of competitors is restricted by external constraints. At one

	Heterogeneous: differentiation	Homogeneous: price competition
One seller: *monopoly*	A	Not applicable
Few dominant sellers: *oligopoly*	B	C
Many sellers: *free entry or encroachment*	D	E

Figure 7.1 Classification of markets and competitive strategies

147

end of the scale a market consists of a single supplier. This is called 'pure monopoly'. At the other end there is free entry, with the market consisting of many competitors, none of them dominant, and all of them price-takers. These are features of the model of 'pure competition'. Between these two extremes there is a range characterized by the presence of several dominant sellers, each able to influence the market price, and each dependent on the others' reactions to their own moves. This is therefore called the 'circular'[8] case, or 'oligopoly'.

- The *distance between differentiated offerings*: the extent to which competing substitutes are different or homogeneous. This concerns the differentiation between competing substitutes, not their number. Again the extreme case of homogeneity meets a feature of the model of pure competition.

The resulting possibilities[9] are set out in polarized form in Figure 7.1. The cases differ as follows:

- One seller (A): Monopoly can arise because either a powerful single buyer (such as a government) or a legal constraint like a licensing system, or the seller's stranglehold on the supply of (say) a raw material restricts a market to a single supplier. In this case the price sensitivity of the offering approaches zero and the seller's market power and profit margins tend to be high.
- Many sellers, none of them powerful (D, E): In this fragmented case there are no dominant sellers, and no external constraints on entry or encroachment, at least in the longer run. The offerings can be heterogeneous or homogeneous. In D the primary influence on margins will be the distance between offerings. E is the case of pure competition.
- Few dominant sellers (B, C): This condition is called circular or oligopolistic. This again is the consequence of external constraints on market entry or encroachment. Here again the offerings can be either heterogeneous (B) or homogeneous (C). These circular cases will be discussed below, after the monopoly case.

This chapter will focus on Boxes B and C rather than D and E. D and E and the essential characteristics of differentiation have been discussed in some detail in previous chapters.

Monopoly

In Box A of Figure 7.1 both the incumbent's and the would-be entrant's competitive strategy must concentrate on the bottleneck factor. The monopolist is concerned to retain and foster its grip on that factor. The holder of an exclusive licence will give priority to the preservation of that privilege,[10] by cultivating relations with the body that grants it. The would-be entrant's focus must be on either loosening or bypassing that grip.

Monopoly virtually excludes price competition. In this respect its effect resembles that of a high degree of differentiation. The difference between monopoly and differentiation lies in their causes. Monopoly is brought about by dominance of supply; differentiation through differences seen by customers.

Pure monopoly, like most limiting cases, is rare, and we need to say no more about it. That leaves us to discuss the circular case, that of oligopoly.

Few dominant sellers: the circular case

The circular pattern is caused by a variety of constraints which restrict markets to few suppliers. Perhaps there are dominant buyers like defence or health ministries, who will only consider a short list of suppliers. Perhaps the dominant sellers themselves restrict competition. 'Few' dominant suppliers means so few that each seller has to consider the likely responses of the others in deciding on price or differentiation.

Oligopoly is often present even where there are many sellers, as long as a few of them are dominant. The word 'dominant' is needed because some markets contain participants of sharply different size or influence. There are of course markets in which all are equally influential, so that either all or none have a circular relationship. Often however, there is a small or large number of minnows in the pond, whom the big fish can ignore. The circular relationship is between those who need to consider one another's likely countermoves before deciding their own moves. If the washing powder market or the market in crossings of the English Channel is dominated by a few powerful competitors, then each must take note of the likely countermoves of the others. These are the big fish. Circularity requires that there is only a limited number (hence oligopoly) of big fish.

In a circular market competitor X's strategic decisions must take account of how X believes Y will respond, and Y's response must likewise take account of X's subsequent reaction. This chicken-and-egg chain is what is called circular.

The circular pattern normally applies to one offering at a time. We shall however in Chapter 16 discuss the phenomenon of the cross-parry[11] where two pairs of competing offerings owned by two rival companies can give rise to circular competitive conduct.

Circularity is a very common phenomenon of competitive markets, and arguably the most important environmental feature of competitive strategy. The reason why it occupies relatively little space in texts like this, is because its indeterminate nature relegates it to the realm of behavioural and especially psychological studies.[12]

The circular nature of oligopoly switches the logic of cause and effect from market forces to competitive psychology. Oligopoly thus introduces an element of indeterminacy[13] and low predictability. A strategist will however ignore oligopoly and its circular pattern at his or her peril.

The offerings can be either homogeneous (Box C) or differentiated (Box B) to varying degrees. The indeterminate balance of forces will have a greater influence on prices than the degree of differentiation. That predominance becomes weaker however as an offering distances itself from the dominant set of competing substitutes by greater differentiation. In other words, differentiation offers a measure of insulation or escape from circularity.

150

Suppose for example there were just three manufacturers, P, Q and R, of up-and-over garage doors, selling an essentially uniform offering. They are in Box C. None of them can change its price or introduce marginal improvements in the appearance or operation of the doors without pondering possible countermoves by its two competitors. Then Q designs the first remote-controlled door with a not easily copiable technology. Q will not remain unimitated for ever, but for the time being its offering is differentiated. Q has moved to Box B, and the circularity of its positioning is substantially reduced.

It is helpful to think of differentiation and circularity as alternative deviations from the model of pure competition. That model assumes homogeneous offerings, unimpeded entry and therefore a large number of suppliers. In those conditions price will settle down at a low, market-clearing level, and all competitors are price-takers. Of the two deviations under discussion,

- differentiation removes the assumption of homogeneity, and
- barriers to entry or to encroachment limit the number of competitors, possibly to the point where there is circularity.

A small increase in the intensity of either of these forces, in the absence of any other change, will marginally reduce the sensitivity of a seller's volume of sales to price changes. In any case, any element of circularity makes it harder to predict whether margins will be high or low.[14]

In a market characterized by differentiation the seller needs to give priority to the offering and its positioning, rather than to its price. On the other hand, in a market characterized by circularity, the seller's focus must shift towards the reciprocal reactions of its principal competitors.

In the real world pure examples of all three states – pure competition, differentiation and circularity – are rare. It is much more common to find private markets in which differentiation and circularity are present to varying degrees. Markets with a mixture of these two conditions are much the most common. Yet business managers often describe and analyse their markets without that critical distinction.

That however will put not just the analyst, but also the practitioner off the scent. Managers will take better decisions if they analyse their part of the galaxy by isolating these two quite different conditions. It matters a great deal to the success of a competitive strategy whether the strategist has understood to what extent the offering will be (a) a price-taker, (b) differentiated and unique, and (c) subject to circularity with the need to anticipate competitive reactions or countermoves.

Circularity and the formulation of competitive strategy

The principal strategic issue is not so much how to deal with a circular pattern after entry or encroachment, as whether and how to enter or encroach in the first place. Competitive strategy seeks to decide the future positioning of the offering, and one of its central questions must be whether a circular position is desired or not. Is it desirable or undesirable that margins should depend on the decisions and reactions of a few dominant competitors?

The first question therefore is: should we get into a circular position? As we cast around for a profitable future position in the galaxy, should we prefer or shun oligopolistic areas? This issue also concerns operations in dirigiste regimes, where heavy regulation restricts the freedom of markets, causing oligopolistic conditions. Many offerings have done extremely well in oligopolistic markets, but perhaps a greater number have not. This high-risk game suits those who have both the financial strength and the skills needed to win it.[15]

Much has been written[16] about the winning skills. The main principles are painstaking research into the mentality and bargaining strengths and weaknesses of the key competitors, adroit exploitation of one's own strong points, and a flair for predicting, anticipating, and turning to one's own advantage the countermoves of competitors. This excellent advice applies to any offering intended for an oligopolistic market.

The skill of predicting and anticipating countermoves greatly benefits from the study of game theory.[17] That is where circular competitors can learn how to anticipate the likely behaviour of competitors, and how to influence it to their advantage. All types of games can be instructive in circular conditions, from zero sum games of pure conflict to those of complete coordination. In the zero sum case a player wins only if others lose; in the coordination case all can win. A small private market with strong economies of scale is apt to lead to a zero sum game, in which only one large seller can succeed. On the other hand where there is room for several dominant sellers, coordinated price policies may benefit all.[18]

All these valid points tend however to be made on the assumption that oligopoly and circularity occur in a *public* market. The prevalent world of *private* markets[19] modifies that picture, because each such private market, i.e. that of each and every offering, will contain a differently constituted small group of dominant sellers. We saw in Figure 4.4 that offerings A and E, for example, had different, only partly overlapping sets of competitors. This makes our competitor's circular puzzle more complex. It also dilutes it in the sense that the reciprocal relationship is with different opponents in at least marginally different, only partly overlapping private markets.

Generally, a circular market will suit our business if we are well equipped to dominate it. This requires such low unit costs as to enable us to dictate the terms on which the whole circular group will do business.[20] It means entering the circular market in such a way as to bring about and exploit that dominance.

If on the other hand we are unlikely winners in the circular game, our best strategy may be to keep away from those parts of the galaxy where few players are likely to dominate. Putting a distance between them and us is of course differentiation. Differentiation helps a seller to avoid or mitigate unwelcome circularity.

So much for entering circular markets. What about the case where we are already in such a market and perhaps too committed to depart from it? In this case if we are dominant, the aim must be to stay dominant. In a dynamic business world that means never resting on our laurels, always keeping at least one step ahead of the rest. If we are not dominant, then the options are:

- the hard slog to develop the means of becoming dominant or at least avoiding domination by others,
- cutting that process short by acquisition,[21] or
- differentiating in order to reduce our vulnerability.

Oligopoly and strategy implementation

The circularity of a market also has a decisive influence on the way a competitive strategy needs to be implemented. A manager's moves and signals must be calculated to trigger desirable reactions from competitors. In some cases the best move is invisible and invites no countermoves. These moves and signals can be designed to either inform or misinform, to warn and threaten, to bluff and mislead competitors, or to communicate commitment and determination to both competitors and customers.

The interrelation between circularity, differentiation and price

Figure 7.1 classified competitive *markets*. We are now ready to adapt that classification to show how the competitive postures of *offerings* can be represented in a continuum. Whereas markets vary between homogeneity and differentiation, offerings compete with either more or less differentiation, as well as more or less circularity, as in Figure 7.2.

An offering can appear in any position such as p, q, r or s, where conditions of differentiation or circularity can be present or lacking to any degree and in any combination.

In general, the seller's strategic and tactical decisions will be more powerfully influenced by the vertical dimension, circularity, than by the horizontal dimension, differentiation. This is because a change big enough to change a market to

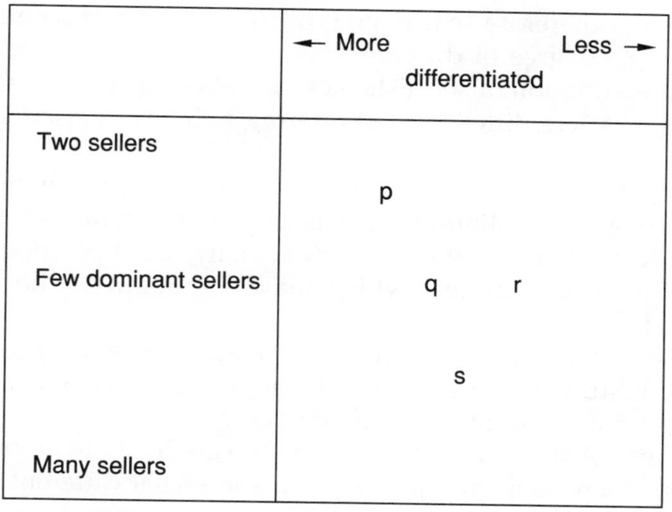

	← More Less → differentiated
Two sellers	p
Few dominant sellers	q r
	s
Many sellers	

Figure 7.2   Interrelation of differentiation and circularity

circularity suspends all the normal rules about price sensitivity which apply in a market with no dominant players.

On the other hand, a sufficient degree of differentiation does offer a measure of immunity to the indeterminacy of circularity, if an escape is desired. Position q is much more immune than r. In any case, where circularity is absent or weak enough, differentiation tends to outweigh the impact of price competition.[22]

These are the principal interactions of the three forces of circularity, differentiation and price competition.

Summary: Differentiation, circularity and price

Differentiation is a central concept of competitive strategy. Chapter 6 has explored the meaning of differentiation as the measure of the insensitivity of an offering to price comparisons. Differentiation is much the most important – if not the sole – influence on the degree of the insensitivity of an offering's sales volume to price changes. For practical purposes therefore that degree of insensitivity measures the offering's degree of differentiation.

Differentiation also distances an offering from its substitutes. A less differentiated offering will have closer substitutes.

An offering is designed ex ante to have a high or low degree of differentiation; how its ex post differentiation turns out, depends on how customers actually see it positioned in relation to substitutes, which may not be what the seller intended.

The purpose of differentiation is to enable the seller to have more latitude in pricing. This includes the choice of charging a higher margin, often for a smaller volume.

Oligopolistic or circular markets too are likely to be private ones, where each competitor has a somewhat different set of key competitors from the next. Where an offering is in a part of the galaxy which is not only characterized by differentiation, but also by circularity, margins will be subject to both sets of forces. This is a very common condition, but encroachment should be contemplated only by those who have reason to believe that they have the winning advantages and skills to exploit it profitably.

The characteristics of an offering's market are largely determined by the combined degrees of oligopoly and differentiation. Price is for this purpose mainly a dependent variable, dependent on that combination.

The competitive positioning of an offering is defined mainly by its differentiation, but also by price to the extent that the seller can decide the price. Oligopoly occurs irrespective of whether offerings are differentiated or undifferentiated. Generally the degree of differentiation has less impact on profit margins than the outcome of the circular game of powerplay. Nevertheless, the margins of a highly differentiated offering should be less open to that impact.

Notes

1. The difference between these terms was discussed in Chapter 2.
2. The concept of entry into an industry as a threat took off with Bain (1956).
3. Caves and Porter (1977).
4. See Chapter 4.
5. See Chapter 4 and the first box in Chapter 11.
6. Bain (1956) classified entry barriers as consisting of product differentiation, absolute cost advantages and economies of scale. These barriers are further discussed in Chapters 10 and 11, where it will be argued that a more appropriate and comprehensive term is 'protective armour'.
7. The framework follows that of Triffin (1940), Chapter III.
8. Triffin (1940).
9. Adapted from Triffin (1940) p. 143. Triffin was only concerned to classify markets, and used just 'heterogeneous' and 'homogeneous'. We have added 'differentiation' and 'price competition'. These are of course the corresponding contrasting competitive strategies.
10. In Chapter 11 the competitor's tenure of this privilege is treated as a 'key resource'.
11. Porter (1980) Chapter 4, Karnani and Wernerfelt (1985). 'Cross-parry' was Porter's original expression; more recently it has been referred to as 'multi-point competition'.
12. It does however receive a lot of attention in some texts, notably Porter (1980, 1985). Kay (1993) brings game theory to bear on circular market conditions. The indeterminacy is inherent in circularity itself. In a *non-circular* market of homogeneous offerings by many sellers of modest size, a single equilibrium price is established if each seller maximizes its own profit. If the offerings are heterogeneous, equilibrium will result in a clear pattern of relative prices. In a *circular* market there is no single price/volume equilibrium, because each seller must make assumptions about the ensuing behaviour of its oligopolistic competitors, and there is no single logical assumption for it to make. This lack of a single equilibrium makes the situation indeterminate.
13. The indeterminacy is again psychological. Each party has to take a view on how the others will act and react. For example, are the others rational enough to behave as game theory might predict?
14. This does not imply that a circular market will not settle down to an equilibrium, a state in which no competitor has an incentive to change its position. It merely implies that a number of alternative equilibria are possible, depending on the psychology of the contestants.

15. One of the many hazards is the reluctance of losers to exit, due to exit barriers, described by Porter (1980) pp 259–265.
16. For example, Porter (1980), Chapters 4, 5 and 9, Kay (1993) Chapters 3–7, 16.
17. Kay (1993), Oster (1990), Dixit and Nalebuff (1991), Schelling (1960).
18. Chapter 8 will refer to some limitations of game theory in this context.
19. See Chapter 4.
20. See Appendix 8.2.
21. Discussed in Part Five. See also discussion of market share in Chapter 8.
22. See Chapter 6.

Part Three   Competitive Strategies for Profit

Part Two has sought to bring about an understanding of different types of competitive strategy. It looked at what competitive strategies are and what defines a given competitive strategy. What has not yet been discussed is how a strategist sets about choosing between alternative competitive strategies. Part Three begins to tackle that question, relating the nature of competitive strategy to the financial raison d'être of business. Chapter 8 does this in static, Chapter 9 in dynamic terms.

8 Competitive strategy: (e) What makes it profitable?

Introduction: strategies are selected for their financial value

Chapter 2 stressed that the central purpose of all business is to create financial value. Financial value is therefore also the overriding purpose of business strategy. All strategies, competitive or corporate, have to be measured, assessed, ranked and finally selected by the criterion of how much financial value they add to the company. Chapter 2 also discussed how that overriding function of a business fits into the ethical picture. Financial value is not to be seen as conflicting with the objectives of human and social welfare.

This chapter discusses the interrelation between profitability and competitive strategy, and how the strategist uses that relationship when choosing a competitive strategy.

Accounting profits versus financial value

Profitability is the manager's practical proxy for financial value. Financial theorists tend to steer clear of accounting concepts like profit or earnings which are not even designed to measure growth in financial value.[1] Managers on the other hand find it difficult to use a language without accounting concepts, for three reasons. First, managers are legally required to report on their stewardship in accounting terms. Secondly, many of their contracts, especially loan instruments, impose important limits on them, expressed in accounting terms. Thirdly, as a result of those legal requirements the accounting framework is deeply embedded in the

161

manager's information system. Without accounting information, without profit-related measurements, the manager may have no integrated means of controlling or analysing the business. Moreover, if strategy A is more *profitable* than strategy B, the chances are that it will also be of greater *financial value*.

However, that correlation is fragile. Financial value is measured as the net present value of expected future cash flows. The cash flows are discounted at the risk-adjusted cost of capital of those cash flows, using the risk factor appropriate to each specific strategy or project.[2] Accounting concepts are seldom safe to use as a proxy for that valuation without some modification.

Differences between the accounting and financial frameworks[3]

The principal differences between the accounting and financial value concepts are the following:

- The accounts look backward. The financial markets by contrast are concerned with their estimates of future cash flows rather than with the past.
- The accounting framework takes no account of the cost of capital and the risk factor, or of the time value of money.
- The accounting approach contains the concept of the *margin* between price and cost in a given period. This concept is indispensable to the manager as a control ratio. However, margins, let alone period margins, play no part in defining financial value. For this there are three reasons. Financial value:

  (a) deals not with surpluses in any one period, but with the discounted net present value over the life of the project;
  (b) does not in each period match sales with costs incurred, but cash receipts with payments;
  (c) accounts for cash changes in fixed assets and working capital, which do not affect margins.

- The historical accounting convention values a business at its net asset value, derived from historical cash transactions and accruals. Financial value looks at the net present value of future cash flows rather than past values and non-cash adjustments like depreciation and transfers to provisions.
- Accounting earnings ignore the investment of cash in fixed and working capital.
- Inventory valuation, accruals and the treatment of acquisitions, mergers, disposals and restructuring leave a great deal to the judgement of those preparing accounts. Some of the more flexible or cosmetic accounting practices are, since 1990, in the course of being disallowed in a number of countries. In the UK financial reporting standards are being reformed by the Accounting Standards Board.

The estimation of future cash flows, and especially the residual value which has to be treated as a receipt at the end of the forecast period, do of course also require estimation and judgement, but under more disciplined rules.

In practice therefore managers face a dilemma. On the one hand there is their legal and often contractual duty to report in accounting terms, using the data available in their accounting systems. On the other hand they know that their ultimate critics, the financial markets, apply a very different approach, even if market participants are restricted to the same reported numbers as raw material for their estimates.

Stockmarkets have largely learned to see through the illusory features of accounting conventions. That reinforces the need for managers to attempt to make the same calculations as are made by stock market analysts, and to direct the business towards the creation of financial value.

Subject to these substantial reservations, managers can cautiously use profitability as a proxy for financial value. Profitability is of course the ratio of profit or return earned on the funds invested.

The impact of competitive strategy on profitability: targeting profitable customers

Some managers tend to think that managing for profit consists of tight control of expenditure, and maximizing sales and profit margins. These measures are the weaponry available to improve current, *short-term* results. They are of little relevance however to strategy.

The impact of competitive strategy on profitability is widely underestimated. There is only limited scope for improving this year's results for an offering which has a poor competitive position. A poor competitive position inevitably means low operating margins. We can and should tighten our cost controls, redouble our sales effort, and generally strive to produce the best possible short-term results. Yet all this fire-fighting, necessary as it is, can at best bring about marginal improvements. It cannot make an uncompetitive offering competitive. We could and should have attended to its competitive position some years ago when we made either bad strategic decisions or none.

Much more can be done for the profitability of our offering at the time of its design:[4] in the framing of the competitive strategy. A competitive strategy positions an offering in a unique triangular relationship with customers and competitors. The measure of its attraction is its financial value. In this sense the job of a competitive strategy is to target profitable customers. This positioning of the offering will affect profits much more powerfully than any short-term measures that can be taken after the triangular relationship has become a commitment.

Competitive positioning is for tomorrow

Chapter 6 briefly stressed the distinction between intended and achieved differentiation. What a competitive strategy positions, is a *future* offering: *tomorrow's* triangular relationship with *tomorrow's* customers and competitors, not today's. Today's competitors and their present positions, and today's customers and their preferences are of interest only as pointers to tomorrow's configuration.

Let us for example assume a time-lag of three years. In that case if we run into losses in year 0, it is too late to remedy strategic mistakes or omissions made in year –3. We are left with fire-fighting measures like cutting costs, closing down activities, or desperate and often self-defeating efforts to win market share[5] away from competitors.

One lesson is to start at once on ensuring that the story will not repeat itself in year +3. There is of course a grave risk that the company under its present management team will not survive to year +3, but will go insolvent or be taken over before then. Yet if it is to have any chance of real recovery, the action programme *must* include the adoption of viable competitive strategies. Fire-fighting is unavoidable here and now, but it is not a road to real recovery. A palliative is not a solution. Histories of successful corporate turnarounds invariably include the adoption of good competitive strategies, often for the first time in years.[6]

It is difficult to overstress this point. Too many managers take a broad brush approach. Surely the radical upgrading of my own offering will automatically see to it that tomorrow's customers see it as repositioned? No, not automatically. Not if any or all competitors make identical improvements. If they do, then there is no change in my or their competitive positioning. Tomorrow's configuration will be the same as today's. If all had been offering commodity-buys yesterday, they would all still be selling commodity-buys tomorrow, not system-buys. The only correct benchmark for competitive strategy is competitors' offerings tomorrow, not our offering today.

In any case, the appraisal of a new competitive strategy[7] must factor into its projections the likely cyclical changes in the market for the new offering. This obviously matters more in cyclical trades like civil construction than in food retailing.[8]

As is widely recognized,[9] the task of developing a competitive strategy must include a searching analysis of competitors. What is not usually stressed is that the task is:

- to analyse year +3's competing substitutes,
- to identify those future substitute *offerings* by researching the *companies* likely to offer them,
- to do this for each of our offerings, not collectively for all offerings.

The task is to formulate a clear scenario of the private market expected to be faced by the offering now under review. That market is likely to differ substantially from today's markets, because either we ourselves or one or more of our competitors may destabilize the market between now and then.[10] The competitive scene is not static.

The time-frame

How distant is 'tomorrow'? There is no universal answer: it depends on competitive logistics. We saw in Chapter 2 that if our offering requires a new nuclear power station or the designing and setting up manufacture of an entirely new motor-cycle, it may take seven or more years to launch that offering in the market. If on the other hand it merely means today's washing powder coloured blue instead of white, it can be in place in a matter of weeks.

The forgotten truism: the source of profits

The fact that profits come from competitive strategy is self-evident when put in these simple terms. Yet it is quite startlingly different from the way profitability is widely discussed. It is not common to read in directors' reports to shareholders, or in chairmen's reviews of the year, that the toilet soap division had taken a bath due to the lack of good competitive strategies three years earlier. It is much more common to read about tough trading conditions, failure of governmental macroeconomic policy, unfavourable cost changes, or unfair dumping by a foreign competitor.

Financial value is of course created by corporate as well as competitive strategy. For example, successful turnarounds, like those of Courtaulds and TI in the 1980s, were the fruits of brilliant *corporate* strategies. What must not be overlooked is that a good corporate strategy serves to produce a well chosen and monitored cluster of competitive strategies. This will become clearer when we discuss corporate strategy in Part Five.

Competitive strategy and the determinants of profit

The financial value created by a competitive strategy depends on six main factors:[11]

- the net operating cash flow margin,
- fixed and working capital investment, less divestment,
- the economies of scale (which depend on the proportion of variable to fixed costs),
- the volume of sales to be generated,
- the duration of that volume,
- the offering's cost of capital.

Variable costs are those which do, and fixed those that do not, vary with the volume of units sold. Materials are a variable cost, office rent a fixed one.

The determinants of fixed and variable costs are well understood in conventional terms of management accounting. In formulating competitive strategy, we must of course look hard at whether the resources available to us for the new offering are available at competitive costs. This is emphasized by the resource-based approach to competitive strategy discussed in Part Four. However, cost of capital apart, the principal effect of competitive strategy is on margins, volume and duration. To that effect we must now turn.

Effect of competitive strategy: differentiation and circularity

Chapters 6 and 7 have set out that the key influences on prices and volumes are the degree of differentiation and the degree of circularity.[12] Chapter 7 put forward the view that circularity, caused by the presence of just a few dominant sellers, is potentially the stronger of the two influences. In the context of competitive strategy two things need to be remembered. One is that in general terms the effect of circularity is indeterminate. Any equilibrium of competitive forces in conditions of circularity is psychological, and therefore depends on the parties involved in each case. Game theory models are of some interest, except when they assume an unrealistic degree of rationality. The other thing to remember is that a seller can seek a degree of immunity to circularity by a sufficiently high degree of differentiation. The present discussion will leave it at that, and focus on differentiation, not because it is more important, but because its effects, unlike those of circularity, can and must be analysed in general terms.

Chapter 6 noted that the all-important *margin* depends on the degree of differentiation. Differentiation increases the seller's latitude in setting prices. The more differentiated the offering is, the higher is the margin that can be charged. This favourable effect is often, but not invariably, counteracted by reduced volume. However, the loss of profit from reduced volume can be either greater or smaller than the gain from the increased unit margin.

Whether or not a given change in the degree of differentiation improves profitability, is therefore a question of fact case by case. It depends on how price-sensitive customers are. It follows that all generalized axioms, like 'the more differentiation the better' or 'zero differentiation is fatal' or 'differentiation means higher cost', are unhelpful oversimplifications.

This benign effect of differentiation, this greater freedom in pricing policy, has two implications, one strategic, one tactical. The strategic opportunity is the scope it gives for a pricing policy. The seller can either set price at the level where it maximizes current profit, or set it a little lower so as to 'buy' more longer-term market share by means of that discount. It is a form of investment, forgoing cash flows now in order to have better cash flows later.[13]

The tactical opportunity exploits the fact that price is one of the few outputs which can be changed at short notice. Price can generally be changed faster than other outputs can be re-differentiated. As we have seen, this normally takes some planning ahead.

The effect of differentiation on volume

Differentiation normally has the effect of reducing volume. Exceptional cases where a new offering would displace most substitutes even without a lower price are discussed in Chapter 6 under the heading 'Very successful new offerings'. An example discussed there is the case of the Honda motor-cycle around 1970.[14] In these rare, but important cases, the volume-curtailing effect of differentiation is swamped and reversed by other factors.

In the more common case, an increase in differentiation results in reduced volume. Volume depends partly on the size of the targeted customer segment, and can therefore among other things depend on the degree of differentiation.

Durability of margins and threats to durability

The combination of differentiation, volume and margin is one important strategic determinant of profitability. The other is the duration of a given combination. The volume per unit of time determines the period needed to recover the fixed costs and earn the cost of capital. We therefore now turn to the durability of a competitive position. A fleetingly profitable offering is clearly unlikely to meet the requirement.

Competitive threats

There are two sets of threats to that durability. The most common threat is competition. When others see our attractive competitive positioning, they will attempt to offer close substitutes to our offering, thus eroding our combination of margin and volume.[15]

Autonomous, non-competitive threats

The other threat is that customer preferences may autonomously move away from our offering. Normally, customer preferences desert an offering because new competing substitutes tempt them away. That is the first of the two threats. This second threat is that customers might move away under their own initiative, not prompted by the actions of our competitors. Customers may for example go 'green', rebelling against ecologically harmful life-styles or offerings. Again perceptions may change of what is healthy or ethical. Examples are reactions against food additives, asbestos materials and exports from apartheid and other racially discriminatory political systems.

This second class of threats can only be met by vigilant anticipation. It pays strategists to scan the horizon for signs of this type of change in preferences.

Responses to competitive threats

The response to the first type of threat, those from new substitutes, is dealt with in Chapter 11. Briefly, an offering can itself be armoured against new substitutes by what in Part Four will be called key resources. In other cases the *investment* in a resource can be protected by a planned series of successive further innovations which continue to exploit the initial investment.

That task of ensuring such protection is an integral part of the design of our competitive strategy for the offering. Appendix 8.1 discusses Porter's[16] famous five-forces framework. The usefulness of any such model should not however be overestimated. It mainly serves as a check-list of threats to profitability.

When is a commodity-buy strategy profitable?

An undifferentiated offering can be very profitable where one competitor has a sustainable advantage over its rivals in unit costs. This needs either a superior resource (Part Four) or better economies of scale, or a combination of both. As such a strategy tends to invite more intense competition than one of differentiation, special care needs to be taken to ensure that the advantage is sustainable.[17] The strategy therefore depends for its success on the ability to maintain that cost advantage. If the market is a price-taker market with no circularity, the cost advantage can be exploited either by simply enjoying a better margin at the market price, or by cutting the price so as to attract a larger share of the market. If the market is sufficiently circular, it may be possible to go for the prize of becoming a price-setter; in other words for the most advantageous form of what Appendix 8.2 calls 'price leadership' (it discusses cost and price leadership). Cost leadership (like price leadership) can occur in private markets with differentiated offerings, as long as customers compare prices in terms of value for money.[18]

Volume and scale economies

Volume and scale economies are central to many disciplines like microeconomics, management accounting and marketing, and managers are universally mindful of them.

In the framework of this book the significance of economies of scale is twofold. The first is their well-known beneficial effect in reducing unit costs. The second is that economies of scale are often sacrificed by differentiation. In Chapter 6 we saw that differentiation can in some rare and felicitous cases result in high volumes, but this requires some degree of market failure.

In the more normal case there is a tradeoff between differentiation and economies of scale. Those economies reduce unit costs. Lower unit costs give the seller the opportunity to reduce prices. To the extent conditioned by customers' price sensitivity, price reductions will raise the seller's market share and volume. This in turn reduces unit costs yet further. The process is a 'virtuous circle'. This must be traded off against the attractions of a differentiated offering with higher margins and lower volumes and scale economies.

Market share and its benefits

The popular model and the evidence

Market share has been a popular concept with writers[19] and managers. Its pursuit was a favourite strategic goal of the 1970s. In the market share model a rise in market share,

- cuts unit costs through the volume effect, i.e. through economies of scale,[20]
- reduces competitive pressures on prices and margins from competitors, thus giving the company more pricing freedom, and
- may make the offering more attractive to customers wherever a leading market position makes customers more aware of it or more confident in it.

The association of high market share with high profitability is well established.[21] Empirical work, such as that described in the box, suggests however, that it is far from certain that market share itself is the cause of the observed profitability. If a school has simultaneously improved its standard in mathematics and football, it does not follow that better mathematics produces better football. A new maths teacher who also coaches football may be responsible for both improvements.

All this empirical work assumes that shared markets are public ones. The difficulty of defining markets,[22] noted in the box, becomes much more critical in the framework put forward in this book, in which markets are private rather than public. Private markets are not only much smaller, but also defined for just one competing offering at a time.

As for the simple market share model itself, it makes a number of often tacit assumptions:

- Even apart from the difficulty of defining a market in the first place, its expected size and shape is assumed to remain unchanged.
- Competitors are assumed to make no successful counter-moves.

Szymanski, Bharadwaj and Varadajaran[23] in a meta-analysis of other empirical studies find that the simple statistical relationship between market share and profitability does not do justice to the causal chains involved. Much of the effect on profitability is due to other causes, such as product quality and 'firm-specific intangibles'[24] which affect both market share and profitability: '... omitting product quality from the model is shown to bias the market share elasticity upwards, and ... the estimate of market share elasticity all but disappears on average when firm-specific intangibles are specified in the profit model.'[25]

The authors also stress that the definition of the market has a significant influence on the statistical association. For example, it seems plausible that studies derived from PIMS data might turn out to show higher correlations than those using whole-company data.

- The cost of bringing about the rise in market share is assumed not to dissipate the benefits. Otherwise the cost of capital would not be recovered.

Above all, the simple model does not usually specify whether the implied time-frame is short or long, or indeed long enough to recover the cost of capital. All this therefore describes the effect of a rise in market share in terms which are not explicitly strategic. It often seems to treat the rise in market share as the sole change, assuming that all other conditions are held steady. For example, competitors are assumed to make no countermoves. Such assumptions can at best hold very fleetingly. It is certainly not safe to conclude that any offering 'without a competitive advantage *will* increase its profitability by increasing its market share through price cutting, advertising' and the like.[26]

The strategic model

Those who advocate a competitive strategy of raising market share, ought to have in mind a move which repositions an offering in relation to customers and competitors for a strategic time-span, a time-span long enough at least to recover the cost of capital of the effort.

That is clearly how such a strategy ought to be viewed. In fact, however, market share has often been treated almost as a goal in its own right. It is as if it went without saying that more market share will in all circumstances improve profit. Kay[27] and the recent empirical work quoted in the box have refuted the assumption of this automatic causal link.

How a strategy aimed at raising market share can generate financial value

A strategy of raising market share can create financial value in one of four ways:

- by substantially raising the degree of monopoly. In this case the rise in market share deters, eliminates or weakens some competitors. The result is to make the demand for the seller's own offering significantly less sensitive to price: this leaves the seller freer to move its own price up or down. It often gives the seller better than competitive margins.
- by giving the seller a cost advantage. This can enable the seller to enjoy higher margins or cut the price and attract yet more market share away from competitors, or – better still – to dictate pricing policy – again up or down – to its competitors.[28] This requires a substantial advantage in unit costs, and therefore usually in economies of scale. On the other hand, compared with the raising of the degree of monopoly, the attainment of this cost advantage does not require nearly such a high market share or such a high degree of insensitivity to price changes.
- by enabling the seller to become part of the dominant group in a circular or oligopolistic market, where this is to the seller's advantage.[29]

- by enhancing the prestige and familiarity of the offering and thus raising its differentiation.

These four routes to extra financial value are effective only if certain conditions are met:

1 The market (private, public, or quasi public)[30] is clearly definable.
2 The market can be relied upon to retain its expected size and shape for long enough to recover the cost of capital of the effort to increase market share. In other words, the strategy presupposes no shrinkage in the market during the strategic period, and correctly anticipates and meets any counteraction by competitors.
3 The financial value to be generated must not be swallowed up by the cost of the move to increase share.

How valid is market share as an intermediate goal?

In the framework put forward in this book, market share is not a valid goal in its own right. It is at best an intermediate goal, which may or may not produce the desired benefits. The well documented association[31] of higher market share with higher profitability has to be ascribed at least in part to the fact that successful competitive strategies often also raise market share. It does not follow that the extra market share was the source of the extra profit. Wet grass does not prove that it must have rained.

To sum up, how valid is the pursuit of market share? It has to be said that the assumptions and conditions listed in the previous section are not likely to be met together in many cases. Unfortunately the failure of any one of them is likely to invalidate the pursuit. However, in some slow-moving, not too heavily differentiated parts of the galaxy the conditions may well sometimes be met.

Supermarket food retailing might be an example. The market as a whole is fairly distinct from its substitutes. It is unlikely to shrink suddenly. That would require a significant switch from private cars as a mode of transport, which is not likely to occur overnight. If one chain succeeded in buying another cheaply enough, there is no inherent reason why it should not retain the customers of the acquired chain. There are economies of scale, for example in provisioning, and the opportunity for price leadership in some neighbourhoods.

This is only a brief survey of a very popular doctrine. The main conclusion is that in a modern dynamic and largely differentiated world, its validity may be rare, but by no means non-existent.

Summary

This chapter has reviewed some practical difficulties in understanding competitive strategy, and especially what makes a competitive strategy profitable enough to add financial value.

The main key to profitability is the competitive positioning of the proposed offering. The job of competitive strategy is to target profitable customers.

Competitive strategy adds financial value mainly by the way the offering's positioning influences volumes, margins and their duration and its risk profile. That combination of factors is powerfully influenced by the degrees of circularity and differentiation. Threats to duration can come from the actions of competitors, from autonomous changes in customer preferences, or from adverse developments in the company's resources or the markets for those resources. Changes in customer preferences can only be countered by intelligent anticipation; the response to the other threats is discussed in Part Four.

Market share is a more complex phenomenon than is often supposed. Its efficacy in delivering financial value depends on a number of difficult assumptions and conditions being simultaneously met. This unusual combination is most likely to occur in a few relatively slow-moving parts of the competitive galaxy.

* * *

Appendix 8.1

Profitability analysis and the five-forces framework

Porter's (1980) framework is famous amongst other things for its five-forces model of industry analysis. In his industry-centred framework it forms the key, the starting point and the central tool of competitive strategy. Its main purpose has been to assess the robustness of the value to be generated by a competitive strategy.

One difficulty with that five-forces framework has been its central preoccupation with industry analysis. Industry analysis has caused much headache. Its shortcomings were reviewed in Chapter 4.

Another difficulty is that the framework has often been applied to the multioffering firm.[32] This can of course be appropriate on the supply or cost side, as many offerings share common costs. It is however inappropriate on the demand side, where only each single offering confronts customers and competitors.

Porter's famous diagram shows threats to profitability from:

- Buyers, especially those with strong bargaining power.
- Suppliers, again especially those with strong bargaining power.
- Three kinds of competitors:

  (a) present members of the industry,
  (b) potential entrants to the industry,
  (c) substitutes outside the industry.

As we are not concerned with the industry, we can simplify this to

- buyers
- suppliers
- incumbent and potential competitors.

To that list of three threats we might wish to add a fourth: the threat from those who do not compete for our customers, but for our key resources, a point which will be developed in Part Four. Our optical business may for example own a warehouse on a site which others might wish to develop into a supermarket.

The five-forces model is helpful in its intended use, as a check-list of threats to the profitability of a *given* proposed offering.[33] Its usefulness in that role has however prompted some practitioners to apply it much more widely, for example as an aid to the design of a competitive strategy. That however is to misuse it. It is not a complete analysis of such a strategy, nor does it cover all aspects of its evaluation.

The things which the model is not intended to do, include the following:

- It does not take account of the cost of investing in the strategy, such as acquiring necessary assets or skills, systems and other resources.
- As a static analysis, it ignores the time-lag between the adoption of a competitive strategy and its presence in the market.
- Similarly, it fails to highlight the duration for which profit margins need to be maintained to recover the cost of capital.
- It does not directly refer to the degree of differentiation, or to the consequent effect on volume and price sensitivity.
- Nor to any degrees of circularity.

Finally though it focuses on customers and competitors, it fails to bring out the basic asymmetry between the demand and supply sides, with only the offering competing for customers, but the business as a whole competing for resources.

Appendix 8.2

'Cost leadership' and price leadership

Porter (1980) contrasts a strategy of 'overall' cost leadership with one of differentiation. In the framework of this book, with its private markets, the concept of cost leadership is still instructive, although it does not here amount to a strategy. Cost leadership can be defined as having lower equivalent costs than competing substitutes. 'Equivalent' is needed because customers will pay less for what they see as a less good offering, and that lower quality may be due to cost savings. Hence if offering A is dearer to produce and more attractive than B, then its higher costs may still be consistent with cost leadership.[34]

In its own right, cost leadership does not position an offering in relation to customers and competitors. Cost is not an output. In this framework cost leadership is a necessary condition of price leadership, which can be a competitive strategy. The concept needs to be viewed in terms of value for money.

Price leadership needs a durable capacity – not necessarily exercised – to attract customers away from competitors by means of prices low enough to make competing offerings unattractive, given the degree of differentiation. This formulation enables us to discuss cost leadership in a system of private markets. Porter's concept of cost leadership was of course formulated for public markets.

Price leadership is most effective where the price leader has the power – again not necessarily exercised – to affect the prices of its competing substitutes.

Notes

1. Rappaport (1986).
2. See for example Brealey and Myers (1991).
3. For a full account of the shortcomings of the accounting framework in this context see Rappaport (1986). See also Stewart (1991).
4. This shorthand statement is not of course to assert that a competitive strategy is cast in stone at a single point in time when it is

'designed'. Competitive strategies are modified from time to time in the light of changing news, as is argued by Mintzberg, and discussed in Chapter 1.

5. The significance of market share is investigated at the end of this chapter.
6. Slatter (1984).
7. See Chapter 12.
8. See also Chapter 1.
9. Porter (1980).
10. See the discussion of rearranger and transformer firmlets in Chapter 9.
11. Rappaport (1986) lists seven 'value drivers': sales growth rate, operating profit margin, income tax rate, fixed and working capital investment, cost of capital and value growth duration, but they are not formulated for an internal appraisal of a specific new offering.
   Appendix 8.1 discusses Porter's five-forces model.
12. Triffin (1940).
13. See the critical discussion of the objective of market share at the end of this chapter.
14. Chapter 9 refers to this case as one of market transformation.
15. This process is analysed in Chapter 10. The response to that success-aping pressure is the central theme of Chapter 11.
16. Porter (1980).
17. See Part Four.
18. See Appendix 8.2.
19. The best known propagator of the market share view was the Boston Consulting Group. Their view was influentially reinforced by Buzzell, Gale and Sultan (1975) who found a strong empirical relationship in the PIMS database between market share and return on investment, but qualified their findings by stressing that the correlation varied with industries, with how frequently offerings were purchased and other factors. Subsequent reviews of the Boston Consulting Group's model and of the market share view generally were more sceptical. Examples are Porter (1980), Buzzell and Gale (1987), McKiernan (1992) and Kay (1993).
20. The cumulative experience effect, preferred by the Boston Consulting Group, is normally highly correlated with scale economies, and likely to provide a better explanation only in rare, technologically advanced cases.
21. Best sources are Buzzell and Gale (1987) and Szymanski, Bharadwaj and Varadarajan (1993).
22. Kay (1993).
23. Szymanski, Bharadwaj and Varadarajan (1993).
24. These are the subject of resource-based theory, discussed in Part Four.

180

25. Szymanski, Bharadwaj and Varadarajan (1993) p. 14.
26. Kay (1993).
27. Kay (1993).
28. These are the two stages of price leadership set out in Appendix 8.2.
29. Circularity is discussed in Chapter 7.
30. See Chapter 4.
31. See for example Buzzell, Gale and Sultan (1975).
32. Or its divisions or other sub-units. See page 52.
33. Porter does not refer to an 'offering', but to the 'firm' which he treats as a proxy for its offering.
34. Porter (1985, p. 13) uses 'equivalent' and goes on to make this same point. He also there talks about 'either parity or proximity in the bases of differentiation'. In other words the product must either have proximity (i.e. be very homogeneous) with its substitutes, or have parity with them (i.e. be equally price-sensitive), where parity 'implies either an identical product offering to competitors, or a different combination of attributes equally preferred by buyers'.

9 Competitive strategy: (f) Dynamics

Introduction

An account of competitive strategy is bound to begin with a static description. This chapter sets out to redress the balance by describing some of its dynamics, and how those dynamics can be harnessed in the pursuit of financial value or profitability.

In particular this chapter describes:

- the transaction life cycle: a strategic counterpart to the 'product life cycle' and
- the distinction between rearranger and transformer strategies: rearranger strategies aim to win customers from competitors without significantly changing the market or area of the galaxy. Transformer strategies on the other hand radically destabilize the affected market area.

The generic offering

An individual offering is defined in this book as one which has a unique triangular position in relation to customers and competitors. If we therefore modify an offering like a soft drink, say by giving it a new advertising slogan or package which will make it more attractive tomorrow, its triangular positioning will change. That makes it a new offering and a new firmlet. Similarly, if we take an otherwise unchanged offering and extend the territory where we market it, say from the USA to Canada, it may have different competitors there, or be seen in a different competitive light by customers:

once again, it will have a new competitive positioning, and will be a new offering. This strict use of words is helpful and necessary to a full understanding of competitive positioning and strategy.

On the other hand it is very occasionally in practice useful to have a term which can be held steady for a series of versions of an offering which retains a great deal of continuity along with minor changes in space and time. We call that a **generic offering**. Such a generic offering is strictly that of a single seller, but where several sellers offer something substantially similar, that too can be included in the term, by way of extension.

McDonald's restaurants may serve as an example of a generic offering. Their market position is somewhat different in Moscow, Paris and Boston, but the offering has strong common outputs in all three places. Similarly when the offering changed from manual to computerized ordering and billing, it retained a considerable degree of continuity of other outputs.

The term 'generic offering' can serve to acknowledge these continuities across space and time.

The transaction life cycle[1]

It is a truism that the pace of economic change in the modern world is accelerating. Technologies are changing ever faster, and so are consumption patterns. Consequently the markets served by business are in a constant state of flux. Business can never afford to stay still.

Most microeconomic change is unidirectional, for example towards lower unit costs or higher quality. However, when it comes to competitive strategy for a generic offering, change can oscillate between less and more differentiation. The swing can be from commodity-buy towards system-buy, as well as the other way.

These features can be neatly illustrated in the model of the transaction life cycle (Figure 9.1). It must be stressed that this model is merely illustrative of how markets can evolve; it does not predict what will actually happen in any particular case.

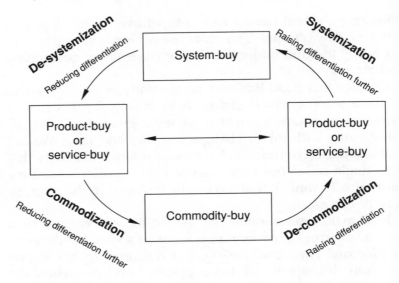

Figure 9.1 *The transaction life cycle*

First an illustration: the very first desk-top publishing software. When such radical innovations are widely marketed for the first time, they are usually transacted as system-buys. The vendor must not only supply the new software, but also unique support to enable it to be integrated and used effectively. The package is differentiated in both dimensions – it is the novelty and uniqueness of both its merchandise and support attributes (Figure 5.1[2]) that give the customer the full benefit of the purchase.

As the new software gains popularity, new players enter the arena – they offer their own desk-top publishing software. They may only be distant competitors. Their merchandise and support target different specialized customer segments and compete from a distance.

Competitors start moving closer to the pioneer. Some match the merchandise of the pioneer, but vary the support they provide. This move may receive its impetus from the behaviour of customers. Starting with the most knowledgeable customers, an increasing number of buyers learn and often improve the way the merchandise can be integrated and used.

The application know-how and support provided by the pioneer is no longer a critical part of the purchase. Some competitors respond by restricting the support element of their packages. Buyers begin to need less support, and become more price-conscious. Other competitors may offer even more sophisticated support to target those customers who require even more hand-holding. From these types of competitors the pioneer now finds itself differentiated not in both dimensions but only in one – that of support. It thus finds itself conducting service-buy transactions. The process of **de-systemization** has started.

Other competitors may match the support of the pioneer but vary the merchandise they provide. They may supply simpler desk-top software or more advanced or sophisticated software. From these competitors the pioneer is now differentiated only in the merchandise dimension; it finds itself reduced to conducting product-buy transactions.

The process of desystemization is now fully under way. The pioneer who had started out transacting system-buys has had its level of differentiation dramatically reduced. Competitors are moving in; some in the support, some in the merchandise dimension, some in both.

If the process of evolution is allowed to continue un-hindered or if conditions enable one competitor quickly to match the merchandise and support of the other, then the pioneer's generic offering is well on its way to being traded as a commodity-buy. The process is best described as **commodization**.

Of course the pioneer need not be a passive player watching helplessly as its differentiation disappears. It could at any stage resist the onslaught of competitors and distance itself by differentiating its generic offering. It could fight the trend towards desystemization by introducing a stream of more advanced packages. Even offerings that have attained the status of commodity-buys can be modified to differentiate them from competitive offerings. Perhaps either the merchandise or the support dimension can be differentiated, enabling the pioneer to conduct product-buy or service-buy transactions. That process can be labelled **de-commodization**.

It may pay to differentiate both merchandise and support to produce a significantly different package of benefits. De-commodization has now become **systemization**. The whole cycle may now recommence, perhaps at a higher level of technical sophistication.

In a well-established market it is quite likely that the customer will encounter all four types of transactions. Some competitors may offer system-buys. Those who focus on differentiating along the merchandise dimension, may offer a variety of features and refinements until a class of product-buys emerges. Parallel developments may lead to the emergence of a class of service-buys.

Markets would be defined and redefined as competitors jostle for position. These various processes tend to be reinforced and sustained by the entry and exit of competitors at any point of the cycle. All this encourages the growth of some generic offerings and the decline of others.

The transaction life cycle is no more than an illustration. Yet it brings out two important lessons in competitive strategy. First, an entire generic offering, an entire patch in the galaxy, such as desk-top publishing, may go through these phases. If customers collectively move from one preference to another, then any competitor who for cultural or other internal reasons finds it hard to make the transition, say from system-buy to product-buy, will lose out.

Secondly, if some customers fail to shift, or can be attracted away from such a collective shift, then the transaction life cycle can teach an individual company that it does not have to move with the herd. On the contrary, it can profit, perhaps by standing still, or again perhaps by moving in a different direction by innovating and either raising or reducing the degree of differentiation of its new offering.

All these shifts are motivated by the jostling of all competitors for profitable positions in their part of the galaxy. Needless to say, each transaction shift in the cycle creates a new offering, possibly even a new generic offering, by modifying the competitive configuration.

The model of the rearranger

The second dynamic topic of this chapter is to distinguish between two types of competing offerings: the **rearranger** and the **transformer**. A rearranger is a new offering, the arrival of which changes the existing configuration of its private market, but without radically transforming that market and its surrounding landscape. It may for example aim to capture some extra market share in its private market, without however radically disturbing the composition or configuration of that private market. The rearranger is relatively conformist. The transformer on the other hand sets out to destabilize and reshape its part of the galaxy, so as to leave its landscape unrecognizable.

Chapters 6 and 8 noted that what a competitive strategy plans for an offering, is its *future* triangular relationship with competitors and customers, not its present or past positioning. That picture was nevertheless still that of the relatively conformist firmlet. It looks at the present configuration of the target space in the galaxy, modifies this for forecast changes including competitive retaliation, and then positions the new offering profitably in that target space.

The tacit assumption is that the arrival of the new offering will not radically transform the target neighbourhood. The landscape will not change very much, customers will not find their choices radically disturbed. Many competitors may lose some customers, but most of them will survive. The pattern of sellers and their interrelationships will not have changed beyond all recognition: the newcomer is either not close enough to them, or not big enough, or not sufficiently novel to transform the neighbourhood.

The key continuity here is the map of customers' choices and preferences. Preferences include for this purpose potential preferences for what is not currently on offer. None of these will show any radical discontinuity with the past.

Differentiation and the rearranger

In the rearranger model offerings with different degrees of differentiation are traded within the same neighbourhood of interlocking private markets. The new rearranger offering, let us assume, achieves a less price-sensitive competitive positioning. It does this by virtue of the originality of its concept and by its choice of a more specialized customer segment, with fewer customers and fewer close competitors.

The rearranger model allows for two kinds of dynamics:

- Change induced by external forces, such as changing technology, tastes and fashions, or macroeconomic cycles or encroachment by individual offerings. An example might be the 1990s fashion favouring ethical unit trusts and other ethical investment media.
- Decisions by the rearranger itself to serve previously existing, but latent customer segments, or to reposition its offerings either closer to substitutes or further away from them. Examples might be the original 'singles' package holidays or Braille newspapers.

Price competition and the rearranger

Alternatively the rearranger may choose to compete just on price. It will position its offering so close to its competitors' offerings that its sales volume will depend almost entirely on its pricing policy. In that case it must normally charge a price low enough to make inroads into the sales of its competitors, after allowing for any residual differentiation from their offerings. The competitive focus switches towards costs.

The model of the transformer

However, a competitive strategy can cause a much greater disturbance in its environment. A transformer offering is one whose arrival radically transforms the configuration of markets in its part of the economy. It is not uncommon for a new offering to bring about an explosive transformation of its neighbourhood; to change and realign preferences. Its arrival can be cataclysmic. It can *destabilize and reshape* the markets of its neighbours, perhaps beyond recognition. Customers come to see their choices in an entirely new light. Preferences are created or awakened for which no seller had previously catered. The strategy transforms rather than rearranges its part of the galaxy.

A firmlet which destabilizes its part of the galaxy with a differentiated offering, changes the configuration of the area by disturbing the given pattern of customer preferences; some distinctions may be blurred while others cease to be relevant. The new offering may detach some preferences from the rest and thereby split off a profitable private market in which competition is less intense. It illustrates that the best way to compete can be to compete[3] as little as possible: i.e. to differentiate. The first competitor to market a 'green' cosmetic attempted precisely that, as did Direct Line, the first UK insurer to offer motor, and then other insurance cover by telephone.

In some cases the separation into new private markets will not be complete; the new offering will in those cases still be seen as a substitute, though a less close one, for the other offerings in a radically redefined private market. In other cases however the separation may be so complete that a distinct private market is fashioned, remote from the others.

Destabilization of market systems is evidently a matter of degree. The degree depends on the extent to which customers have to readjust their view of the choices facing them, and therefore their preferences. Destabilization occurs where changes in the choices faced by customers are radical.

A market can of course be destabilized by price as well as by differentiation. Japanese motor-cycles destabilized markets in the 1960s more by their lower prices than by their differentiated outputs. Float glass destabilized the market in plate glass. Heavy discounting in cigarettes forced Philip Morris in 1993 to slash the price of its Marlboro brand so as to regain some lost volume.

However, differentiation is a much more common desta-
bilizer than price. This is what the compact audio disc did
to vinyl discs and audio tapes, and word processing to typewriters.

If a rearranger strategy is one of differentiation, if its
offering is targeted at a specific group of customers, then it
often – but by no means invariably – targets a smaller volume
of sales, but at higher margins. More differentiation seldom
means more sales for the rearranger. The transformer on the
other hand in rare cases achieves a high volume of sales in
a completely realigned and reconfigured market environment.

The important lesson for managers is not to regard markets
as given, i.e. as having an unchangeable definition and
composition, but as inherently pliable or even fragile.
Virtually all markets can be destabilized, either by ourselves
or by competitors. The lesson is both aggressive and defensive.

Even the most established market system can be totally
reshaped by a well positioned offering. Good examples of
market transformation are:

- Mars' transformation of the humble choc-ice into the ice-
  cream bar in 1989,
- Häagen-Dazs introduction of the premium 'adult' ice
  cream,
- The effect of the information super-highway on a large
  proportion of communication and information businesses.

The trick is to outmanoeuvre competitors by destabilizing a
part of the galaxy in one's own favour, and being prepared
to do this as quickly and as often as required.[4] For even when
the configuration of the local markets suits us, we may still
wish to destabilize the area again, if only to maintain and
increase our lead by pre-empting or wrong-footing competitors. Customers *can* move away from offerings of their own
accord, but much more often they are attracted away by
nimbler competitors who reshape markets, merging some and
splitting others.

190

The importance of this transformer strategy is hard to exaggerate. It goes far beyond the usual model in which a market is an inert black box, something out there, something given, which the business either conforms with or exploits. Destabilization acts on neighbouring offerings as nuclear fission acts on atoms and molecules.

Moreover the transformer holds the initiative. If its vision of the fallout is correct, it will have a profitable and prolonged advantage, prolonged because competitors have a process of mental adjustment to go through as well as mastering the physical and financial logistics of mounting an effective response.[5] In the UK Häagen-Dazs had few close competitors for several years. The threat from Ben & Jerry for example came after five years of dominance by Häagen-Dazs.[6]

Summary

This chapter has shown how the pursuit of financial value must take account of the dynamic character of markets.

The transaction life cycle is a useful model which illustrates that neither competitive markets nor competing businesses need to go on shifting in the same direction: either away from or towards greater differentiation. Parts of the galaxy can oscillate from system-buy to commodity-buy and back again.

The distinction between rearrangers and transformers is the distinction between adaptive and destabilizing competitive strategies. Transformer firmlets can completely destabilize their market areas, often reaping handsome rewards. Destabilization changes the map to such an extent that the originator can enjoy good margins and high volumes unless and until competitors regain their balance.

Notes

1. Earlier versions of this model are contained in Mathur (1984 and 1988).
2. Rather than the more complex Figure 5.4.
3. 'Compete' is used here in the colloquial sense of offering an identical or very close substitute.

4. In Chapter 11 this type of process will be called serial innovation.
5. The concept of the transformer has a long history. It is older than the world of predominantly differentiated offerings. In that older context it was part of Schumpeter's (1934) concept of creative destruction.
6. *Financial Times*, 11 August 1994.

Part Four   Resources and Business Strategy

Parts Two and Three have concentrated on the outputs of offerings, on what customers perceive and compare. Part Four restores the balance by focusing on the resources which enable companies to build financial value with their offerings. Their different resource endowments make companies heterogeneous, and enable different companies to bring out different offerings, and to do this successfully and profitably in competitive markets.

10 Corporate resources for sustained value-building

Introduction

This chapter contains more theory than the rest of this book. It unavoidably uses more technical language. However, some prizes await the manager who perseveres with the technical argument.

The question is what the company needs in order to attain durable super-normal performance, here called 'sustained value-building'. The chapter provides a critical piece in the jig-saw of what makes a competitive strategy successful enough to sustain value-building.

A competitive strategy, i.e. an offering, will create financial value only if it has a positive net present value (NPV), discounted at the offering's cost of capital. A positive NPV requires that the NPV of the net cash outflows during the initial investment phase of the strategy is at least matched by the NPV of the subsequent net cash inflows. Those subsequent net inflows may fluctuate heavily from day to day or from period to period, and these fluctuations are included in the appraisal of the proposed new offering.

A new offering which beats the cost of capital in this way, needs to be more successful than most other offerings, and for this reason many people refer to the required above-normal financial performance as 'competitive advantage'. That expression is avoided here, because it does not readily communicate its financial significance, nor more particularly the need to beat the cost of capital. The required financial performance will therefore be referred to as **'value-building'**, and the offering or company which achieves it as a **'value-builder'**.

When we look back at financial performance, the fact that value has been built is enough to show that we have beaten the cost of capital. However, when we plan a new offering or competitive strategy, we need to ensure that the offering can sustain its value-building process until value is actually built, i.e. until its NPV becomes positive. The offering will therefore need protective armour against encroachment or other external threats for long enough[1] to achieve that goal of a positive NPV. In a nutshell, the new competitive strategy or offering needs to become a **sustained value-builder**.

This chapter presents the 'resource-based view' put forward by a number of writers in recent years. That view suggests that in order to become a sustained value-builder, a competitive strategy needs a special kind of company-specific resources, here called 'key resources'.

The chapter also points to an alternative, yet at least equally powerful path to sustained value-building. This path is corporate strategy, i.e. the continual upgrading of a company's cluster of offerings.

Different perspectives of 'sustained'

The resource-based view came as a response to the observed fact that some companies 'simply do better than others, and . . . do so consistently'.[2] In other words, some companies manage to be sustained value-builders. In this context however the expression is first of all applied to a company, not to a single strategy or offering. It is also secondly observed after the event as a sustained historical achievement,[3] not as an expectation at the time of appraisal.

These two perspectives of value-building, one for the company and one for a single strategy, are in fact quite compatible: a company is unlikely to have succeeded in sustaining the generation of value, unless it has over the years adopted and implemented value-building strategies. The *strategy's* value-building needs to be sustained for defensive reasons: it needs protective armour so that its intended net inflows are not upset or cut short by the actions of competitors or other envious parties. The *company* by contrast may

196

need to be more aggressive in pursuing a succession of winning strategies, in order to become a sustained value-builder in its own right.

The resource-based view and its success criterion

The resource-based view has been put forward by a number of writers. The writer whose approach most closely matches the focus in this book on competitive strategies for offerings, is Barney.[4]

All resource-based theorists seek to explain the contradiction between the efficient markets assumption of perfect competition and the fact of sustained value-building by some companies and therefore presumably by the offerings of those companies. If resource and offering markets[5] were as efficient as financial markets are believed to be, then why are all companies not equally efficient? Less successful companies should be able in efficient markets to replicate the resources of the star performers. That process should continue until there is equilibrium, i.e. until no company has any further incentive to shift its position. At that point all companies should have equal resources and perform with equal success.

The evident fact that some companies perform significantly and persistently better than others, strongly suggests that resource and offering markets are not efficient, and that companies have different resource endowments. Barney focuses on what kind of company-specific resources will ensure the success of a competitive strategy. Success is called 'competitive advantage', for which we substitute 'value-building' in this book.

Barney[6] defines the duration for which competitive advantage must be sustained. He suggests that in order to be sustained, it must continue until 'efforts to duplicate that advantage have ceased'.[7] We do not adopt Barney's criterion in this book, as we are concerned with achieving a positive net present value, i.e. with beating the cost of capital.[8]

Success-aping pressures

Resource-based theory was, as we saw, a response to the puzzle of persistent unequal performance by companies. If resource and offering markets were efficient, such a state would be a disequilibrium, and therefore unstable. Companies with less efficient resources would successfully seek to ape the success of others, by acquiring the same or equivalent resources in the efficient resource markets. Just as nature abhors a vacuum, so efficient markets abhor superperformance by some competitors. Moreover it is not just Champion's own competitors who would seek to ape its sustained value-building, but any company that might profitably exploit Champion's resources in other offering markets.

This success-aping[9] pressure should force prices and margins down to the point where the successful offerings' cash flows revert back to an equilibrium level. At that point its position as a value-builder has been competed away.

Where does sustained value-building occur? In the offering or in the company?

A tacit assumption made in the resource-based view is that sustained value-building comes from competitive strategy, i.e. from the favourable market position of an *individual* offering competing for profitable customers, and not from the company's management of *the composition of its cluster of offerings*.

This chapter however will in turn examine two alternative explanations of how a company's value-building may come to be sustained:

- first through the competing offering, and
- then, at the end of the chapter, through the company's management of its cluster, i.e. its prowess in corporate strategy.

Sustained value-building in customer markets: the resource-based view

First, then, the puzzle of sustained value-building by offerings in customer markets. As the puzzle is formulated, the critical assumption is that competition occurs in efficient markets.[10] In such efficient markets, i.e. in the model of pure competition, there is unimpeded entry. 'Firms', customers, offerings and inputs (factors of production) are all operating or traded in free and well and promptly informed markets, in which competitive forces will tend to produce homogeneous suppliers and customers. All agents in such markets are price-takers. None of them is dominant: there is no oligopolistic circularity.[11] Most importantly, this theoretical model has been applied to what a given 'firm' buys as well as what it sells. Consequently competing 'firms' are in market equilibrium assumed to end up with homogeneous resource endowments. In this theoretical model any persistently super-profitable offering is conclusive evidence of a disequilibrium.

Now suppose that the offering's resource markets are less than perfectly efficient, because the offering is protected by an encroachment barrier. At first, would-be encroachers may be unaware of the barrier. They will treat the successful offering as evidence of a disequilibrium. However, once they have encountered and recognized the barrier, they may accept the barrier as a fact, and cease their success-aping efforts. There is then an equilibrium in a less than efficient market. The previous erroneous perception turns out to have been that of an apparent, not a real disequilibrium.

Those who use the pure competition and efficient markets model as their starting-point have of course never claimed that it faithfully mirrors the world as it actually is. Economists have however widely and often tacitly assumed that even when real-life impurities are allowed for, the model still retains much of its power to explain how markets work and how prices are determined.[12]

The 'resource-based' school of strategy[13] has, as we saw, questioned the assumption of efficient resource markets, and attributed the observed fact of sustained value-building to heterogeneous, company-specific resources.

Resources, their types and classification: key resources

'Resources' are in this context a subset of inputs.[14] Resources are a stock,[15] representing unexhausted value from past expenditures. The wider term 'inputs' denotes all expenditures, irrespective of whether they are an accumulated stock of unexhausted and continuing value.

Barney[16] helpfully classifies resources into physical capital, (individual) human capital and (collective or social) organizational capital resources.

Similar distinctions are made by those who use terms like 'competences' or 'core competences' or 'capabilities'. Capabilities have been distinguished as skills in coordinating other resources.[17] Some of these interactive resources are a subset, but an important one, of what this book calls 'key resources'.[18] However, 'key resources' are very special, and exclude those higher level resources which later in this chapter we shall classify as 'pure management resources'.

The resource-based view above all distinguishes resources not by their nature, but by their economic properties. These are:

- the ease with which they are bought or otherwise acquired, and
- the extent to which they enable a company to conceive and implement competitive strategies that create value.[19]

The resource-based view[20] is only concerned with resources which can persistently build value. Writers attach to them a variety of terms, such as 'critical resources', 'strategic assets',[21] 'specialized and difficult-to-imitate resources', or 'firm resources'. Our preferred term for resources capable of (a) creating value and (b) sustaining it long enough to defeat success-aping attempts is 'key resources'.

A key resource needs to be *capable* of meeting that second requirement, even though we shall see[22] that it will not always be required in practice. This tighter specification is needed because:

(a) even if the ability to see off all emulation attempts is not needed for this offering today, it may be needed for this offering tomorrow if the going gets tougher, or
(b) it may in any case be needed for other offerings served by the same resource.

A relaxation of this requirement may be appropriate for a particular strategy, not for the generic definition of a key resource.

The resource-based view was developed as an explanation of deviations found in the real world from the success-aping tendency of the efficient markets model. That is why it concentrates on those features of key resources which cause those deviations.

A central topic of the resource-based view is just what characteristics are needed by key resources. There are almost as many accounts of that central topic as there are writers. A most useful integrating framework which takes account of most of them has been put forward by Peteraf.[23] Peteraf's framework can be taken as representative of a number of others.

Unlike Barney's, Peteraf's definition of value-building (called 'competitive advantage') is returns which exceed breakeven.[24] That means that the returns more than cover costs, including the cost of capital. The concept is therefore one of period cash flows rather than net present value, but that distinction is immaterial to the attributes of the required resources, which is our interest in this framework. All that matters to that discussion, is that the resources create and sustain returns exceeding those in the efficient markets model. In the account below the expression 'value-building' will therefore be used in the sense of 'better than breakeven returns' when the context requires it.

Peteraf's resource-based framework: the four cornerstones

Peteraf's starting point is that a company achieves the sustained creation of value by means of what are here called key resources. Key resources need to have four characteristics, which Peteraf calls *the four cornerstones*. Key resources must be:

- heterogeneous,
- subject to ex ante limits to competition,
- subject to ex post limits to competition,
- imperfectly mobile.

('Ex ante' describes how an event or project looks before it occurs, i.e. an intention or expectation. 'Ex post' describes how the same occurrence appears after the event, i.e. its realized outturn.) It will presently be seen that heterogeneity is fundamental to value-building, that ex ante limits prevent the value generated being swallowed up by the costs of acquiring the resource, and that the other two cornerstones in various ways mainly serve to sustain the building of value.

Chapter 11 will apply the cornerstones to the task facing the manager, who may need some briefer and less technical labels: diverse, felicitous, matchless, inseparable. These labels are shown in the headings below in brackets.

Heterogeneous (diverse)

The requirement of **heterogeneity** is a fundamental departure from the assumption of efficiency in the market for the resource. It simply recognizes that companies are not in fact homogeneous, but endowed with different resources.[25] This heterogeneity is both general and specific. Companies which appear to belong to the same industry, such as steel or automobiles, are not equally strong in R&D resources, distribution, automated manufacturing processes and so on. However, even when two such companies have comparable total R&D resources, these may in their turn differ in their specific scope. For example one company may be specialized in product research, the other in process research.

By a more efficient resource we mean one which delivers better value for money. The resource either helps to produce a superior or more attractive offering, or it produces an offering which matches its substitutes in quality, but does so at lower cost. In that last case the cost advantage may either be retained by the seller as extra cash flow or be passed on to the customer as a price reduction.[26]

The resource-based view has thus explicitly[27] removed two implied assumptions in the model of efficient markets. They are:

- that competing companies' resources are homogeneous, and
- that those resources are tradable[28] in efficient markets, so that any differences between individual companies' resources are purely short-lived, as any company will smoothly replicate the best resources used by others.[29]

The two assumptions do not of course bear much resemblance to the real world of most resource markets. After all, many of the resources are human skills and capabilities.

A direct *effect* of resource heterogeneity (Peteraf points out) is on profit margins. Different companies will have resource bundles of different levels of efficiency. Company A with resources of marginal efficiency will break even, Company B with more than marginally efficient resources will do better than break even.

The general condition of resource heterogeneity is market imperfection. Without a degree of market failure it could not persist. In the short term at least, the resources must be in limited supply. If supply were unlimited, success-aping would lead all companies to acquire the most efficient resources, and thus erode the successful competitor's value-building position. An extreme example might be a uniquely positioned site for an oil refinery. That site can only be available to one, not to all interested companies.

Ex ante limits to competition (felicitous)

Ex ante limits to competition stop the value to be generated by a key resource for its owning company being swallowed up by a rise in its cost due to a competitive auction. Suppose Companies A and B expect resource X – say the uniquely positioned site – to generate the same value and are equally endowed to exploit that value-building potential. Then their competitive bidding for X would lift its price to the point where its cost would cancel out its prospective value-building to either A or B. The entire intended gain would go to the previous owner of the site.

Ex ante limits to competition are a condition which can be met in one of two ways: foresight or luck.[30] **Foresight** consists of differences between one company's expectations and another's; differences which prompt them to place conflicting values on a given resource. These differences constitute a market imperfection in the demand for the resource, whereas heterogeneity is an imperfection in its supply. The company which places the higher expected value on it, and thus outbids others at a cost which still generates value, is said to have superior foresight.

By a different route, luck also avoids the erosion of value-building from a competitive rise in the cost of the resource. **Luck** describes the case where the key resource is or had been acquired as it were inadvertently, without triggering an auction. Perhaps it had been acquired before present opportunities became apparent, or perhaps it is acquired now, with both the company and its potential rivals undervaluing it.[31] Of course, if an already owned resource could now be sold for more than the value it can build for the company, it should be sold: its opportunity cost exceeds its value-building potential.[32] However, markets for such key resources are not often perfect enough for their opportunity cost to rise that high.[33]

Ex post limits to competition (matchless)

Ex post limits to competition, together with imperfect mobility, are the principal means by which value-building can be sustained.[34]

Margins can be eroded by competitors or others, bent either on encroaching on a market position, or on depriving the incumbent of the use or the full value of a resource.

The specific function of ex post limits to competition is to prevent the value-building of an offering being eroded by encroachment from competitors attracted by its advantageous position. The competitors in other words have an incentive to emulate the success of the offering. Ex post limits obstruct such encroachment. They take the form of both (a) imperfect imitability and (b) imperfect substitutability.

Imperfect imitability makes it hard for a competitor to copy the resource and thus the competitive strategy to which it is instrumental. Possible obstacles to imitability are:[35]

- Social complexity: the resource may depend on skills or knowledge of company-specific teams rather than of individual managers or employees.
- 'Causal ambiguity': competitors would like to copy the strategy, but have an inadequate grasp of the causal chain between the key resource or the process of creating it and the competitive success.[36]
- 'Time compression diseconomies': e.g. crash R&D programmes tend to be less successful. Switching costs fall into this category. Porter defines switching costs as one-time costs facing the buyer of switching from one supplier's (offering) to another's.[37] There may for example be unfamiliarity on either side in dealing with the idiosyncrasies of the other.
- 'Asset mass efficiencies': these are illustrated by the advantage held by a company which already has greater experience of successful R&D, or a larger customer base and reputation: this superior stock of a resource constitutes a barrier for competitors with inferior stock accumulations.

- Complementarity of resources: the value of an R&D capability is enhanced by the company's better distributor network which passes back reactions from customers.
- Commitment as a deterrence to encroachment: imitators are deterred by the incumbent company's show of commitment to get tough with encroachers. A good deterrent is spending on a 'stock' resource like capacity or brand loyalty rather than on a 'flow' expenditure like volume or advertising. Flow expenditures can be adjusted at will in the event of encroachment by a competitor.[38] Only stocks are resources, and thus a credible commitment.

Imperfect substitutability blocks an avenue for bypassing imperfect imitability. A competitor who has difficulty in imitating the resource could bypass that obstacle by devising a *substitute* offering, using a different, more accessible resource.[39] Thus satellite or cable TV can bypass local broadcast channels. Imperfect substitutability impedes or prevents such substitution.

Imperfect mobility (inseparable)

The employer of a resource needs it to be imperfectly mobile to prevent:

- either its loss to a competitor or to some other outsider,
- or the loss of the value it builds; that value is vulnerable to claims by an owner of the resource, who might for example be an employee with a special skill, or some member of the 'inner team'.

The threats against which this cornerstone protects a company, come not just from its competitors, i.e. companies offering substitutes to its offerings, but also from non-competitors which could derive value from the same key resource. An investment bank may be interested in poaching a uniquely successful catering team from a luxury hotel.

Imperfect mobility differs from ex post limits to competition in that it concerns the employer's degree of control over the resource itself or its value, rather than competitors' ability to match it. Imperfect mobility protects against removal rather than replication. What it has in common with ex post limits to competition, is that both mainly serve to sustain value-building, rather than to start it in the first place.

The two threats, of losing control either of the resource or of its value, are quite separate and will be separately discussed.

Imperfect mobility: (a) To keep the resource

Imperfect mobility counters the threat to the company's control over the *resource itself*. It takes two forms: the resource can be,

- non-tradable: this prevents other parties bidding it away from the employer, or
- tradable, but less valuable to others than to the incumbent employer; this removes or impairs other parties' bargaining power rather than their physical access to the resource. Valuable here means worth more than its opportunity cost, which in this narrow context Peteraf defines as its value to its next best employer.[40]

An example of a non-tradable resource[41] is a company's reputation for excellence: the reputations of Boeing or Rolls-Royce are not capable of being bought or sold.

Examples of the more-valuable-to-the-employer category are resources which are,

- *company-specific* (in the sense of less useful outside the company), like an information system for just-in-time provisioning, designed by a retailer like Marks & Spencer, for working with its particular set of suppliers,
- *a sunk cost* to the owner, like the intimate knowledge acquired over time by a hospital receptionist of the organization, its communication channels and its members,
- subject to switching costs, like a legal adviser's thorough familiarity with the special needs and the external and internal relationships of a large industrial client,

207

- co-specialized with another company-specific resource, like NEC's skill in integrating computer and telecommunications technology,
- transferable only with very high transaction costs: Reuters' or Datastream's expertise in financial market information would be costly to exploit by a company which lacks Reuters' or Datastream's high and specialized skills in information technology.

Imperfect mobility: (b) To keep the value of the resource: appropriability

The second type of imperfect mobility responds to the threat of the total or partial loss to an inner team member of the value which the resource builds. It is sometimes labelled 'appropriability'. **Appropriability** describes the ability of either the company or the team member to 'appropriate' that value. It therefore looks at this type of imperfect mobility from the point of view of a claimant to the value created by the resource.

The significance of the inner 'team'

The greatest threat of loss of the value of the resource comes from the inner team of resource owners, like key employees, who intimately share in the creation of a valuable offering. For a successful offering a company often heavily depends on a resource which it creates by a joint effort with its inner team of key suppliers, customers, and especially key employees. These inner team members are often well placed to snatch away from the company the value generated by the resource.

Suppose a software house supplied software for the control systems of a communications satellite to a satellite operator. The task would not have been possible without the intimate participation of another subcontractor, which manufactured and supplied the satellite itself. The inner team includes the key designer employed by the software house, as well as the supplier of the satellite and its operator. If any one of these had too much bargaining power, the software house could lose the generated value or profit to that party.

Mr Peter Wood in 1985 brought to the Royal Bank of Scotland an innovative way of processing motor insurance proposals very cheaply by telephone. The venture was funded as a subsidiary of the bank under the name of Direct Line Insurance, run by Mr Wood. From 1988 Direct Line was wholly owned by the bank, and Mr Wood's equity in the concept became a bonus entitlement in his service contract, geared to the profits of Direct Line Insurance. In the early 1990s this business took off to such an extent that for the year ended 30 September 1993 Mr Wood's bonus escalated to £18.2 million. This caused media comment. In any case there were other business changes at this point. The bank therefore agreed to buy out Mr Wood's bonus entitlement with payments (including a £7 million pension contribution) totalling £24 million. That figure was a professional valuation of those bonus rights. Under this freely struck series of bargains each party was evidently able to 'appropriate' some of the value of the resource, which in this case was Mr Wood's brilliant concept and his ability to implement it.

How the framework fits together

This completes the account of the four cornerstones and of Peteraf's framework. What this book calls key resources, are resources capable of (a) building value and (b) doing this for a sustained duration. The second of these requirements means that a key resource must be capable of defeating all success-aping attempts. To meet those two requirements, they must have all four of Peteraf's cornerstones to some degree; degree, that is, of market failure.

Peteraf stresses that the four cornerstones are not independent of one another or mutually exclusive. Nor are they of equal rank. Heterogeneity (diverse) is the most fundamental condition of value-building; if companies had homogeneous resource bundles, they could not be a source of value-building. Ex ante limitations (felicitous) to competition are necessary because no resource could generate value

if it were wiped out by its acquisition cost. These two conditions are needed primarily for value-building itself, rather
than for its sustaining. Sustainability comes mainly from the
other two cornerstones, ex post limitations (matchlessness)
and imperfect mobility (inseparability).

Using the resource-based framework

Resource-based theory suggests some useful points about the
way companies should go about finding and identifying key
resources. These and other practical questions are discussed
in Chapter 11.

Why no customer market failure?

One apparently odd assumption implied in the resource-
based set of theories is that sustained value-building is
exclusively due to market failure in key resources. Could
failure not also occur in the market into which the offering
is to be sold?

For example, would there not be such market failure if
(say) BSkyB bought out its only competitor (as it has done)
for satellite TV and its dishes in the UK, or if Euroclear, one
of two Eurobond registrars, bought out Cedel, its sole
competitor?

In any such case it seems improbable that competitors
would not be able to devise an offering close enough to win
customers away from the monopolist, using either similar or
quite different resources. Any temporary market failure
achieved by BSkyB is unlikely in the longer term to preclude
either encroachment or any other erosion of value-building.
It is of course quite conceivable that BSkyB might succeed in
persistently building value, but its success would be due to
an input market failure, i.e. to a resource monopoly.

Customer market failure could of course come about in
'seller's market' conditions. These occur when buyers
compete for suppliers instead of the other way round.
Supplier's markets come about through some interference

with free market forces. The interference could come from governmental price or physical controls like production quotas or licensing; or through the exercise of monopsony or 'single buyer' power by a dominant player. Such monopsonists may typically be governments who exercise a 'flag preference' by placing defence or other procurement orders only with favoured domestic suppliers. In such cases sustained value-building may result from a failure of customer rather than resource markets. Chapter 11 will however show that in rare conditions there may be scope for suppliers too to create profitable market failure of this kind by developing their own key resources, instead of merely exploiting monopsonistic customer initiatives.

Sustained value-building by companies

Markets abhor real or apparent disequilibria. That tendency for competitors to move in to compete away value being generated, concerns individual *offerings*. However as already noted, the empirical data showing sustained value-building all tend to relate to *companies*.

The resource-based view has so far been put forward in the literature only to explain sustained value-building in customer markets. It therefore helps to explain successful *offerings*. However, practically all empirical observations of sustained value-building relate to the performance of *companies* or *profit centres* within companies. Sometimes it relates to major sub-units of a company, identified as its 'lines of business' in different 'industries'.[42] The data do not normally relate to single offerings.

The available evidence therefore does not demonstrate that offerings or firmlets alone account for empirically observed sustained value-building. It seems likely that much of it concerns companies.

Now suppose that what sustains the generation of value was attributable not to resources which cheapen or differentiate individual offerings, but to the company and its corporate strategy, then there would be no competitors to move in! Value-building by each offering may be eroded by

211

competitive moves, but the company might still in that case create sustained value.

If sustained value-building were the work of corporate strategy, the most obvious explanation is that excellent corporate managers will pursue excellent corporate strategies.[43] They will again and again add profitable offerings and divest unprofitable ones, thus bringing about a continuing stream of above-normal earnings. A super-profitable offering may well attract success-aping competition, but by the time its margins cease to build value, it will be under different ownership: the excellent corporate managers will have divested it!

A company's excellence in corporate strategy consists of a flair for picking winners among offerings and for felicitous timing of additions to and divestments from its cluster of offerings. Continuing skill in corporate strategy may therefore be a major explanation for the sustained value-building that has been observed.

Competitive strategy must in fact be seen in context. It receives so much attention, because the task of identifying valuable offerings is complex. However, corporate strategy is important because it asks two vital extra questions, to be explored in Part Five:

- Is this the right company to have this profitable offering?
- Is this offering continuing to add value to this company?

Does the company encounter a success-aping process?

The owning company, the head office, is not in direct competition for customers in any market. The landlord of the cinema is not in competition for filmgoers. The landlord does of course have an indirect stake in the prosperity of the cinema, but the landlord does not compete for filmgoers. Only the cinema does that. If the cinema becomes unprofitable, the landlord may well turn it into a leisure centre.

The company's corporate strategy, as distinct from its firm-lets' competitive strategies, does not therefore run into those success-aping pressures which the resource-based framework discusses.

Nevertheless, does the company and its corporate strategy run into some other success-aping process? The question must be asked; for if it does not, then apparently corporate strategy can win the kind of free lunch that market economics needs to be sceptical about. So in what other market or markets could corporate strategy attract a success-aping process, if not in customer markets?

Two candidates spring to mind:

- the capital and other financial markets in which the company funds itself, and
- the market in managerial talent with a flair for corporate strategy.

Yet neither of these candidates looks very promising. If a company is seen to enjoy a consistently high investment rating and therefore a low cost of capital, or consistently successful corporate management, then others will inevitably seek to emulate its success. They may even succeed and become equally prosperous. Emulation however, is not enough to constitute a value-eroding process. To erode value-building, it would need to threaten the company's premium status in the market concerned. In customer markets, from which the analogy is taken, the success-aping process does its damage not by its mere encroachment upon the successful offering's part of the galaxy, but by the consequent erosion of its advantage in prices and margins. A corporate strategy could only run into that problem if the company and its would-be emulators became significant factors in one of the markets concerned. They would have to be able to move prices in the world financial market or in the market in chief executives. That possibility looks remote.

It seems remote because a value-eroding tendency presupposes some scarcity, in the offering's case the limited size of the private market in which rivals compete. Emulation may marginally increase the size of that market, but not enough to stop the success-aping process. In the financial and

213

managerial talent markets it is hard to see any equivalent bottleneck factor. Imitation of its prowess in corporate strategy will not perceptibly raise the company's cost of capital, or the cost of retaining its critical resource, the excellent manager or managers. Funding markets in the modern world are global and huge, not narrow and specific; if a few more companies produce excellent performance, this drop in the ocean will not perceptibly raise the general cost of capital. Again, if a few more companies achieve excellence in corporate strategy, this may not perceptibly raise the general scarcity value of managers with a flair for corporate strategy. Picking winners and a flair for timing are not so specific that a narrow market is likely to develop in which prices, i.e. compensation levels, will be dramatically affected by imitation. Even if it did, that market is not efficient enough to permit a value-eroding process.

It is therefore no surprise that the equilibrium puzzle has only been put forward in the context of competitive markets for customers. Customer markets are much narrower than for example financial markets, especially in a differentiated world. Customer markets present a natural bottleneck to attract a success-aping process. Excellent corporate strategy does not appear to run into any easily identifiable and equivalent bottleneck.

The evidence and the logic

The logic here presented has not so far been tested by empirical research. It does however point to a strong case. First, the empirical evidence for sustained value-building appears to concern companies, not offerings, not economic entities which compete for customer preferences. There is therefore no evidence that competitive strategy accounts for the bulk of the empirically observed phenomenon.

Secondly, the logic suggests that corporate strategy has a much more untrammelled chance to create really durable value. Resource-based theory explains how competitive strategy can lead to a degree of durability due to imperfections in resource markets, but in the case of corporate strategy

214

there is no logical limit to that durability other than human frailty and mortality. There must be a strong prima-facie possibility that corporate strategy may be responsible for much, perhaps most of the observed incidence of sustained value-building.

This is an important conclusion, as it opens up an avenue for sustained value-building, which has hardly been explored in the strategy, as distinct from the marketing literature.[44]

Pure management resources

There is a class of resources which is valuable and important, yet outside the scope of this book. We might call these **pure management resources**. General Electric for example has a flair for structuring itself so as to get the best of central thrust combined with the benefit of decentralized responsibility.[45] That is a most valuable resource, which will be of benefit to the company's business strategies as well as to its day to day management. It is not however specific enough to help the company develop competitive or corporate strategies, or to be identifiable as a resource which has made or will make any one offering valuable. Competitive strategies identify particular sets of profitable customers, and corporate strategies time the addition or divestment of offerings designed to serve those customers. Pure management resources are at too high, too general a level[46] to identify specific profitable offerings. They are helpful to that and many other tasks generally, but at too high a level of abstraction for our purposes. They are not key resources, nor do they include the very special flair for corporate strategy to which we turn in the next section.

Generally, there is a rising awareness of resources which characterize a whole company rather than offerings, and among these it is useful to distinguish between:

- those more general resources which help to direct practically any set of activities, among them pure management resources, and

- those more specific ones which give the company an advantage in particular types of offerings, like a flair for R&D or innovation in pharmaceuticals or electronics.

The next section deals with a more general type of corporate resource. In Chapter 11 there will be a discussion of 'corporate capabilities' (under a variety of similar labels), which largely fall into the more specific category. The two categories are not always neatly separated in real life, but they are worth distinguishing. The more general category cannot protect any one offering against success-aping pressures. The advantage which it confers is not properly *competitive*.

The resource-based framework and corporate strategy

A flair for corporate strategy belongs of course to the more general category of corporate resources. This alone shows that this corporate strategy explanation of sustained value-building cannot itself be a key resource. If it were, it too would be derived from resource-based theory. There are in fact two difficulties in this suggestion.

First, resource-based theory is in essence an explanation for the defeat of success-aping forces in customer markets. Yet we have argued that in corporate strategy there is an apparent free lunch, as it seems hard to find a value-eroding force to defy.

Secondly, at a more practical level, it might be hard to apply the four cornerstones to the flair for corporate strategy. Part Seven will argue that corporate strategy is the inalienable responsibility of the chief executive.[47] That flair must in that case be an attribute of that same chief executive.

It is not possible to generalize how companies recognize, select and evaluate this chief executive resource if the chief executive himself or herself is not the selector or decision-taker. Vacancies in that office are filled for example by committees such as boards of directors, but can they be seen as strategists? This is not perhaps impossible, but hardly common.

216

The question is: who assesses the skills of a chief executive? Who can test them for ex post limits to competition, or indeed for appropriability? This is a difficult area to discuss, but perhaps it does not warrant a detailed discussion in view of the more fundamental lack of a value-eroding force to defy. Without such a force in sight, there is no need to look for ex post limits to competition in order to explain sustained value-building.

Nevertheless, the cornerstones still provide some practical insights for corporate strategy. For example a company will not build value if in order to acquire a brilliant corporate strategist it needs to pay that person's full value. The acquisition cost has in that case swallowed up the whole of the potential value of the move. That is why a valuable flair for corporate strategy is most likely to be acquired by luck. Finally, those who appoint brilliant chief executives, may wish to devise incentives which restrict their mobility.

Summary and conclusion

This chapter has sought an explanation of the phenomenon of sustained value-building and its apparent inconsistency with the success-aping pressures of efficient markets. Where this is created by an offering, we must conclude that the only free market explanation is likely to be market failure in a key resource, as explained by resource-based theory.

This may or may not be a common occurrence. However, sustained value-building is just as likely to be due to the company's prowess in corporate strategy, which is immune to the threat of success-aping forces.

This chapter has been more theoretical than most of this book. Resource-based theory is however insightful and carries a wealth of practical messages. The exploration of what makes sustained value-building possible, has uncovered some fundamental concepts with important practical implications.

Moreover, the phenomenon of sustained value-building has opened up the question whether corporate strategy accounts for some or even most of it. Companies would achieve this through persistent good judgement in selecting and retaining valuable competitive strategies, and a flair for timing. As regards competitive strategy, the resource-based view gives the practitioner a clearer grasp of the central role played in it by resources. This clearer grasp will make it easier to assess and compare the chances of success of alternative competitive strategies.

This chapter, like resource-based theory, has focused on explaining sustained value-building in the abstract. It has not looked at the phenomenon primarily through the eyes of the manager. The next chapter will reverse that priority by focusing on how these insights can help the manager.

Notes

1. The need for durable positive cash flows, and for encroachment barriers, has already been mentioned in Chapter 7, and briefly in Chapter 8.
2. Rumelt, Schendel and Teece (1991) p. 12.
3. A good example is found in Kay (1993), Chapter 2. Kay's expression is 'added value' rather than just 'value' or 'positive value'.
4. See especially Barney (1986) and (1991).
5. Called 'product markets' in the literature.
6. Barney (1991).
7. This is of course a state of equilibrium in an imperfect market.
8. This point is developed in Chapter 11.
9. The expression 'success-aping' is used in this Part Four to characterize forces, pressures or attempts to emulate another company's supernormal returns.

   This incentive to 'enter' a market is described as an equilibrium concept, e.g. by Barney (1991, quoting Hirshleifer) and by Rumelt, Schendel and Teece (1991). The would-be 'entrant' sees the other company's super-normal returns as an opportunity to be imitated, i.e. a disequilibrium. When such attempts cease, equilibrium is said to be restored. Microeconomic writers often treat the super-normal cash flows as 'rents' earned by the resources concerned, whereas Barney (1991) and we treat them as value generated by the offering that uses the resource. 'Success-aping' is used in preference to technical terms derived from either 'rent' or 'equilibrium', which non-economists may find ambiguous or difficult.
10. See Rumelt, Schendel and Teece (1991) and Hunt and Morgan (1995).
11. See Chapter 7.

12. This case has been argued by Friedman (1935).
13. Some of the departures by the resource-based school have their ancestry in the Austrian School of economics. For a review see Jacobson (1992).
14. Defined in Chapter 3.
15. Dierickx and Cool (1989).
16. Barney (1991).
17. Nelson and Winter (1982), Grant (1991).
18. The special importance of some of these narrower categories is developed in Chapter 12.
19. Barney (1991), translated into the terminology of this book. Chapter 11 will stress the practical benefit of this approach.
20. The resource-based view is held in a number of versions. We here follow the version formulated in some detail by Barney, and couple this with Peteraf's systematic synthesis and presentation by means of her helpful cornerstones metaphor.

    The supernormal cash flows created by key resources can be attributed either,

    (a). to each resource as its 'rents' (cash flows in excess of the opportunity cost of the resource), or
    (b). to the projects, strategies or offerings which use the resource so as to generate value (i.e. cash flows in excess of cost of capital, resulting in a positive net present value).

    Barney (1991) and this book adopt approach (b), but many writers, including Peteraf, go for (a). It is worth stressing that there is no one for one relationship between resources and offerings.

    Approach (a) requires a sharp focus on the opportunity cost of the resource, and therefore on its alternative uses. This book with its emphasis on beating the cost of capital favours approach (b), in which the opportunity cost of each resource is only one of many factors in establishing the NPV of a competitive strategy.
21. Amit and Schoemaker (1993).
22. Chapter 11.
23. Peteraf (1993).
24. Peteraf's expression for (positive) value is 'competitive advantage', and her expression for returns in excess of breakeven is 'rents'.
25. 'Heterogeneous' is strictly the antithesis of homogeneous. It means that the *group* is not uniform, but diverse. The *individual* resource is by this cornerstone required to be sufficiently distinctive to command extra margins (rents). It does not need to be unique (Peteraf, 1993), but different from most substitute resources.
26. Conner (1991) p. 132, Peteraf (1993) pp 180 onwards.
27. The strategic management literature, as distinct from microeconomics, had of course implied resource heterogeneity for some

time, for example in the SWOT model. Resource-based theory made the rejection of the assumption of homogeneity explicit and formal.

28. Chi (1994) observes that A's company-specific resource can be acquired by B in a number of different ways, i.e. by acquiring A or part of it, or by buying the service of the resource from A, or by buying from A the transfer of the resource, i.e. getting A to teach B to replicate the appropriate skills and organization routines.

29. Barney (1991).

30. Barney (1986).

31. Barney (1986).

32. The authors are indebted to Professor Robert Grant for drawing attention to this important point.

33. Dierickx and Cool (1989)

34. Discussed in Chapter 11.

35. The list is based on Dierickx and Cool (1989).

36. Lippman and Rumelt (1982), Dierickx and Cool (1989), Barney (1991) p. 107: 'the link between the resources possessed by a firm and a firm's sustained competitive advantage is *causally ambiguous*', Grant (1991) p. 125 (under the heading of transparency).

37. Porter (1980).

38. Dierickx and Cool (1989) p. 1508. The authors describe the commitment as being 'to punitive post-entry behavior', which in this book becomes post-encroachment behaviour.

39. Barney (1991).

40. The opportunity cost of the resource to the incumbent competitor is of course its value in its best alternative use, which is the higher of its disposal value or its best alternative use by the incumbent. In the present context the disposal value is what the resource is worth to its best alternative owner, who may want it either for a different use or for the same use.

   Peteraf points out that the resource here earns a kind of Pareto (or quasi-) rent, as distinct from a monopoly rent, or a Ricardian rent. As long as the resource would be less valuable to any alternative employer, all of the rent could not be swallowed up by its opportunity cost. Companies' valuations of resources can vary (a) because they have divergent expectations about future cash flows from the resource, or (b) because they have different opportunity costs. Barney (1986) focuses on *the accuracy or otherwise* of companies' divergent expectations of the value of a resource. Peteraf focuses on their *grounds* for diverging.

41. Dierickx and Cool (1989).

42. Rumelt (1991).

43. See Chapter 3. The full discussion of corporate strategy comes in Part Five.

220

44. Kotler (1965). The Boston Consulting Group's growth-share matrix did of course stress the importance of divestment, but not in the context of sustained value-building.
45. Chapter 21 touches on these issues.
46. Collis (1994) makes a similar point. The paper analyses, groups and discusses higher level capabilities and the tendency to look for ever higher levels of them ('the capability to develop the capability to develop the capability that innovates faster (or better), and so on' p. 148).

    He calls capabilities 'organizational' in the sense of belonging to the organization, and reviews three types of efforts to categorize them: static, dynamic and creative. In all cases a capability needs to perform better than competitors. Our pure management resources may turn up in any of these three categories.

    Collis regards the mid-1990s fashion for capabilities as exaggerated, because their sustainability, especially in delivering superior performance of specific offerings, is highly vulnerable. He is very sceptical of the normative value of advising companies to build or acquire capabilities.
47. *Decisions* over what changes to make to the corporate cluster of offerings, and when, are the chief executive officer's inalienable function. *Proposals* however for the CEO's consideration can and should of course be generated by all levels of the organization.

11 Resources and the manager

Introduction

This chapter builds on resource-based theory to develop a managerial view of the process of selecting individual competitive strategies. In particular, it examines to what extent the manager needs to apply resource-based theory as it stands, and to what extent he or she needs to depart from it. This chapter deals with the conceptual issues of selection, Chapter 12 with the mechanics of the selection process.

The central themes of this chapter are:

- Managers have to beat the cost of capital rather than success-aping attempts.
- How that insight affects the selection of competitive strategies.
- The central role of Peteraf's four cornerstones in the selection process.
- The critical role of the cornerstones in protecting value-building against erosion.
- The resources which best ensure durability.
- Sustained value-building through corporate strategy.

The cost of capital as the benchmark

Resource-based writings do not address what degree of market imperfection is needed by managers. In fact, the point at which the resource-based and managerial views can diverge, is the purpose of that protective armour, and therefore the measure of how strong it needs to be:

- The manager needs a positive net present value, discounted at the cost of capital.
- Resource-based theorists like Barney[1] by contrast seek to explain how value-building performance can outlast success-aping attempts.

It will here be recalled from Chapter 10 that equilibrium means a state in which none of the agents in the market stand to gain by shifting their competitive positions. This theoretical concept operates even if it is assumed that all other conditions, like technology, tastes, etc. remain unchanged. Unless and until there is equilibrium, markets tend to generate a strong success-aping force which will tend to threaten any successful competitive strategy.

A business offers a notably profitable offering in the market. This sets up a disequilibrium. Competitors have an incentive to seek similarly high rewards with a similar offering. Customers courted by more numerous substitutes will shop around among them. Price competition then erodes the pioneer's margin. At some stage equilibrium is restored. Barney's[2] benchmark in such a case is whether the company's special resources will enable the offering to counteract the market force just described until all success-aping attempts have foundered.

Managers do not in fact concern themselves with the defeat of *all* success-aping attempts; nor should they. Their benchmark must be to beat the cost of capital. True, managers may also not think in terms of building financial value, and sustaining that value-building against success-aping forces. However, that concept might well catch their attention once it was explained that this is the strategic condition of earning the cost of capital, and therefore of the independent survival of the business.

So when we as managers choose a new competitive strategy, we need to make sure that its planned margins, volume and duration will at least recover the strategy's cost of capital. That is our benchmark.

Resources and Business Strategy

Satisfying the benchmark

What practical difference does it make that the manager's benchmark is earning the cost of capital, rather than beating all success-aping attempts? The important difference is that in normal conditions the cost of capital benchmark is likely to be the less stringent of the two. As always, there is need to guard against overstatement or overgeneralization. Short-lived and easily defeated success-aping attempts do occur. There will also be offerings with very long payback periods. Commonsense suggests however, that these cases will be rare, and that for most offerings the pecking order is the other way about.

Normally, the cost-of-capital hurdle is much the easier of the two. Value-building offerings are much more common than offerings able to outlast success-aping forces. Managers do not need margin erosion to be absolutely impossible. Nor do they need to inflict total defeat on all possible success-aping attempts. It is usually enough if the would-be imitator is confronted with a significant cost or delay: long enough for the cost of capital to be recovered. In any case what needs to be protected, is not so much the offering itself, as the investment in it. That investment can sometimes continue to build value in an updated and repositioned successor offering.

Earning the cost of capital is a benchmark, not a cut-off point

It has been much stressed above that when we design a new competitive strategy, beating the cost of capital must be our benchmark. If a competitive strategy falls short of it, we should reject it. We should of course prefer to build value beyond that point – the longer the better. A zero NPV is merely the threshold, the minimum, not a place to rest on our laurels.

Managers cannot afford to 'satisfice', to earn just the cost of capital and not a penny more. Their overriding duty is to exploit every opportunity to add long-term financial value.

224

In any case, their career prospects, bonus and share option schemes and the like, motivate them to aim ever higher. In the small family business, the future prosperity of the family provides the same incentive.

In practice managers will therefore look for the most profitable positioning that they can find, as long as it earns its keep: its cost of capital. Their concern will be with creating value long enough to beat the cost of capital. These processes will be explored in more detail in the next chapter. The principle established here is that beating the cost of capital, not total immunity to success-aping pressures, is the manager's benchmark. This point has been heavily stressed here because it has received little attention in texts on business strategy.[3]

Practical benefits of the resource-based view

Value-building thus has to continue long enough to beat the cost of capital benchmark. This is where the four cornerstones of Chapter 10 are so useful. They comprehensively categorize the threats and how they can be met. What meets the threats is key resources, with a combination of all four cornerstones. Moreover, key resources must be either under the company's control, or at least warrant the company's reliance on them for the required period. The practical strategist will find the detailed illustrations of the cornerstones in Chapter 10 helpful.

Must they always be key resources?

Key resources are comparatively heavy armour. If we follow Barney (1991), then they must be *capable* of defeating all success-aping attempts. That in turn requires all four cornerstones. They must also be sufficiently under the company's control for the company to be able to rely on them for the requisite period. Resource-based theory goes on to describe what kind of resources tend to meet these conditions: for example, collective routines and skills of a company.

Companies' competitive strategies do not always need quite such heavy armour, because they need to recover the cost of capital rather than defeat all success-aping attempts. Effectively, they need degrees of protection which lie along a continuum. At one end they may not need what meets the description of a key resource. Only a very light shield, enough to protect against small arms ammunition may be needed. Further up the scale they may need key resources with all four cornerstones, but perhaps they only need to withstand 90mm shells. That falls short of perfection in key resources. At the far end of the spectrum they will need key resources in the fullest sense, able to withstand bombardment by the heaviest artillery.

How much armour is needed, depends on the offering, its payback period, its competitive threats, and its production logistics. The payback period for example can be anything from a few days to many years. In an extreme and exceptional case it may be shorter than the minimum delay imposed by the ordinary, natural logistics of encroachment.[4]

The threats facing an individual offering may depend for example on how capital-intensive it is, and how great its competitive risks are. Thus a nuclear power station is highly vulnerable because it is so capital-intensive; a fertilizer plant because there tends to be overcapacity in fertilizers.

This chapter suggests that Peteraf's four cornerstones provide considerable practical insights to managers. Managers may find it useful to refer to the cornerstones by the shorter and less technical nicknames in Table 11.1.

The role of the cornerstones: me-tooism is not enough

All four cornerstones are needed in a key resource. All of them help to make the company and its offering distinctive and to preserve the duration of that distinctiveness against threats such as success-aping attempts. The fundamental cornerstone is diverseness, which is of course the essence of distinctiveness. Although all four help the resource to be persistent in building value, duration is most specifically the fruit of matchlessness and inseparability. The degree to which these cornerstones are needed for a given offering, depends

Table 11.1 *The four cornerstones and their nicknames*

Peteraf's names	Nicknames
Heterogeneity	Diverse
Ex ante limits to competition	Felicitous
Ex post limits to competition	Matchless
Imperfect mobility	Inseparable

on its risk and its cost of capital, and on the size of the required investment.

The importance of diverseness is widely ignored in current practice. Perhaps the best example is the herd instinct, the me-tooism that pervades sectors like financial services. Too many commercial or investment banks have explicit corporate objectives of *emulating* their leading competitors. The ambition is merely to become a replica, not to excel in serving either selected customers better, or all customers more cheaply. Nor are the other three cornerstones heeded. Banks routinely assume that all they have to do is to poach some of the leaders' key experts. This is not enough. If poaching is that easy, the experts can be lost again by the same route. Me-tooism badly underestimates the strategic task.

Illustration: the jersey knitters

To illustrate the cornerstones and their nicknames, we take an example of a key resource with particularly robust cornerstones. Three sisters Anne, Beatrice and Cynthia set up a very successful business, called ABC, designing, making and selling knitted jerseys of distinctive patterns and good quality. Between them they had the skill to design distinctively attractive patterns, the ability to organize the knitting process with a small team of employees, to maintain quality control, and a network of social contacts which gave them all the customers they needed. Their workshop was at their home in the Scottish Borders, at a prestigious address, very presentable to visiting clients, but not easy to find.

Each sister with her talents is a key resource. Now suppose that Anne might be tempted to make a career in some alternative business.

Diverse

Anne was the operating manager in the team. Her diversity was the scarcity of the skills needed to produce and sell such distinctively designed jerseys.

Felicitous

'Felicitous' is of course shorthand for acquisition by luck or foresight. In this illustration Anne was clearly not 'bought in' by a commercial contract, but that does not change the concept of the felicitous development. What matters is that she happens to be in the ABC business either by foresight if Beatrice and Cynthia correctly valued her more highly than any alternative bidder, or by luck, if she joined for some other reason, in this case the blood relationship.

Any rival bidder for Anne would have to expect earnings far in excess of those earned from this resource by ABC. The bidder would for example have to recover the once for all initial costs, including the learning process of integrating Anne into her new team. B and C might of course not wish to outbid their rivals, but that does not alter the fact that to her present ABC business Anne is a felicitous acquisition.

The 'felicitous' cornerstone – as we saw – can be met either by luck or by foresight. An example of foresight is where Company A correctly places a higher value on future cash flows from resource R than Company B. Differences between those valuations can be both subjective (different expectations about customer markets) and objective (R has a different opportunity cost for A than for B).

The dice here tend to be loaded in favour of the incumbent owner, who has often acquired the resource by luck, if not by superior foresight. Superior foresight is a less likely explanation: in our case this would have required Beatrice and Cynthia to have placed a higher valuation on Anne than any alternative employer.

Matchless

Matchlessness is not a question of whether a resource can itself be lost, but whether it can lose its value by being copied or bypassed. Matchlessness is achieved through qualities like skill and experience. These tend to be unique either to individual human beings or to a collective team or organization.[5] Anne's special skill and her integration into the ABC team would be hard for a competitor to copy. It would also be hard to bypass the need for her skills by automating the production process.

Inseparable

Inseparability is control over the resource or over the value it generates. It would be lost first if Anne could easily and advantageously defect. This would be protected if Anne were less valuable to another company, due perhaps to the learning costs of integrating her into a different team. In that case, as we had seen before, the poacher could not afford to outbid Beatrice and Cynthia for her. Inseparability could secondly be lost if Anne were able to hold out for so much extra reward as to deprive the ABC business of the entire value contributed by her.

Protective armour

Our discussion of protective armour builds on the repeatedly stressed point that the mere generation of value for a period is not normally[6] enough. The offering's ability to build value must also be durable or sustained. Of the two requirements, duration is generally harder to ensure and less well understood.

Key resources have the built-in capacity to protect an offering against competitive forces eroding the strategy's generation of value. That capacity is what we are calling their **protective armour** (see box).

Of Peteraf's cornerstones, the last two – matchlessness and inseparability – are the predominant generators of protective

229

Protective armour is here a more appropriate metaphor than 'barriers'. Microeconomists since Bain[7] have used the concept of barriers. 'Entry' barriers protected an 'industry' and 'mobility' barriers a strategic group[8] within an industry. In each case what is being protected, is a *group* of offerings. 'Entry' is hardly appropriate in the framework of this book, because there cannot be entry into an individual offering, only 'encroachment' into its galaxy space: offering a close substitute. Moreover, the resource-based view has shown that what protects the competitive positioning of an offering is its key resource (or resources). It is the resource that has and needs the armour.

The threats against which protection is needed are success-aping threats. These, it must be remembered, can also come from those who are competing not for the same customers, but merely for the same resource.

armour. They constitute imperfections in the market either for the resource itself or for its value, or for any equivalents or substitutes.

The serial innovation case

Successive offerings come into the picture where the investment in a new offering contains substantial elements which will continue to create value in subsequent innovative improvements. In terms of their triangular positionings, the improved versions are new offerings. However, the investment may have a strong continuity through the series. An example quoted by Jacobson[9] is Sony's Walkman, which owed its success not to its original introduction in 1980, but to the stream of better models and improved production techniques that followed. Clearly much of the investment in the original model continued to benefit the successive improvements, so that the recovery of its cost of capital must be measured over the successive offerings, not just one of them in isolation. This is one more instance of the big asymmetry already referred to and more fully discussed in Chapter 12. In such cases the protectice armour of a key resource may need to be strong enough to protect successive offerings.

Jacobson observes that the capacity for this serial innovation process is itself an important key resource, as we call it here.

The rapid payback case

This chapter showed earlier that the manager is concerned with earning the cost of capital, rather than outlasting success-aping forces, and that in many cases the cost of capital can be recovered faster. We noted a continuum of cases ranging from those needing the full protective armour of true key resources at one end to those needing only very light armour at the other. One important reason for the reduced requirement at the latter end was the case of an offering with a very short payback. Short payback is not a particularly common phenomenon, nor is it always a reliable one. Competitive innovation can erode the two conditions which make it possible: low investment or high margins.

External impediments to encroachment

Encroachment – competitors coming in to imitate or replicate a profitable competitive position – is one of the most potent threats to value-building and to recovery of the cost of capital.

Companies can use or acquire protective armour against encroachment. Often however, encroachment is impeded not by competitive countermeasures, but by external factors. These factors always amount to some form of market failure such as:

- Restriction of competition by interventionist governments.
- Discriminatory public procurement, especially in sectors like defence or public health services, where authorities impose restricted lists of approved suppliers.
- Inconspicuousness where offerings are bought by few customers. Competitors fail to move in due to sheer unawareness for example of the offering itself, of its attraction to customers, of its potential for wider customer groups, or of its high margins.

A company can sometimes develop a resource to promote and exploit such market obstruction, and in some cases this may turn out to be a key resource. Thus it may cultivate a public authority which restricts or selects shortlists of preferred suppliers, so as to obtain a place on that list. A flagship airline may induce the authority to write the rules in such a way that it has a privileged position, with more landing 'slots' than its competitors. Similarly, UK broadcasters have by auction won a limited number of commercial TV franchises from the broadcasting authority. The winners have won tenure for a stated number of years.

Quite commonly however, such rules are written differently, with the government able to extend or modify the list of competitors at will. In those cases there may still be a potential key resource, capable of ensuring recovery of the cost of capital. However this can occur only if there is a tacit understanding or convention that incumbents can rely on continuity of tenure. It all depends on how the authority exercises and communicates its power to write and operate the rules. The essence of this potential key resource in these not very common cases is the company's ability to *rely upon*, *rather than control* its privileged tenure. This informal, non-legal tenure is less robust than the typical, physically or legally controlled key resource. It may nevertheless meet the cornerstones if the company is satisfied that it can see off any attempts to oust or erode its favoured position. On the other hand it may be an adequate, if less than key, resource if the company can rely on its tenure long enough to recover the cost of the offering's capital. In many cases it will not pass that test. In any event both the incumbent company and its would-be assailant are well aware that it is lighter armour, because it rests on confidence without control.

The inconspicuous offering is a different and interesting case. The company's superior awareness of the favourable competitive position is clearly a resource. The environmental opaqueness of the opportunity is just a market condition, and its adequacy as a protection again depends on how reliable the continuance of that condition is. The company's managers must make a judgement about this. They must assess the threats. These are usually outside the company's control. For example, where the offering is simply not widely known, customers might get enthusiastic and broadcast its existence.[10] The strategy should go ahead only if the company is confident that, if the need arose, it could see off all success-aping attempts. When that condition is met, it has a key resource.

To sum up, for a small minority of rapid payback strategies duration is not a significant issue. In the majority of cases duration is safeguarded by key resources, sometimes for a succession of serially innovative offerings. Key resources can protect the company's incumbency even in some cases where it is not in actual control of the protective armour.

Resources suitable to protect duration

What resources are likely candidates to make good armour for the sustainability of value-building? The list which follows can be narrowed down in two stages.

The *initial* list of likely candidates consists of relatively wide categories of resources which are:

- non-tradable (helps a resource to be inseparable and matchless),
- not under the control of an inner team member like a key supplier or employee (inseparable),
- hard to imitate or bypass by substitution (matchless).

A *short* list consists of resources which are:

- matchless by being company-specific, due to historical accident, social complexity, causal ambiguity, time compression diseconomies, asset mass efficiencies, complementarity of resources, or deterrence through signs of commitment,[11]
- matchless in that they are hard to substitute,
- felicitous, i.e. located with the incumbent employer due to foresight or luck.

Finally, the likely *winners* are key resources rooted either in human knowledge, skills and experience, or best of all in a company's collective routines and procedures, rather than in physical resources. They also tend to be already within the company's control, having been acquired by either superior foresight or luck.

These individual and collective human resources are the backbone therefore of sustained value-building. They are both generated and grown by being used; consequently they can be expected to grow with use or to decline with neglect. They are hard to acquire at an economic cost if they are to be felicitous.

Corporate competences

There is a current fashion suggesting that companies should acquire corporate[12] competences. They are in fact a subset of the collective human resources just discussed.

They are those competences (i.e. skills to coordinate other resources) which are corporate in the sense that they are *collective* skills[13] or routines. They are in other words not lost when individuals die or leave the company. Typical skills of this kind are often technological; for example NEC's pre-eminence in digital technology, Philips' in optical media, and 3M's in adhesives.[14] By successfully fostering and constantly upgrading such a competence, a company can design many successful offerings. The string of such offerings may be marketed both simultaneously and serially, by replacing one successful offering with another upgraded one.

Prahalad and Hamel's 'core competences'

Prahalad and Hamel[15] have investigated some large international companies, mainly in advanced techno-logical businesses. They found that the company which grows most successfully in sales and market share, is conceived by its managers as a hierarchy of core com-petences, core products and market-focused products. In NEC's case, a major 'core' competence concerned semiconductor technology, and semiconductors were its most important 'core' product which enabled it to become a leader in computing and communications. The head office made this central decision, and continues to control the core competences, for success.

This model at first sight differs from the view put forward in this book. In particular:

- core competences are treated as deliberately acquirable,
- the objective is taken as market share or size rather than financial value, i.e. beating the cost of capital,
- market share is not defined in terms of single offer-ings,
- sustainability against success-aping forces is not stressed,
- nor is the need for the combination of all four corner-stones,
- corporate and competitive strategy are not explicitly distinguished.

The authors are not in fact trying to explain sustained value-building (or 'competitive advantage'). They are looking for what core (i.e. company-characterizing) competences have made one company like NEC oust another company like GTE from leadership in a broad range of offerings.

The authors' concept of the core competence is interesting and valuable, especially for large companies at the leading edge of technology. Outside that important field, a multitude of companies have successfully sustained the creation of value without such core competences, with key resources appropriate to individual offerings or groups of them. The core competence only partly overlaps with the concept of a key resource. Some of the said core competences may be key resources acquired by foresight rather than luck, others may be what are here called pure management resources. Yet others, like NEC's (imitable) semiconductor technology may be not key resources, but specific skills acquired as a fruit of a key resource, the more general ability to keep ahead of competitors at the leading edge. That resource is a skill to acquire and update skills, with a nose for the direction in which customer markets are developing.

The emphasis on such resources is helpful, but the current fashion runs the risk of overstating first the need for them,[16] secondly the ease of acquiring them, and finally the advantage of concentrating on just one or two such resources. Broad reasons for scepticism include:

- Many companies have prospered without a corporate competence.
- Other companies successfully deploy several quite disparate competences at the same time.
- At least those corporate competences which are, or are intended to be, key resources can hardly ever be acquired at will, or quickly, given that key resources need to be felicitous.
- The cost of obtaining a corporate competence may well wipe out the value it can create for the company, if its present owners recognize and use their bargaining power: here again the fashion takes inadequate account of the 'felicitous' requirement.

Corporate competences take years to develop, and are not usually acquired consciously. An unusual skill or experience develops without any conscious plan and stays long enough to become embedded in the company's routines. Companies seldom have the chance to plan for so much stability. Could they count on the necessary external circumstances to remain favourable throughout the required period? Corporate competences grow through a combination of persistent good management and good fortune.

Successful strategies are greatly helped by a corporate competence, but fortunately many can be developed without one. It may be difficult for example to attribute the success of a well located cinema to a corporate competence.

Discriminating among key resources

The strategic significance of different key resources varies a great deal. There are, for example,

- those which apply company-wide to all of the company's offerings,
- more specialized ones which benefit specific groups of those offerings, and
- those which generate serial innovation.[17]

Figure 11.1 illustrates how key resources can support varying numbers of offerings, and Figure 11.2 how a given offering may benefit from varying numbers and sets of key resources.

Almost any key resource can be of company-wide usefulness. Typically this might be a brand, or a pharmaceutical manufacturer's excellence in R&D. A more specialized key resource might be a distribution network, or a technology or process plant serving a limited range of the company's offerings. If the resource were the company's culture or reputation, it would be a key resource only if it conferred advantage on specific ranges of offerings, specific enough to make the advantage strictly competitive.

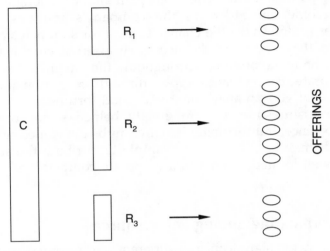

C: company-wide key resource of benefit to all offerings.
R_1, R_2, R_3: key resources of benefit to specific groups of offerings.

Figure 11.1 Key resources may serve varying numbers of offerings

A simpler distinction is that between key resources which are:

• collective skills of the company,
• skills of individual human beings, and
• inanimate.

Collective skills of the company include (a) collective human skills and (b) resources deriving from such collective skills, as a reputation for excellence.

These three categories tend to represent a descending scale of,

• The degree to which the cornerstones are likely to be present.

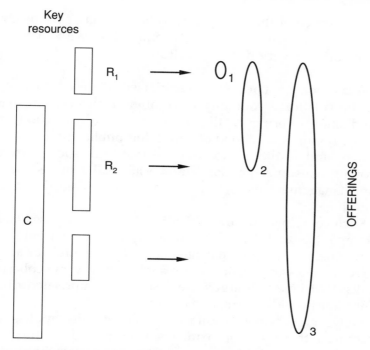

C: company-wide key resource used by most offerings.
R_1, R_2, R_3: key resources used by less than all offerings.
O_1, O_2, O_3: offerings using varying numbers and sets of key resources.

Figure 11.2 *Offerings use varying sets of key resources*

- The difficulty in acquiring the resource from scratch. Collective human skills, experience and routines, or a reputation take longest to breed, are hardest to replicate or detach from the company, and are most likely to be acquired through superior foresight or luck. Inanimate resources like computers and automation equipment are the easiest to match.

Collective skills and routines have three important features:

- They tend to characterize and distinguish the company.
- They grow slowly, but they also change or degenerate slowly.

239

- A resource of this type tends to have strong specific characteristics which can be incompatible with resources requiring a very different culture.[18]

The last point is not always recognized. It may for example be difficult for a company to combine a prowess in mass-production offerings with one in one-off construction contracts. Again, if it is good at supplying public sector utilities, it may find it difficult to combine that with success in fast moving consumer goods. The special skill required of the top management in such a case has been called the 'dominant logic'.[19]

Such combinations are difficult rather than impossible, for example Fiat and the British company GEC have tried them. Nevertheless, the top management may not find it easy to direct businesses which require such very diverse collective skills. Part Five will argue the case against unrelated diversification in wider terms.

However, where this kind of incompatibility applies, the resource either is or approximates to a corporate culture, and pervades the entire company.[20] The reason for the incompatibility is that even top management teams are not universal geniuses, and each excellent company has a limited and idiosyncratic area and spirit of excellence.

All this applies at top level, to resources which characterize the company as a whole. At a lower level however a diversity of key resources may not be incompatible. It is unlikely that a large company with many offerings will need a research and development capability, or a credit control or billing system for 100,000 customer accounts for *all* those offerings.

These perceptions can be used to tackle the further question of whether for its stream of successive offerings a company is likely to choose those which continue to use the same key resources, or whether it will ring the changes, and invest in offerings needing different resources. The answer is that at top level, the successful company is likely to be fairly consistent in using the same company-characterizing resources, with only slow change over time. Lower down, that continuity is much less likely to be needed or appropriate. In any case the need to stay with the same key resource is unlikely to apply to inanimate key resources like hotel sites. The usefulness of a site may have run its course when a given offering comes to the end of its valuable life. At that point the site should probably be divested. Company-characterizing key resources tend to outlast individual offerings. That is not necessarily true of other key resources.

Limitations of the resource-based approach

The resource-based approach has greatly improved our understanding of how sustained value-building comes about in customer markets, but its wider significance needs to be viewed with a sense of proportion.

First, it does not displace the need for a customer focus in competitive strategy. The resource-based view must not blunt our recognition that even the most brilliant resource is worthless if its fruits cannot attract profitable customers. It presents no alternative to the task of finding a profitable position in relation to customers and competitors. On the contrary, its sole function is ancillary to that overriding task. At the stage of finding a profitable competitive strategy, a company needs to be aware of its key resources, and to look for market areas where it can deploy them. At the next stage, implementation, key resources play a vital role in getting the planned offering into the market.[21] Nevertheless, no resource, however pre-eminent among competitors, can create a profitable position without serving profitable customers. Moreover, a resource may enable us to create value today, but be worthless tomorrow if customers no longer prefer the offering for which it is specialized.

Secondly, the resource-based view does not dispense with the need to focus on the individual offering. The company operates in factor markets, but only the individual offering competes in customer markets. The resource-based view advocates *action* in corporate strategy for *success* in competitive strategy: our big asymmetry.[22]

Thirdly, resource-based analysis, strictly defined, only covers the role of key resources with the four cornerstones.

241

Managers sometimes have to focus on resources which do not defy success-aping forces, but are critical to specific areas of business. This is dramatically illustrated by financial service companies, whose capital is an essential competitive resource, irrespective of sustained value-building. This special case is examined below, after the discussion of value created through corporate strategy.

Value-building through corporate strategy

That brings us to the most important limitation: resource-based analysis does not aim to explain the sustained creation of value outside customer markets, i.e. from excellence in corporate strategy. This is perhaps one of the most valuable lessons for managers.

Resource-based theory has essentially restricted itself to competitive strategy. In that theory resources, however distinctive, confer value only when they help to create successful individual offerings. Key resources are the principal tools that shape the outputs of specific competitive strategies.

Meanwhile there is also the flair for managing the corporate cluster of offerings. Chapter 10 described this other company-characterizing resource which enables a company to pursue consistently successful *corporate* strategies. This route to sustained value-building is beyond the reach of success- and value-eroding forces, and therefore outside the scope of resource-based theory. There is no customer market in which the company itself will run into that counterforce. Of course, the company will find its successful offerings challenged by imitators, encroachers and by those who want to detach or appropriate the value of the company's key resources: to erode its creation of value. However, the successful corporate strategist will with perfect timing divest each offering as soon as its expected future cash flows cease to add value to the company, and invest in fresh value-enhancing offerings.

Corporate strategy cannot succeed without value-building offerings. Competitive strategy cannot succeed if corporate strategy fails to divest offerings after they have ceased to add value. In those respects they cover some common ground. They are alternative paths however to the goal of duration, of sustaining the building of value. Competitive strategy seeks to do this by designing offerings expected to be durable enough at the time of investing in them. Corporate strategy can achieve this at a much later stage in the life of an offering, by optimizing the timing of its divestment and replacement. The retain or divest decision has the advantage of hindsight, where competitive strategy has to use foresight.

There are glittering prizes therefore for good corporate management. To this topic we shall turn in Part Five. As we examine it, we shall also describe corporate strategy's role in applying and allocating key and other resources to different offerings.

A special case: the capital of a financial institution

Financial services at first sight appear to place a question mark over the distinction in this book between the functions of the company and those of its firmlets. In a typical commercial bank, investment bank or insurance underwriter, the role of the company and its head office seems to be much greater than a mere ownership role consisting of just cluster management and financing. The head office seems to take a greater part in the management of the firmlets.[23] Nor is this greater part just a matter of supplying expert or functional services which the firmlet might alternatively buy in from an external source. The picture is more interventionist than that. The head office seems to exercise a greater and more detailed degree of control.

The greater centralization is of course an organization issue, but it is merely symptomatic of an underlying difference of substance. The explanation lies in fact in a resource, albeit not a key resource. This resource is the capital of the company, which not only funds its operations, but also represents its capacity to bear risk.

The place of this risk-bearing capacity is more critical in a financial institution of the type under discussion. For such a bank or insurer effectively sells precisely that capacity to its clients. It is a central attraction of its core offerings. This can be contrasted with a typical manufacturing company. A manufacturing company can bear a limited amount of risk. If it incurs risk beyond that limit, it must transfer it to a specialist risk carrier like an insurer or a bank. Its limit is set by its capital. It is not equal to its capital, but geared to its capital. The greater its capital, the more risk can the manufacturing company carry without transferring that risk to a specialist risk carrier.

A bank or insurer is different only in that (a) it happens to be the professional risk transferee whose own risk-bearing capacity too depends on the size of its capital, and (b) its risk-bearing capacity is dramatically more central to its core offerings: that capacity *is* what it sells.

Its capital is however the one resource which a company and its head office cannot decentralize. It can allocate its use among the operating units, but it cannot relax its control over it. In Walter Wriston's memorable words, Citicorp cannot allow a dealer to bet the bank. It must monitor and control the risks of those outer units. This is the reason why the head office of a bank or underwriter must intervene more in the conduct of business of its firmlets.

All this concerns a resource: the company's capacity to bear risk. In a bank or insurer it differs from other resources in that it is the heart of the company, the very essence of its core offering. Its centrality also explains why head offices have much greater management role in this type of financial service than in any other type of business.

Summary

Managers can gain much insight into what kind of resources are likely to be competitive winners by familiarizing themselves with the cornerstones of resource-based theory. Key resources must be diverse, felicitous, matchless and inseparable. The failure of any one of these conditions would in most cases either prevent the process of creating value or risk its premature interruption. Key resources can be viewed as achieving and protecting the building of value, whenever the sustainability of that process is a material condition of its success.

The main divergence between the manager's task and some resource-based theory lies in the benchmark of how strong the four cornerstones need to be. This is because managers need the value-building process to last long enough to recover the cost of capital. On balance this is likely to be a good deal less than the duration needed to defeat all success-aping attempts, which is the benchmark of at least one resource-based view. Where the payback period is very short, key resources may not be needed at all.

The most important type of key resource is the company-specific type which tends to consist of collective human skills and routines. These resources tend to have the cornerstones to a high degree; they often characterize the company; they are hard to acquire; they develop and decay slowly and some-times outlast generations of specific offerings.

Notes

1. Barney (1991).
2. Barney (1991).
3. Important exceptions are Grant (1995) and Kay (1993).
4. To defeat all success-aping pressures would almost invariably take longer than these natural logistics; hence a resource-based writer like Barney (1991) had no need to allow for this case if his bench-mark was to outlast success-aping attempts.
5. The importance of collective human resources, and especially organizational routines and experience is described and analysed in Nelson and Winter (1982), Dierickx and Cool (1989) and many other texts.
6. The exception is the offering with a very fast payback, already referred to.
7. Bain (1956).
8. See Chapter 4.
9. Jacobson, (1992) p. 799.
10. This must be distinguished from causal ambiguity, described by Dierickx and Cool (1989) or uncertain imitability (Lippmann and Rumelt, 1982). Causal ambiguity describes the case where the would-be encroacher is aware of the opportunity, but cannot find out how to encroach. In the present inconspicuous case the encroacher is not even aware of the opportunity.

11. All these terms are described and discussed in Chapter 10.
12. There is also the phrase 'core' competences. The two expressions are sometimes used interchangeably. In other cases 'corporate' is used to mean simply 'belonging to the company' and 'core' to mean 'characterizing the company (rather than the resource)'. See also Collis (1994).

    Prahalad and Hamel (1990) use the expression 'core competence' in a way which only partly overlaps the meanings used by the resource-based school. See the box later in this chapter.
13. These are typically what Barney describes as organizational capital (see Chapter 10). They are also the focus of Nelson and Winter's (1982) attention.
14. Prahalad and Hamel (1990).
15. Prahalad and Hamel (1990).
16. As Collis (1994), p. 151 puts it, 'to attribute normative value to capabilities . . . is inappropriate'.
17. Discussed earlier in this chapter.
18. See Leonard-Barton (1992).
19. Prahalad and Bettis (1986). Chapter 16 argues that a dominant logic is not necessarily a key resource.
20. Goold and Campbell (1987b) make a similar point about corporate styles, discussed in Chapter 16.
21. These stages are further explored in Chapters 12 and 21.
22. See Chapter 12.
23. Chapters 13 and 21 deal with the centralization of management functions in a multioffering company.

12 The 'scissors' process of choosing a competitive strategy

Introduction

Parts Two to Four have so far described:

- favourable competitive positions, and
- corporate resource endowments which are likely to make such positions profitable for a given company.

Building on the insights in the preceding two chapters, this chapter examines the *process* of choosing a competitive strategy. More particularly it discusses the coordination and integration of the two sides of the task. That means finding an offering which:

- has a winning competitive positioning in relation to customers and competitors, and at the same time
- requires a resource endowment in which the business has a competitive edge.[1]

The former side of the task can only find prima-facie profitable customers. Whether they will actually be profitable enough to be value-builders, nearly always depends on whether our company has access to the necessary key resources.

The chapter will thus explore how outputs and inputs or the demand and supply sides interact in the task of identifying and adopting a competitive strategy. Neither of these two requirements can on its own ensure financial success.

The exceptional case of the rapid payback offering[2] which poses no duration problem and thus needs no key resource, will be almost entirely ignored in this chapter.

The big asymmetry

Much practical and theoretical work on competitive strategy has been difficult to grasp and use, because it fails to distinguish whether the competitive agent is the company or the offering. This was discussed in Chapter 3. One reason for the neglect of this distinction may have been the major asymmetry between,

- the demand side, where the single offering alone can be chosen by customers, and
- the supply side, where it normally takes more than one offering to share a key resource and other inputs at competitive unit costs.

This asymmetry has particularly caused confusion around the word 'compete'. In the sense of acquiring, identifying, maintaining and deploying key and other competitive resources, a company plays a major part in the competitive process. It does not however 'compete' for customers, in the sense of seeking to be chosen by them: only the individual offering is chosen. Competitive action – unseen by customers – is confused with the offering of competitive choices to customers. This linguistic trap is greatly encouraged and compounded by the big asymmetry.

It is seldom economic to exploit a key or other resource in just a single offering. In order to reap the economies of scale, resources commonly need to be shared between offerings: they are thus in that sense corporate. They belong to the *company*. This does not mean that a key resource or competence must actually reside in the head office. It may well be located elsewhere in the company, used specifically for one or several offerings.

We have not yet described and discussed corporate strategy in detail, but we have defined it as the management by a company of the composition of its cluster of offerings. It covers decisions to add, retain or divest offerings.

The two options

What we shall call the scissors process of selecting a competitive strategy, can be approached in one of two ways, from key resources to a competitive position, or vice versa:

- One way is to identify the company's existing key resources first, and then to look for offerings which best exploit those existing key resources.
- The other way is to find an attractive competitive position in the galaxy[3] first, and then to see whether the company happens to have the right key resources for it or even whether in a special case it might be able to acquire them. As the resources needed for a profitable competitive strategy must, amongst other things, be felicitous, they must be the result either of past corporate strategies, i.e. of luck, or of special foresight enabling the company to acquire them now for less than their value to the company.

All these processes belong not only to competitive, but also to corporate strategy. It is precisely at this point that these two kinds of strategy overlap.

The choice process

To simplify this account of the selection process, we unrealistically assume that the strategist starts with a blank mind.

Volume apart, value-building depends on margins and their duration. The selection process therefore requires identification of:

- the future offering and its degree of differentiation, which governs that margin, and
- the required key resources, their cost and what protection they confer on expected margins and for what duration.

249

Any market impediments to encroachment[4] are an important, but given, background in the chosen area of the galaxy.[5] Whatever protection they give to margins may reduce the residual protection needed from key resources. They are part and parcel of the scenery which may attract the strategist to a given part of the galaxy.

The task of looking for seemingly attractive positionings in the galaxy has already been described in Part Two. Its main concepts are those of differentiation and circularity.[6] We therefore now have to describe how a manager can gain an insight into the company's key resources.

An inventory of key resources?

At first sight it may appear easy to identify our own company's key resources. After all, as insiders we know them, don't we? Well, not many experienced managers will believe that. The question is not whether resources are good, but whether they persistently generate value, also called 'competitive advantage'. Or rather whether they will do that in tomorrow's competitive markets.

That is the general difficulty. Individual key resources are elusive, and not always obvious to those who have them. A highly professional credit control team, with an innovative system for collecting cash from late payers, may know more about key customers' purchasing procedures than the sales force. Will it occur to them to alert the sales force to the possibilities? More important, will sales and higher management be aware of the resource and how it might be used?

Strategists might perhaps think about making an inventory of the company's competitive resources, so as to identify the key resources among them. That too sounds easier than it is. Taking an inventory is easy if we know what we are looking for. However, here we are mainly looking for intangibles, preferably collective or team capabilities or routines, because they are less mobile and more company-specific.

Where do we start? The first thing to bear in mind is that from this practical point of view resources can be categorized two ways, by the nature of the resource or by the way it is acquired and held. If we want to have a good prospect of identifying them, we must use both routes.

Resources can first of all be categorized by their nature. In Chapter 11 we categorized them as (a) collective company-specific, (b) individual human, and (c) inanimate.[7] In a little more detail we can distinguish such categories as:

- a prime site or location,
- a physical installation like a specialized large process plant,
- a distribution or supplier network,[8]
- technological or scientific know-how,
- operating know-how,
- soft skills like the ability to attract high class managers or specialists,
- a company's reputation,
- a brand.

They can secondly be categorized by how they are acquired or held. Here we should distinguish between:

- investment in assets,
- knowledge held in formulae or on computer files,
- knowledge, skills, etc. specific to an individual,
- knowledge and skills held by a team or wider circles in the company,
- routines specific to the company.

A resource like excellent credit control procedures might be discovered under operating know-how in the first list, or (more likely) under routines, or skills held by a team in the second. The risk is that it might well escape discovery altogether. That is why more than one search path is helpful.

What it comes to, is that the compilation of an inventory may be worth attempting, but is at best an unreliable way to set about the selection task. In any case, the difficulties are instructive.

This discussion has reviewed resources generally. The next step is to refine the list down to key resources, with the four cornerstones.

A short cut

Fortunately however, resources and their competitive applications are intermeshed at varying levels of detail. In practice the search for a suitable resource can be curtailed by the nature of the offering that may be contemplated. Process plants are likely to be more relevant to a petrochemical offering than to an accounting practice, and a good European distribution network may be more valuable to an exporter of plastic components than to the operator of a nuclear power plant or a local newspaper in Alaska. Highly specialized production know-how is more necessary to a maker of microchips than to a fishing fleet operator.

The two selection routes: which comes first?

The task of identifying a value-building new offering is like the two blades of a pair of scissors. One blade searches for supply side advantages and the other for demand side ones. The demand side blade looks around the galaxy for offerings to exploit the company's existing key resources. The supply side blade looks for resources to exploit specific favourable spots in the galaxy.

Some writers[9] believe that the resources blade should invariably be used first. This is proposed on two grounds:

- Key resources are already under the company's control and few in number. The writers further assume that they are easily identified. If this were correct, then it should with little time and effort be possible to define a short list of exploitable market areas.
- By contrast the effort to locate favourable market areas in the galaxy is potentially unlimited because the field consists of the entire world economy.

These reasons for starting with the resources blade are strong in some cases, and will in those circumstances prevail. However, its proponents are surely claiming too much if they believe them to apply universally.

The case for reversing the order and beginning with the markets blade rests on the following grounds:

- First, as mentioned in Chapter 11, offerings with an exceptionally rapid payback do not require key resources at all.
- Secondly, as argued earlier, few companies are aware of the full range of their key resources, or of all potentially profitable applications of those resources. Consequently, if managers were to confine their attention to offerings for which they know the company to have advantageous resources, they would miss a lot of opportunities.
- Thirdly, there are entrepreneurs with a special flair for spotting favourable market opportunities. A brilliant insight into such an opportunity can often be implemented with resources which are less hard to find than the opportunity.

To sum up, it can in some cases be more effective to identify favourable parts of the galaxy first, and then check whether the company has the key resources for each such offering.

The task of looking for a favourable market area consists of a number of steps. The strategist will look at promising regions of the galaxy as they now are, and will then visualize how the dynamic of the markets, and indeed the likely actions of actual or potential competitors, will change those regions.[10] The next step is to look for what will be a favourable area within such a region. This can be either an uncrowded area or gap for the new offering, with the desired degree of differentiation or distance from substitutes, or an opportunity for a winning commodity-buy. It is particularly worthwhile to look for areas that lend themselves to transformer strategies discussed in Chapter 9.

In any case, it is wrong to assume that there is just one correct order of search. The intermeshing of output and input factors can be extensive, as we saw earlier, and in practice it may well be easier to apply the scissors approach piecemeal over a limited market area or a limited set of resources, before proceeding to wider market or resource sets. What matters is that the input and output sides are both explored for a good and profitable match. That is what the scissors approach means.

There is thus no invariable rule. The best answer will vary case by case. Whether it is more effective to concentrate first on one or the other, is a matter of horses for courses. These are the considerations:

- The length of the list of key resources. If there are only few, then it may save time to list them first. The longer the list, the stronger is the case for beginning with a search for favourable market areas.
- The *degree* and precise nature of any causal ambiguity[11] concerning the relationship between a resource and how it creates valuable offerings. On the one hand it may be harder to identify all the potential market applications of the company's key resources. It is possible to have an excellent distribution network, for example, without knowing all the possible offerings for which it might have a competitive advantage. On the other hand, it may be harder to be sure what key resources are needed to address identified favourable spots in the galaxy. We may be sure of a good market for a cure for baldness, without knowing how to produce it at an economic cost.
- The company's skill in spotting favourable market areas. The greater that skill is, the greater the chance that the market blade is the better starter.

The steps in the process

If in a particular case we assume that it is worth beginning with the company's key or near-key resources, then the steps are as follows:

- Ascertain the actual or potential key resources of the business.
- Identify broad areas in the future galaxy where these might generate value.
- Scan those promising market areas for private profitable gaps: potential offerings with a suitable distance, of some

duration, from close substitutes, or opportunities for profitable commodity-buys, where our company has a sustainable cost advantage.
- Then use ordinary demand and cost curves to determine the net present value of each potential future offering and their rankings, so that the most attractive can be selected. The effect of varying degrees of circularity and differentiation on profitability was described in earlier chapters.
- Note whether any candidate competitive strategies are mutually exclusive: a given perfume cannot be positioned as both romantic and independent.
- Finally, conduct a financial analysis of the apparent winner to ensure that it meets the requirements. This will be described in Chapter 17.

How sustainable must the value-building process be?

The financial analysis described in Chapter 17, among other things ascertains what duration is needed to achieve a positive net present value, and therefore that the protective armour is adequate. Up to that point the selection process has not explicitly brought in the issue of sustainability.

This final stage will fine-tune the fit of resources with market area, to check whether the selected competitive strategy meets its financial objective.

Back to the great asymmetry

We have come back to a central insight into the structure of business strategy. Profitable business strategies are those which design value-building future offerings. We have seen that the process of selecting a profitable competitive strategy is like a pair of scissors. Blade 1 focuses on favourable regions in the competitive galaxy, blade 2 on the company's actual or potential resources, to see what valuable single offerings they are suited to deliver. Whereas blade 1 is searching for profitable opportunities for *single* offerings, blade 2 is concerned with the *plurality* of actual or potential offerings that might be made valuable by the company's resources.

Together, the two blades design and formulate a new and profitable competitive strategy, but this has brought us back to the fundamental asymmetry: the positioning of outputs concerns *only what customers choose, and therefore only one offering at a time*, but the internal resources and other inputs which help to determine the profitability of any given positioning, concerns the company, i.e. more than one offering, and therefore corporate strategy. Corporate strategy does not merely pick competitive strategies, it also contributes to them. The company's role is so big that we do well to stress again that the company is not itself a competitor for customers. This asymmetry is a feature of the business world as it really is; it is not just a way of looking at it.

Why lay so much stress on the distinction between the firmlet and the company? Would it not be easier to simply talk about 'the business', and to leave the context to determine case by case whether this is the firmlet or the company? The difficulty is that a great many writers and practitioners have misdirected their analysis of competitive strategy by attempting it for more than a single firmlet or offering. It is only too common to see attempts to describe competition between two domestic appliance manufacturers, as if competition for customer choices were possible between entities with multiple offerings. Domestic appliance makers can compete in washers, dishwashers, freezers, refrigerators, cookers, microwave ovens, irons and toasters, but in each of these offerings they are likely to have different customers, different competitors, different competitive positions. The company as a whole has no definable competitive position, only its individual offerings or firmlets have that. Yet its information system, its manufacturing know-how, its marketing and distribution skills and its reputation for quality, to mention just a few resources, serve most if not all its offerings. We have already seen that the same point can be made about investment or merchant banks.

Summary of the scissors process

The selection of a competitive strategy can and should follow two parallel routes: looking for profitable spaces in the economic galaxy of offerings, and looking inwards towards the key resources which make a profitable new offering possible. These are more likely to belong to the company than to any one of its firmlets. This means that corporate strategy makes a critical contribution to competitive strategy, by putting together offerings which can collectively and economically muster the resources needed for value-building.

Summary of Part Four

Part Four has filled in an important part of the framework of business strategy. A company can add long-term owner value either by making key resources available to individual offerings, or by developing a continuing flair for corporate strategy.

Key resources are those which are specific to the company and give it a capacity for sustained value-building in customer markets. In sustaining the building of value, i.e. preventing its premature erosion, they constitute protective armour. Key resources must be diverse, felicitous, matchless and inseparable; the four cornerstones of resource-based theory.

Companies offering financial services are a special case in that they also critically depend on their capital as a risk-bearing resource, in addition to key resources.

Resources tend to be assembled for more than one offering. This is therefore a task for corporate strategy, which is the subject of Part Five.

Notes

1. The SWOT analysis was also designed to align advantageous market positions (opportunities and threats) with advantageous resource endowments (strengths and weaknesses). It did not however explicitly address (a) the distinction between the offering (concerned with the former) and the company (concerned with the

latter), (b) the criterion of financial value, or (c) the causal framework of Peteraf's cornerstones.
2. See Chapter 11.
3. See Chapter 4.
4. See Chapter 11 under 'External impediments to encroachment'.
5. The concept of the galaxy is introduced in Chapter 4.
6. See Chapter 7.
7. Barney (1991) similarly classified resources as physical, human or organizational (see Chapter 10).
8. These relationship resources Kay (1993) calls 'architecture'.
9. For example Grant (1991).
10. See Chapter 9 for a discussion of the dynamics of competition.
11. See Chapter 10.

Part Five   Corporate Strategy

Corporate strategy is the management by a company of the composition of its cluster of offerings. Each of these represents of course a competitive strategy. Its task is made up of decisions to add, retain or divest offerings.

Its most distinctive function is the continual review of existing offerings, at a late stage in the life of each offering. By that stage much of its biography and track record is a historical fact. The offering may for example be past its peak. It may no longer have a positive net present value. A shrewd decision to retain or divest, and skilful timing of a divestment can add much value to a competitive strategy.

Corporate strategy's main issues are:

(a) what types and combinations of offerings make a value-building cluster,
(b) the timing of additions and divestments,
(c) the process of managing the cluster,
(d) the strategic allocation of resources to offerings for maximum value.

As suggested in Part Four, corporate strategy can be a sustained value-builder in its own right. This is not the conventional view, which assumes that sustained value-building occurs only in competitive strategies.

Part Five • Corporate Strategy

13 Corporate strategy's task is to build financial value

Back to first principles

This chapter begins the examination of corporate strategy by looking at its nature and purpose.

The object of all business strategy is to add financial value to the business. Chapter 2 clarified that this is *long-term* financial value: the qualification 'long-term' is therefore always implied when financial value[1] is referred to as the object of business strategy.

Earlier chapters have made the following points:

- Competitive strategy designs and creates individual profitable offerings.
- Corporate strategy assembles, maintains and upgrades a profitable cluster of individual offerings for the company.
- In that very process corporate strategy makes a significant contribution to individual competitive strategies. It enables offerings to share resources and other inputs so as to realize economies of scale and reduce unit costs.

Corporate strategy is a function of the head office

A popular question of the 1980s and 1990s has been what value the head office adds. In other words, what net gain do firmlets derive from not being independent? It does not ask whether or not head offices perform any valuable services. The question whether the head office adds value, is a reaction against the fashion for diversification in the 1960s and

1970s. The pendulum has swung from 'big is beautiful' to 'small is beautiful'.

The term head office is of course simply a graphic metaphor for the fact of diversification, of one company owning several offerings or firmlets. In the single retail store which has two offerings, food and photocopying, the owner-manager is the 'head office'.

As long as the large diversified company[2] was in vogue, it was widely believed that head offices were useful *vehicles for centralizing* many services. These might for example cover transport, distribution, purchasing, risk management and insurance, research and development, patents and trademarks, real estate, legal and personnel services, health and pensions. The main arguments for such functional centralization were economies of scale, improved market power or clout, and coordination. An example of clout was that central purchasing might obtain better discounts, one of coordination was that a single pay structure would prevent unions picking the best deal in a particular plant as a lever for raising other plants in the company to the same level. There was also at one time the belief that by directly improving the cost of capital, sheer size[3] and financial clout could reduce the threat of hostile takeover.

There is also a highly respected group of economists who study the relative 'transaction costs' of making investment and other decisions, either (a) inside the company by experts close to the problems, or (b) outside the company in markets.[4] Managers are no strangers to that issue. However, they tend to be unfamiliar with this meaning of 'transaction costs'.[5] In managerial language 'transaction' tends to mean a purchase, sale or remittance.[6] 'Transaction cost' therefore tends to convey a reference to such items as bank charges or despatch costs, which arise from individual sales.

Now that the pendulum has swung the other way, head offices tend to be viewed as having very few inalienable corporate functions that cannot be delegated.[7] This rock-bottom list may well consist of just two, corporate strategy and finance. Finance here means funding in the main financial markets. In addition to these functional tasks, there are of course also the line management tasks of appointing senior operating management and monitoring performance against budgets, targets or milestones.

Views about the functions of the head office change from time to time with fashions and doctrines. In any case the need for centralization varies between different kinds of business, and for much more deep-seated reasons. Banks and insurance underwriters for example need highly centralized risk management.[8] There is no set list of head office functions valid for all times and for all kinds of business.

On the other hand, the expression 'head office' does not necessarily mean whatever activities are located at the same address as the head office. If a divisional head who has to visit government departments regularly, finds a desk in the central London head office the most convenient office location, that does not make him or her part of the head office. By the same token however, if the UK parent company can save tax by holding shares in its foreign subsidiaries through an intermediate holding company located in The Netherlands, that Dutch company and its staff are part of the head office.

It is risky to get carried away by fashions and pendulum swings. The main need is to avoid too much generalization. The important principles are:

- A head office by its mere existence cannot help imposing considerable costs on its operating units, by adding a layer of management, by lengthening communication chains, by bureaucratic controls, and by requiring dysfunctional uniformities. Those extra costs may be justified by cost savings or other advantages, but justified they must be.
- No single structure suits all types of commercial operations. Different operating profiles need different internal structures.

Managing the cluster

Corporate strategy's management of the cluster of offerings is an essential head office function. The head office has the

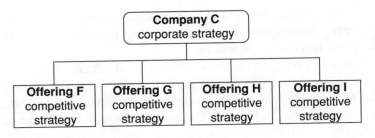

Figure 13.1 Company and offerings (firmlets)

task of constantly monitoring opportunities to improve the financial value of the company by decisions to add, retain or divest offerings. The cluster which the head office manages is illustrated in Figure 13.1.

Additions or divestments can take various forms, such as:

- acquisitions and disposals,
- organic growth by internal investment projects,
- closing down or running down existing offerings.

Table 13.1 contrasts competitive and corporate strategy.

Managers do not always make a sharp distinction between corporate and competitive strategy. Consequently it is not common for them to think of their task as that of managing a cluster of competitive offerings. The usefulness of that model is illustrated in the example of Courtaulds in the box.

Table 13.1 Competitive versus corporate strategy

	Competitive strategy	*Corporate strategy*
Concerns	Offering (firmlet)	Company
Selects	Offering and its positioning	Cluster of offerings to own
To win in which market?	Competitive commercial	Financial

In the second half of the 1980s Courtaulds transformed itself by shifting its emphasis away from
capital-intensive and cyclical commodity businesses
towards those with scope for distinctiveness in product
and process technology, technical service, marketing and
distribution. The process included many acquisitions
and disposals. It culminated in the demerger of 1990
which created two independent publicly quoted companies. Courtaulds plc, one of the two, emerged with
a cluster of businesses with substantial affinities in
technology, in the science of polymers and surfaces for
high quality specialist materials, and in markets.

A number of other UK companies like Bowater, Racal and
ICI have similarly added corporate value by demerging. In
each case the stockmarket has placed a higher combined
value on the two demerged companies than on the single
diversified predecessor.[9]

Its *immediate* effect on stockmarket values is not of course
necessarily what measures the success of a corporate strategy.
Its time-frame is at least medium term. Whether stockmarkets immediately adjust to a strategic move, must depend on
how well informed they are or can be.

The primacy of financial markets: agency conflict

Financial value

The only yardstick by which the success of any function of
business management can be measured, is the financial value
which it adds to the company. Corporate strategy is more
directly related to this goal than competitive strategy, which
pursues it indirectly via success in commercial markets.[10]

For example if a successful competitive offering has a
net present value to the company of n, but can be sold for
$n + x$, then the correct corporate strategy is to enhance owner

value by *x*, i.e. to divest the offering so as to realize $n + x$ cash now. The test of whether an offering should be retained is not whether it is 'profitable' or not, but whether it will *from now on* add further financial value to the company.

The tool which ensures the creation of financial value in cluster management is the 'better-off test' described in Chapter 14.

Agency conflict

Managers[11] need a clear view of their goal, and the overriding goal is to add financial value. In a simple model managers are the servants of the owners; owners want the financial value of their company to be maximized; managers therefore serve their job prospects best by maximising that value. Interests and goals are in perfect harmony. The goal is *financial*, and its test is success in the financial markets.

This harmonious model runs into the difficulty called 'agency conflict'. The expression means that the self-interest of company managers can and does conflict with the interests of shareholders. Agency conflict may occur in all types of financial systems.[12] However, the particular form which has been observed, is peculiar to those modern stockmarket systems in which hostile takeover bids are common, as in the US and UK and perhaps a dozen other countries.[13] In other words, where there is a market in corporate control. In such systems relations between investors and managers are relatively impersonal and distant.

Conflict of this kind has notably been suggested by Jensen and Meckling[14] and characterizes much financial theory. Reservations about its importance have however been expressed in strategy theory.[15]

At normal times, when no takeover bid is in sight, the disaffected shareholder with a relatively small holding can only sell his or her shares. Takeover bids occur infrequently, and for years between such bids managers are left in control, with inadequate incentives to change policies which are not, or are no longer in the best interests of investors.[16] This may occur because after some time in office, managers find it difficult to disown or reverse their own past decisions or indecisions. When managers fail to act in the investors' interests, they will reduce the value of the company. Such conduct conflicts with the simple harmonious model.

Agency conflict affects corporate strategy mainly through a tendency of managers to acquire or retain offerings and major assets which do not, or do not any longer add value to the company, or could be better used elsewhere. Head office managers may feel that their own importance[17] and status varies with the number and sizes of the firmlets they direct. Managers also have a motive to preserve the managerial independence of their company and to resist a takeover bid even if acceptance would be in the best interests of its investors.

Agency conflict: motivation

Managers have in the past embarked on cluster-boosting diversification programmes for two now widely discredited motives. One is *'risk diversification'*. The other is *size*.[18] Chapter 14 will discuss why these two objectives fail to promote financial value. What concerns us in the present chapter, is simply that both these motives superficially seem to serve the self-interest of managers. Size may appear to increase their importance and value, and perhaps their pay, whereas risk diversification appears to make their jobs safer. If both fail to serve the interests of the company's investors, then on the face of it there is agency conflict.

The function of the hostile takeover (or proxy fights) is to wrest control from managers whose continued stewardship conflicts with investors' interests. The threat of hostile bids therefore gives managers an incentive to take their decisions in the interests of the shareholders. If they do this successfully, there will be much less scope for hostile bids, or for conflict between owners and managers.

It has however been argued that the existence of the takeover market actually causes agency conflict. Appendix 13.1 discusses one of the most serious criticisms of hostile

267

Agency conflict: Savoy Hotel

A long-standing example in the UK of shareholder and agency conflict is the Savoy Hotel during the period beginning with the 1960s. During that period this public company had a capital structure which gave the management, backed by the trusts set up by the founding families, voting control with a minority of the equity investment. The Savoy Hotel company owned the Berkeley Hotel in Mayfair, which had under-performed its potential for many decades. Shareholders would have gained much value if new management had come in and enabled that site to be redeveloped inside or outside the Savoy Group. The board consistently opposed any such policy, and blocked takeover bids by means of the two-tier voting structure. The controlling group of directors and shareholders thereby pursued a set of goals which was not always regarded by commentators as consistent with the directors' agency duties towards the majority of shareholders. The Forte Group, which for many years was the major financial shareholder, was powerless without voting control. The controlling group acted against the *financial* interests of all shareholders, their own financial interests included.

---

takeovers, the charge of 'short termism': fear of hostile takeovers is said to cause managers to avoid investing for long-term financial value, and even to take concealed – and therefore unethical – disinvestment action. The appendix sets out the alleged imperfections of the market and their possible mechanics. Any such imperfections would not change the overriding principle that the job of managers is to create financial value for the company's investors.

Corporate and competitive strategy distinguished

Corporate strategy is the continuing task of reviewing the cluster of offerings. It looks at whether:

- The cluster would gain value from additional offerings.
- Existing offerings should be retained or divested.

The reader will recall that in this framework the repositioning of an offering, is its removal and replacement by another. As noted earlier, in the selection of a new offering, competitive and corporate strategy overlap.

It is the second task, the decision to retain or divest, which is the distinctive function of corporate strategy. It is distinctive in two respects:

- Corporate strategy reviews the expected future financial results of any given offering at a later stage. The offering was selected some time ago. At the time of the review either its own track record or at least subsequent developments in its market are known with hindsight. Corporate strategy reviews a forward period which is both shorter and less uncertain.
- Corporate strategy by constantly monitoring the value that is still to come, ensures that each offering is divested before it ceases to add value. This pruning function adds value in its own right. If it is successfully applied to all offerings, then the company may successfully sustain its value-building even if its individual offerings do not.

The fact that top managers with a talent for this pruning function can thereby become sustained value-builders, must not be misunderstood. Strategists must still adopt only those competitive strategies which are at least expected to earn their cost of capital. Pruning decisions come much later in the biography of an offering.

Nevertheless, corporate strategy adds and deletes competitive strategies, and the skill of the corporate strategist must include a good nose for what is or remains a profitable set of customers. There is no strategic task which does not require some customer or market orientation.[19]

Summary

Corporate strategy concerns the management by a company of its cluster of offerings. It constantly plans what offerings should be added, retained or divested. Its yardstick for each decision is always financial value. This goal is served indirectly by competitive strategy, but directly by corporate strategy.

Corporate strategy is one of the essential functions of the head office, one of the very few ways in which a head office as such can add value to the company.

Diversification,[20] the adding of offerings, is only justified if it adds value. Chapter 14 will show that neither risk diversification nor physical size add value. Chapter 16 describes the types of diversification which are capable of adding value, all of which will be categorized as 'related'.

When head office managers act in the interests of shareholders, they will eliminate agency conflict. This in turn will reduce the risk of hostile takeovers.

* * *

Appendix 13.1

Short termism and the market for corporate control

Introduction

Managers are described as 'short termist' if they are excessively concerned with short-term results, at the expense of the long-term prosperity of the business, making them,

- reluctant to spend on the seed-corn of future returns, especially on capital investment, research and development, and other revenue investment items like training or effective and pleasant working environments,
- risk-averse: abnormally reluctant to contemplate the possibility of significant losses or reductions in profits.

To be short termist, the concern with short-term results needs to transcend the discount factor which is properly used to assess the net present value of cash flows. Short termism represents a dramatic overestimate of the discount factor, sharply in excess of a proper assessment of the time value of money.

The existence of short termism is assumed in this appendix, although it has not been conclusively demonstrated by empirical research. For the US it has been strongly asserted by Porter.[21] There is a fair weight of anecdotal evidence. This suggests that short termism is more prevalent in countries like the United States and the United Kingdom, Canada and Australia than in other developed countries like France, Germany or Japan.

Much has been written about the possible causes of short termism. There is almost certainly more than one cause. The main explanations that have been put forward, usually take note of national differences, as the apparent greater incidence of the phenomenon in certain countries is the best clue to be pursued. Such explanations include:

- The social environment of business management in different countries.
- The institutional organization of corporate governance: countries like Germany and Japan have a more corporatist system, with less emphasis on the power of the general body of shareholders.[22]
- The way financial markets operate, and particularly the market for corporate control.

This appendix deals only with the last of these possible causes. It attempts to set out a model which would explain

271

how the market for corporate control[23] might induce short-termist behaviour in countries where it plays a major role.

The stockmarket as a cause

The distinguishing feature of the Anglo Saxon group of economies, where short termism is believed to be prevalent, is the role played by the stockmarket. Most developed countries have stockmarkets, but only in the Anglo Saxon group is that market the *critical* financial institution, on which a listed company's independent survival depends. By a critical financial institution is meant that institution which can 'pull the rug' by wresting control from the incumbent management team. Only in the Anglo Saxon group do hostile takeovers present a serious threat. Hostile takeovers may not be wholly unknown in some of the other countries, but in those countries they were too rare even in the mid-1990s to preoccupy the minds of chief executives of listed companies. In France, Germany, Japan and most other countries, a company's critical institution is typically its principal bank or banks.

The contrast is between (a) fragmented and ever-changing stockmarket investors and (b) the company's more personally involved main bank. The relationship with stockmarket investors tends to be more[24] impersonal, discontinuous and distant, that with the bank often one-to-one, close and continuing.[25] When a bank is the critical financial institution, it will be closer to the decision-making process on the investment projects being financed, and more dependent on their success than fragmented, distant shareholders. Unlike investors, who are and want to be free to sell their shares at short notice, banks can and will be consulted. Nor can a company's principal bank normally exit from its commitment at will. Consultation, as well as significant financial exposure, tends to entail commitment.

It is therefore helpful to distinguish between a *stockmarket-driven* and a *bank-driven* environment. The former is a much more impersonal system, the latter more like a patronage system. Only *listed* companies in the English-speaking group have the former.[26]

We are looking, it must be recalled, for an explanation of *excessive* concern with the short term. If the threat of takeover merely caused managers to manage in the interests of their investors, it would motivate them to boost the properly discounted net present value. That would not be short termism. Short termism gives not its proper weight, but excessive weight, to the immediate future.

So if the threat of hostile takeover is a cause of managers' overpreoccupation with short-term results, how does that causation work? People who study financial markets have seen this suggestion as a denial of market efficiency. If the stockmarket motivates managers to deviate from the interests of investors, then (they argue) the stockmarket must be mispricing the shares of their companies.

Such mispricing is relatively easy to refute. Professor Paul Marsh[27] demonstrates that the stockmarket price of an equity share represents the risk-adjusted net present value of the future expected cash flows to its holder: of *all* future cash flows, not just the shorter-term flows. At the end of August 1990, estimates Marsh, only 8 per cent of ICI's stockmarket price could be attributed to the current year's dividend, only 29 per cent to dividends expected over the first five years, and only 50 per cent to those expected over the first ten years.

Such a calculation is merely illustrative, but it confirms what most informed observers intuitively believe. There are no grounds for believing that the stockmarket values companies myopically.

Mispricing is therefore an unlikely explanation of short termism. However, answers like Marsh's assume,

- that the problem must lie in the day-to-day stock price of a company like ICI, and
- that the day-to-day market and the potential takeover market are one and the same.

This last assumption is not easily compatible with the known facts about the share price of a typical takeover target. In the UK that price has been found on average to gain 30 per cent[28] in the six months beginning four months before a bid, with 22 per cent of that 30 per cent gain occurring in the month of the bid.[29]

If the price four months before the bid was 100, the bidder typically has to offer a price of about 130 per share of the target company (T) in order to be successful, a premium of 30 per cent. Typically, during the offer period the market price may be in the region of 120 to 130, depending on how confident the market is about the success of the bid. Later, if the bid fails, it may fall back to about 105–110.

This pattern suggests that the takeover market trades something more valuable than the day-to-day market, and so it does. It trades potential *control*[30]. The day to day market trades small *non-controlling* parcels of T's shares. A buyer might typically buy 0.1 per cent of the voting equity. This entitles the buyer to a dividend every half-year, to any capital gain on selling the shares, to a share of any surplus if T is wound up, and to attendance at general meetings. What the buyer does not obtain, is any effective voice in the management of T, about dispositions of its assets, not even about the size of the annual dividend. The 0.1 per cent vote will carry little weight, and is seldom exercised. Typical parcels of shares which are traded day by day are non-controlling and powerless.

The takeover bidder by contrast is bidding for control, for the power to break T up, to sell its assets at a profit, restructure what remains, appoint new management, improve profitability. Control is what is worth 30 per cent more per share than the powerless parcel traded in the day-to-day market. T's existing shareholders will not part with their shares unless the bidder offers them a significant slice of the total gain expected by the bidder.

In other words, there are *two markets*,[31] the day-to-day market and the market for corporate control. They each trade a different commodity, with a substantially different market value. It is a misnomer to call this 'dual pricing'[32], as if the *same* item were traded at two different prices. There are *two* items, with substantially divergent market values.

The oddity of this is that these two markets can never function simultaneously. A holder of 1000 T shares can only sell into the one stockmarket. It is the stockmarket in T shares which abruptly changes from trading fragmented parcels at 100 to trading control at 120–130, and possibly back again if the bid fails. Moreover, the market in control only operates rarely, for short periods. The vast majority of the time it is dormant as a market, though possibly alive as a threat.

This split identity of the stockmarket does not by itself explain short termism. For an explanation we must look at the nature and motivation of T's shareholders.

Concentration of institutional shareholdings

We are seeking to explain a short-termist phenomenon which is believed to be prominent in some Anglo Saxon stock-markets, of which the two most prominent ones are New York and London.

In the London market the percentage of institutionally held voting capital has steadily risen over the last half century to nearly 70 per cent. Institutional shareholders are pension funds, unit and investment trusts, and other large portfolios managed by professional fund managers, such as the Church Commissioners. The high concentration in London means that the larger funds have holdings in all companies above a certain size. It also means that 70 per cent of the major equity stocks are controlled by a few dozen institutional fund managers. In the US the corresponding percentage had risen from 8 per cent in 1950 to 60 per cent by 1990.[33]

In London the performance of these fund managers tends to be measured quarterly by their employers. That quarterly performance may therefore have implications for their status and pay. This makes it reasonable to suppose that fund managers are concerned with their performance over that three-monthly time-span.

The short-termist incentive

What follows, is a simplified hypothesis of how a fund manager may be motivated in a hostile bid for a company in which the manager's fund has a share stake. It is not

275

suggested that the hypothesis is an exact or widespread, let alone exclusive, portrait of how decisions are made.[34] It merely illustrates the logic of cause and effect, of what incentives and pressures might influence or bias a fund manager's decisions.

Once the market in T shares has been transformed into a market for control, Pearl Prudent, manager of a fund with a holding in T, has three choices during the couple of months from the time a bidder is first known or believed to be interested until the final day of that bidder's offer:

- sell in the market at the higher price, or
- wait until she is convinced that the offer is at its final price, will succeed and will not be topped by a counter-offer, and accept the bid, or
- reject the bid.

In the last case, if the offer is successful and 'goes unconditional', Pearl's holding must normally be bought out by the bidder at the offer price. However, she runs the risk that the offer will fail, in which case her refusal is likely to leave Pearl with only a small gain against the pre-bid price.

We again assume the pre-bid[35] share price was 100p, rose to 120p during the first two weeks after the bid, and that the bidder's offer later came at the typical 130p.[36] Pearl should then expect the price of T shares to fall back to 105–110p if the bid fails. What will she do?

Timing and tactics apart, Pearl has three basic options: to accept the offer, to sell in the market, or to sit tight. Her nightmare shows her sitting at the next quarterly review with an unsold holding worth 110p a share when her competitors have sold in the market at 127p. This gives Pearl a powerful bias against holding out against the bid. She may decide to accept the bid or sell in the market. If she sells in the market at the current bid-induced higher level, her purchaser no doubt intends to accept; the purchaser would otherwise be aiming to risk a substantial loss. If Pearl or the purchaser accepts the offer, the bid is that much more likely to succeed. Pearl's incentive is to hold tight only if she expects to do still better that way, and if she can afford to wait for better performance. If Pearl's performance is assessed quarterly, has she got that time?[37]

Pearl's dilemma stems from the fact that the market in corporate control operates for such fleeting, discontinuous periods. In this assumed scenario therefore the split market loads the dice in the bidder's favour. As we have described it, Pearl's unequal choice is not predominantly swayed by the merits of the bid. Whether the company will be more profitable if the incumbent managers are replaced, has little to do with the arithmetic of her three alternatives.

What makes that bias possible, is the concentration of holdings and voting power in so few short-term-motivated hands.

Pearl's dilemma is of course just one illustration of how one decision-taker may plausibly be motivated to approach her decision. In practice even Pearl's decisions will be tempered by how she sees the effect on the reputation of the institution.[38] In any case bids are in fact frequently turned down when a bidder fails to convince the market that the target company is more valuable under the bidder's management or broken up. Enterprise Oil's bid for LASMO in 1994 suffered that fate. In such cases Pearl's short-term incentive fails to sway the market as a whole. Some bad bids succeed, but by no means all.

Managerial reaction

Our task is however to explain *managerial* short termism. We asked how the takeover market can cause it. What we have so far explained, is that managers may be rational in expecting the market in corporate control to be biased in favour of bidders. Biased means that the market is not a completely even-handed arbiter of managerial stewardship, but weighted against incumbent managers by factors other than how good or bad their performance has been or is expected to be in the longer run.

Mr Ian N. Cumbent, chief executive of T, will in the light of that knowledge seek to boost T's short-term results. He will do that in the belief that this will boost T's share price and thus make T less vulnerable to a hostile takeover bid.

Short-term results must mean reported accounting profits. Some financial theorists claim to have found empirical evidence that mere accounting changes will not mislead the stockmarket into boosting the share price. They have shown that a change in an accounting standard, such as the basis of stock valuation, has no significant effect on share prices.[39] An announced change in accounting conventions is not however what I.N. Cumbent means by 'boosting the results'. He means genuine, but undisclosed reductions in expenditures which yield longer- rather than shorter-term benefits: training, R&D, building maintenance, environmental protection. Such economies amount to concealed disinvestment. They are not immediately transparent to the stockmarket and analysts. In the very short term they may well temporarily help the share price and make the company less vulnerable. Over any longer time-frame they are of course value-destructive and make the company more vulnerable to a hostile bid.

Summary

This appendix has described short termism and put forward one hypothesis of how the market in corporate control may cause it. The suggested links are the preponderance of institutional voting power, the short-term motivation of fund managers, the split market with its major discontinuity, and the not irrational reaction to that market bias by corporate managers. This is only an explanatory model. The model has not been empirically tested. It is in any case unlikely to be the sole explanation of short-termist conduct. It applies only to listed companies in an Anglo Saxon financial system where hostile takeovers are a real threat. It does not for example explain the behaviour of those who manage unlisted companies in the US or UK. Its dependence on high concentrations of institutional holdings is however a feature of the financial systems of those countries. What it does seek to do is to assert that neither the day-to-day nor the takeover market is inefficient. Mispricing plays no part in causing the problem of discontinuity between the two markets.

Notes

1. Copeland, Koller and Murrin (1990) discuss the meaning and practical implications of the concept of a company's value.
2. An expression which includes of course the group of companies, i.e. parent company with subsidiaries or affiliates.
3. See Exclusion Four in Appendix 3.2 and the distinction between financial value and financial size in Chapter 2.
4. Coase (1937), Teece (1982), Williamson (1975). For a critique of Williamson's thesis that the head office may be a more efficient allocator of funds than the financial markets (a view which favours the formation of conglomerates) see Hill (1985). Another critique is that of Demsetz (1991). See the section entitled 'Do all firmlets need a head office?' in Chapter 16.
5. See Demsetz (1991) for a critique of the language and applicability of transaction cost theory.
6. Also 'cost' tends to mean a specific expense, not a less effective organization structure, or even a missed profit opportunity.
7. Minor relaxations of this principle are mentioned in Chapter 21. That chapter also describes the much wider meaning of the expression 'parenting', a central concept used by Goold, Campbell and Alexander (1994).
8. See Chapter 11.
9. Sudarsanam (1995) Chapter 15.
10. See Chapter 3.
11. Readers are reminded that in this literature the word 'managers' is used to describe senior managers, or perhaps the head office, sometimes with special reference to the CEO as distinct from heads of profit centres. There does not appear to be any satisfactory alternative word. For example, 'directors' or 'the board' are by no means coterminous with those who direct the company as a whole, as they are formal legal terms.
12. Hart (1995) gives a full description and assessment of agency conflict.
13. The market in corporate control does not exclusively operate through hostile takeover. Especially in the United States, poorly performing management can be ousted by other market processes such as proxy fights.
14. Jensen and Meckling (1976).
15. Castanias and Helfat (1991).
16. The literature discusses alternative disciplines: Mitchell and Lehn (1990) p. 373, Walsh and Kosnik (1993) pp 671–700, Bethel and Liebeskind (1993) p. 16.
17. Jensen (1989), Murphy (1985).
18. The Savoy case (page 268) has nothing to do with these two motives.
19. Hunt and Morgan (1995).

20. 'Diversification' simply means the addition of offerings to the cluster, irrespective of whether the new offerings are related or unrelated to the cluster as it was. The derivation of diversification from 'diverse' has misleadingly caused some people to equate diversification with the addition of unrelated (i.e. diverse) offerings.
21. Porter (1992).
22. Charkham (1989) and (1994).
23. That market is of course concerned with corporate governance.
24. This point should not be overstated. In the UK for example a few institutional shareholders like M&G have relatively high stakes in some (perhaps not the largest) listed companies, which they regard as long-term. In these cases the relationship with the company can be as close as stringent insider rules permit.
25. Charkham (1989) and (1994).
26. See Franks and Mayer (1992) for a review of this. The authors call the Anglo-Saxon system an 'outsider' system, and the continental European/Japanese system 'insider'.
27. Marsh (1990). See also Dimsdale and Prevezer (eds) (1994), Chapter 3.
28. Sudarsanam (1995) p. 217.
29. Franks and Harris (1989). The research examined 1900 mergers in the UK.
30. Dimsdale (1994) p. 23.
31. Charkham (1989) calls this a 'double market'.
32. For example, Marsh (1990). Also Marsh in Dimsdale and Prevezer (eds) (1994).
33. Porter (1992).
34. For example, decisions about contested bids are not usually made by one individual, as here assumed, but collectively by the investment team.
35. The 'pre-bid' price here means the last price uninfluenced by any rumour or leak of a specific bidder's intention to make an offer. How long before the bid this price is quoted, varies substantially from case to case. This imprecision is what makes researchers adopt a start point as early as four months before the bid is announced.
36. Or was subsequently raised to that figure.
37. Charkham (1989) makes the same point.
38. Dimsdale in Dimsdale and Prevezer (eds) (1994) points also to the legal duty of UK fund managers to act in the interests of the beneficiaries of the fund, and sums up 'There must be a presumption that shareholders will take advantage of the generous premium offered by a bidder and that a bid will, in these circumstances, generally succeed' (p. 25).
39. Kaplan and Roll (1972).

14   False and valid tests of corporate strategy

The diversification binge

The 1960s and 1970s witnessed a huge wave of corporate diversification in the US and some other Western countries. It mainly took the form of mergers and acquisitions, many of them unsuccessful. '**Diversification**' here simply means *additions* to corporate clusters of offerings. In the 1980s there were further waves of diversification, but that decade also saw the first stirrings of a countervailing fashion. It thus became the decade of management buyouts, of divestments generally, and of a belief that maybe after all 'small was beautiful'.

This countertrend was encouraged, or perhaps even triggered by a number of academic studies which questioned the benefits of diversification, and especially indiscriminate diversification. Studies originated in the two fields of strategy and finance.

Studies in the field of *strategy*[1] showed the disappointing results of much of this burst of acquisition[2] activity. They suggested that a majority of acquired businesses have either:

- reduced the acquirer's financial value, or
- been retained after they had ceased to add to it, or
- been redivested after a relatively short time.

Redivestment is not of course conclusive proof of failure: it is conceivable that a successful diversification had yielded its full intended benefits before the business was redivested.

However, this is unlikely to have been the normal case in the period under review.[3]

Financial research has tended to show that investors in targets have benefited from takeovers, and that *investors* in bidders may also have derived some smaller net benefits.[4] Moreover, in a significant proportion of the cases in which the bidder's shareholders gained, the bidder was itself subsequently taken over, or became the subject of a management buyout, or divested the target again.[5] These findings may[6] vindicate the pricing judgements and the social benefits of the market in corporate control. What they do not vindicate, is the original diversification strategies.

The diversification wave occurred mainly in those English-speaking countries whose stockmarkets were characterized by significant hostile takeover activity.[7] 'Significant' here means that managements of listed companies were seriously sensitive to the possibility that they might become targets of hostile bids. This was not the case in Germany, France, Japan, or most other non-English-speaking countries.[8]

Diversification was less prevalent in the rest of the world, even in the continental EU countries where there was fear of imminent overcapacity in the approaching single market. At the same time diversification in the English-speaking group of countries was not entirely confined to listed companies.

The first false god: risk diversification

The contention is therefore that in the English-speaking group of countries there was a mistaken rush into excessive and perhaps unselective diversification. It would be strange if such a fashion had not been stimulated by some doctrinal belief. We have briefly in Chapter 13 suggested that there were two false gods, risk diversification and size.[9]

The idea behind *risk* diversification stems from the central role of risk in the valuation criteria of financial theory. The cost of equity capital or of any other funds varies with the risk of the project which is being financed. Especially in the case of equity finance, the central preoccupation is with the commercial risk, i.e. the risk of volatile, and particularly cyclical future returns. The cost of capital is much higher in civil construction than in multiple food retailing, which is a good deal less cyclical.

Some managers concluded from this that they could reduce their companies' cost of capital and thus improve their financial value by reducing the overall risk of the companies' activities. As a caricature of this, a civil construction company might decide to acquire a food retail chain and thus 'diversify' (average out) the risk.

The reasoning behind it is fallacious, because it looks at the risk factor in the financial valuation without regard to the fact that investors tend to hold portfolios rather than single company investments. Investors in the real world hold portfolios of equities in which they can diversify their risks more efficiently than can the company internally. In their portfolios they can do this by simple market transactions. Shareholders in a construction company can add shares in retailers to their portfolios. If the diversification is instead performed within the company, it causes the heavy extra costs of less specialized top management. Construction managers may not be the best possible managers of a food retailing business. The stockmarket is therefore very likely to value the combined construction and food retailing company at less than the sum of its previously separate parts. *Risk diversification* is unlikely to add value, and may well cause agency conflict.

Risk diversification is incapable of adding investor value in its own right. A related[10] diversification may of course add value, and at the same time diversify risk. In that case the addition of value happens to coincide with risk diversification. The financial success of this move should however be ascribed to the relatedness, not to the risk diversification.

Risk diversification may also be valuable to owner-managers of small businesses. However, the benefit in that case is to the job security of the owner-managers in their capacity as managers, not as investors. If a self-employed building contractor wishes to diversify his or her investment by also investing in retailing, the best way is to buy shares in a listed retailer like Sears Roebuck, instead of owning a shop.

The second false god: size

The second discredited motive is that of *size*. Those who diversified for the sake of making their company bigger, did not always very clearly define what they meant by 'size'. The word was used from time to time with any one of these implied meanings:

1 Number of line management units. An increase in that number normally results in diversification.
2 Physical size: tonnage of plant, area of real estate, turnover, number of employees.
3 Financial size: market capitalization.
4 Economies of scale.
5 Market power in buying markets, including markets in supplies and in intangible and human resources.
6 Market power in customer markets; this covers both reduced competitive pressures and improved acceptance by customers.

The last three of these are of course genuine potential sources of financial value, and likely to be positively related to changes in a company's size under the first three meanings. Nevertheless, whereas the enlargement of a company *may* increase its market power or economies of scale, that result is not inevitable. A civil contractor may not derive appreciable extra scale economies or market power of any kind from acquiring a television production company.

In other words, the last three meanings are possible consequences of size: they are not the same thing as size. Only the first three meanings (more units, extra financial size or extra physical size) are measures of the company's size.

One widespread reason for the quest for size was the belief that size protects against hostile takeover. For this to make sense, size must mean financial size, such as market capitalization, rather than physical size. In the context of hostile takeover bids, market capitalization is the share price multiplied by the number of voting shares issued. The view that a financially larger company is more bid-proof, has some empirical support[11]. It also finds a measure of support in commonsense logic. A $100 company is hardly a credible bidder for General Electric.

On this view, a lower market value makes the company cheaper to bid for, and brings it within the range of the artillery of a wider set of potential bidders. If this relative immunity of larger companies was ever a reality, it has been undermined in the 1980s by the junk bond market, which enabled some smaller companies to take over larger ones.

In any case, the main weakness of this view is more basic: it fails to distinguish between,

- financial value: the value of an individual investor's stake, and
- financial size: market capitalization.[12]

If anything were capable of protecting against takeover, it would have to be financial value, not financial size. A bad acquisition, undertaken to boost size, will be self-defeating if it fails to enhance the company's financial value. To take an extreme case, the acquisition may be so bad that it will depress the bidder's share price enough to diminish rather than enhance its market capitalization. If so, the pursuit of size has reduced both financial value and share price and made the company more vulnerable to takeover. Chapter 2 has similarly shown that the same structural move can push financial value and market capitalization in opposite directions.

Immunity to takeover is not the only case that has been made for increasing a company's financial size or market capitalization. Financial size is widely believed to give a company clout in financial equity and debt markets,[13] and thus to reduce its cost of capital. The point is not free from doubt, but size may reduce the cost of borrowing from some lenders. What is free from doubt, is that at various thresholds extra size opens access to listing on public bond and equity markets. This reduces the cost of capital by a step function.

285

Extra financial size therefore brings a clear, if rare benefit at the thresholds, and a problematical benefit at other levels. This must not however blind strategists to the large, yet not easily quantified costs of diversified operation which are described below. Size can in some cases have benefits, but these do not justify a diversification which fails to pass the various criteria proposed in this chapter and Chapter 16. What has ruined many companies, is the notion that size can in its own right justify diversification, irrespective of whether the diversification can be justified on other grounds.

The view taken in this Part Five is that business strategy creates value only by targeting profitable customers, and that any diversification proposal must give priority to that aim. If offerings or firmlets are added for non-competitive reasons, their benefits are likely to be outweighed by the extra costs. The extra costs are (a) the extra burdens of diversified operation, discussed below, and (b) the distraction of top management from its areas of excellence.

The damage can however be even greater, if the aim of size is interpreted in terms not of financial, but of *physical* size. Physical size is not even loosely related to financial value. Where there is no value-enhancing reason for adding an offering to the cluster, physical size will help neither companies or managers. More tonnage of machinery or more acreage of land may raise or diminish financial value. That depends on how the future cash flows from the extra assets relate to the cost of acquiring them. In other words, on their value and their cost.

We began this section with a list of six possible meanings of the objective of size. We can now see that in our context only the first three aim at size proper, yet may fail to create financial value. The last three do not in fact aim at size itself, but at value-creating properties which may or may not result from greater size. They are among the 'related' links described in Chapter 16.

The importance of internal diversification

The subject of diversification is often discussed as if all diversification took the form of acquisitions rather than organic additions to the cluster from internal investment.

In fact the overwhelming majority of diversifications are internal and organic. This must be so, because every new offering is an addition to the cluster, and economic life witnesses a myriad of new offerings all the time. Every addition is of course a diversification.

The reason why acquisitions receive so much more attention is that more of them are notifiable to stock exchanges. They also tend to entail much larger structural changes to the diversifying company and to bring more and larger disasters in their train. A misconceived new internal offering like Rolls-Royce's RB211 can be equally ruinous, although fewer of them attract public attention at the time of their launch. Acquisitions are more newsworthy.

The costs of diversified operation

Chapter 16 distinguishes between related and unrelated diversification. For the moment we can define relatedness as a potentially value-building, and therefore valid category of diversification, in contrast to risk diversification or size.

An *unrelated* diversification – and that is what the quest for physical size tends to bring about – will always entail some loss of financial value. This loss is due to the extra costs of diversified operation.[14] The mere organizational separation of the head office imposes extra costs of communication, of bureaucratic uniformity and of demotivation of managers and employees.

These added costs of any diversification are not easily quantified, but are likely to be substantial, irrespective of how well the company is structured.[15] Now without relatedness, these costs are not balanced by any benefits. As the drop in financial value will make the company more vulnerable to a hostile takeover, neither managers nor investors stand to gain from such a diversification. If both take a rational view of this, there will be no agency conflict.

There is reason to believe that many acquisitions of the 1960–1990 period were undertaken with the aim of increasing physical size or risk diversification, or both.[16]

The natural bias towards overdiversification

We have noted the general evidence of past overdiversification, and the case for suspecting a deep-seated human tendency towards it. Its psychological elements are likely to be a search for power, for the security and status believed to be conferred by power, and a sense of living in a jungle in which management teams must either kill or be killed.

These factors tend to blind managers to:

- the need to add value in the sense of beating the cost of capital,
- the risks of a proposal, especially the future competitive pressures on a new offering like countermoves by competitors, and changes in customer preferences,
- the costs of implementing the project,
- the skills, efforts and expenditures needed, and the difficulties of motivating or even retaining key staff in the acquired business,
- the costs of restructuring, of harmonising information systems and the like,
- the very substantial hidden and largely unquantifiable costs of diversified operation, discussed in the previous section.

Evaluations of diversification proposals are particularly vulnerable, because they rest on projections of future cash flows. Past experience shows that those projections tend to be compiled with rose-tinted spectacles. Diversification proposals tend to generate a measure of excitement.

The decision criteria

If risk diversification and size are not suitable reasons for adding or retaining offering F, how should a company decide what to hold in its cluster of offerings?

The answer is that a proposal to *add* an offering should be adopted only if it passes four criteria.[17] They are the better-off test, to be discussed next, and also three filters:

- the contractual alternative filter,
- the best-owner filter, and
- the robustness filter.

A decision to *retain* rather than add an offering in the cluster would have to meet only three of these four criteria. It would not need to pass the robustness filter.[18] If the offering fails any one of the other three, it should be divested. The four criteria and their logic will now be described.

The better-off test

The better-off test as here defined simply requires that company C must be financially more valuable[19] with than without firmlet F.

The rules for measuring financial value are very important to this test:

- For a decision to add F to the cluster the comparison is between the net present value of the entire cluster (a) with, and (b) without firmlet F. The calculation compares cash flows with and without F over the relevant future period.

  The control value of the unchanged cluster without F must of course be calculated with due allowance for likely environmental changes, such as the acquisition of F by a competitor.
- Similarly, for a decision to retain or divest, the comparison is again between the net present value of the entire cluster (a) with F, as at present, and (b) without F, assuming the

most advantageous practicable disposal: selling F to M, selling F to N, or liquidating F.

- Value is measured by the *criteria* of the financial markets. The resulting value is not necessarily identical with day-to-day market capitalization in a stockmarket: the decision-takers may well have a fuller information set than is available to the market. They must assess value as would the stockmarket, if it shared their extra information.
- Financial markets are assumed to assess financial value as the net present value of the expected net after-tax cash flows.
- The transaction costs of acquisition or divestment must be accounted for, as well as the purchase or sale price.[20]
- An acquisition normally acquires more than the targeted firmlet or activity F. The cost of F must allow for the total cost of what is acquired, less what is realized from disposals (net after the costs of disposal), less the value to the company of what may be neither wanted nor disposable.
- Account must be taken of the extra costs of diversified operation, which would be caused by an addition to the cluster or saved by a divestment. We have already stressed the considerable extra operating costs which a head office by its mere existence imposes on its sub-units. These are added by an acquisition or not saved by retention, yet saved by a divestment. These costs are not only heavy, but very hard to quantify. For this reason, it is important either to allow a conservative contingency amount for them, or (much less satisfactorily) to use a conservative cost-of-capital discount factor. The dominant need here is to guard against optimism.
- Sometimes the test must be applied to more than one offering F, if F is too interdependent with one or more other offerings, such as G. In such a case,

  (a) F cannot be added to the cluster without G, as G brings advantages to F which the existing cluster lacks, or
  (b) F cannot be divested unless G is also divested, as G will not be valuable if it remains in the cluster without F.

A typical cause of such interdependence is that F and G both use a valuable resource not needed by the rest of the cluster. F's use of that resource would not on its own exploit adequate economies of scale.

An instance of this might be the Land Rover Defender and Discovery[21], which use a number of common resources, which might well be underemployed with just one of the two offerings.

Another cause of interdependence is when customers can be expected to switch from offering G to offering F, if F is added to the cluster. Any adverse effect of this kind must be taken into account in the decision to add F. It may also make it necessary to reposition G when F is added. The simple rule is again that the value of the cluster must be managed as a whole, not piecemeal.[22]

Chapter 16 will suggest that the better-off test can only be passed by what is there defined as 'related' diversifications.

The contractual alternative filter

We now come to the three filters. All of them are suggested as absolute correctives to two tendencies. One is the natural bias of managers towards adding or retaining offerings. The other is the strong tendency to ignore or underestimate the costs of diversified operation, which are in any case very hard to quantify. Unlike the better-off test, the filters, as absolute bars, do not rest on analytical logic.

The first of the three filters is the **contractual alternative filter**. This filter requires that a supplier-customer relationship (called 'contract') should only be internalized when there is no economic way of obtaining the same business benefit by competitive dealing at arm's length. The essence of the filter is its strong preference for competitive dealing in markets. Neither party should lack the carrot enabling it to shop around for the most economic counterparty, or the stick compelling it to be and remain competitive itself.

The word 'contract' is not here used in its legal sense, which covers a wider set of relationships. In the literature on this issue 'contract' invariably means a *competitive* deal between buyer and supplier. The concept does in our present context extend to arm's-length franchising and licensing deals.

An illustration of a contractual alternative is provided by a small brewery with an excellent, but underloaded bottling plant. It could boost its profitability by finding an extra outlet for its spare bottling capacity. The managers considered acquiring another brewery so as to realize the extra economies of scale. They decided instead to achieve that aim by selling bottles to neighbouring competitors, entered into the appropriate contracts with them, and made their brewery one of the most profitable over a wide area.

The comparison here is between (a) supplying the other breweries at arm's length, by contract, and (b) internalizing that supply by acquiring those breweries – a diversification. The advantages of this contractual route over the diversification route of buying other breweries, are significant:

- The extra costs of diversified operation are minimized. The brewery with the bottling plant acquires a handful of extra customers: it does not need to become a much larger company.
- The new bottling customers remain free, subject to any notice periods and penalties in their contracts, to buy from other suppliers. Similarly the brewery with the bottling plant remains free to switch to other customers if they offer better prices: both sides retain the motivation to remain competitive. All are kept on their toes. This spur would disappear with an internalized relationship under common ownership.

The contracting arrangement is thus a lot more profitable than ownership of the bottling customers.

Wherever the benefit of a diversification proposal might alternatively be attained by competitive contract, this filter should therefore be applied. If that benefit, like the extra load on the bottling plant, can be obtained by competitive contract, the diversification should be turned down. Similarly, whenever an existing firmlet can be divested and replaced by a competitive contractual arrangement, it should be divested.

Joint ventures and the contractual alternative filter

However, what exactly does ownership mean in this context? For example, does ownership include the case of the 'joint venture' where brewery A does not acquire 100 per cent of brewery B, but becomes a part shareholder in B's brewing subsidiary S, with B holding the remainder? Joint ventures of this kind can take many forms, with A being anything from say a 10 per cent to a 90 per cent shareholder in S.

The criterion which matters here is not the formal ownership structure, but whether the operating relationship between A and S becomes internalized. The test is whether A and S are now to treat each other just as they treat each other's competitors or not. Can each of them still shop around and conduct business with the most profitable counterparty? Or are they under an instruction from head office to work with one another? In that last case the competitive criterion would be ousted.

Internalization is the test whether a particular joint venture amounts to ownership or to the contractual alternative. The extra costs of diversification are caused precisely by the internalization of operating relationships. Internalization is what is in principle inferior to competitive contractual relationships. Internalization is however either unavoidable or a lesser evil in certain defined cases. In Chapter 16 we shall include these cases among valid forms of relatedness.

The best-owner filter

The second filter, called the **best-owner filter** is equally stringent. It requires company C to be the best possible owner of firmlet F which C proposes to add or retain. So brewery C must not acquire brewery F if F would be more valuable either independent, or owned by some other owner C_1. Moreover, if C already owns F, it should in that case divest it.

293

The robustness filter

The purpose of the third filter, called the **robustness filter,** is a precaution against adding (not retaining) offerings to the cluster which may cause loss of value even if the analysis shows an expected recovery of the cost of capital.

The robustness filter is a form of sensitivity analysis, testing how robust the offering's market position and protective armour are if things go wrong. It requires the offering to be a value-builder for the greater of two time-spans:

- the payback period needed to recover the cost of capital, and
- the lead time needed to abort or divest the offering, in the event of shock news. Action would be needed irrespective of whether the shock news comes before or after the cost of capital has been recovered. Failure or delay in divestment could cause serious loss of value at either stage.

The rationale of the three filters

All three filters, it is here suggested, should be treated as absolute requirements, except that the robustness filter does not apply to a decision to retain or divest. Unlike the better-off test, the filters therefore bypass or short-circuit the valuation principles of the financial markets. They are not intended as analytical calculations. If F would itself be more valuable under some other ownership, or if the benefits of owning F could be obtained by contract, or if it would fail the robustness filter, then it should not be acquired, *not even if C's calculations show that F would add value to C or its offering G.* The objective of adding financial value is of course left intact and indeed served by the filters. They are needed because the normal calculation techniques do not successfully ascertain that value, given the strong tendency to ignore or underestimate the heavy extra costs of diversified operation.

The erroneous tendency to overdiversify which the three filters are intended to pre-empt, was described earlier in this chapter. All three filters have the function of discouraging the heavy and normally greatly underestimated costs of diversified operation.

The individual filters are formulated in fairly categorical and practical terms. Otherwise they would become pious platitudes, prompting lip-service rather than effective compliance. Their strong business benefits are now set out.

Reasons for the contractual alternative filter

The *contractual alternative filter* corrects for the tendency to diversify when the same business objective can be attained without internalizing the relationship. It saves bureaucratic costs and discourages uncompetitive drift. Contracting at arm's length keeps both parties on their toes, motivates them to become and remain competitive. Each party ultimately stands to lose its contracting partner if it remains or becomes uncompetitive.

Reasons for the best-owner filter

The *best-owner filter* is best seen as correcting for either complacency or optimism.

- Where the filter suggests the divestment of an existing member of a cluster, it acts as an antidote to complacency or reluctance to question the status quo.
- Where it rejects an addition to the cluster, there must be grounds for healthy scepticism about the estimates which showed it to add value. There must be a nagging doubt whether the proposal was built on rosy rather than realistic assumptions, for example about the likely competitive opposition.

In both cases this filter reduces the vulnerability of a listed company to a hostile bid from the best owner, or from a raider who can make money by selling the firmlet to its best owner. After all, if firmlet F fails this test, it is an under-exploited asset. The greater the underexploitation and the greater the proportion that F is of C's total value, the greater is C's vulnerability.

Reasons for the robustness filter

The *robustness filter* ensures that the profitable competitive positioning of a new offering is not just fleeting.[23] The filter strengthens defences against two risks:

- The risk that even if the expected mean or modal outcome recovers the cost of capital, there is an unacceptably high chance of significant shortfalls from that aim.
- The risk of failure or delay in divesting the offering, for cultural reasons, in the event of unexpected news making its divestment necessary.

What is the cultural cause of failure or delay in divesting? Companies other than corporate raiders or catalysts[24] have deep-seated cultural and competitive inhibitions about acquiring with a view to early subsequent disposal – it gives them an image of less than caring employers. Moreover, public opinion will tend to suspect such an intention even where the early redivestment was genuinely unforeseen. Many an acquisition is rapidly seen to have been a disaster, yet divested only after years of blood-letting, due to precisely this resistance to U-turns. The test should not however be used merely to discourage offerings whose divestment would disrupt the employment of people. Even 'bloodless' U-turns may give a company an image as potentially volatile, and thus make it a less attractive employer and investee. Employee relations are not the only inhibition to prompt divestment. Managers are often reluctant to admit failure or mistakes, or to appear accident-prone in the eyes of customers or investors.

An example of the first risk is a 30 per cent expected chance of the proposal resulting in serious loss. An example of the second is that at a very early stage (long before recovery of cost of capital) competitive conditions make it imperative to divest the offering promptly, to prevent a loss of say twice the cost of capital. The risk is that the company will nevertheless resist or delay the divestment decision. The case is not much better if this need to divest becomes apparent after recovery of the cost of capital. If the investment was £10 million, and the company recovers this plus another £5 million, but then loses £20 million, the offering will not have improved the company's value.

The application of this filter requires a judgement in which the following criteria play a part:

- *the risk profile*: the chances of unacceptable loss of value.
- *duration*: how long is the offering expected to go on building value?
- *cost of capital recovery period*: how long will it take for the offering to achieve a positive net present value, i.e. to become value-building?
- *financial commitment*: how big will the loss be if the strategy has to be aborted, and the firmlet divested, at an unexpectedly early stage, or later?
- *cultural commitment*: what inhibitions might obstruct or delay divestment when it becomes desirable, and for how long?

The root cause of both risks is the lack of robustness of the offering's competitive position, and the remedy is to apply this filter which requires qualifying offerings to have that extra degree of robustness. The better-off test on its own does not require this extra robustness.

Internal (e.g. 'green field') diversifications are often more competitively vulnerable than acquisitions, whose present competitive positioning can be observed and evaluated.

All three filters bypass cold quantitative analysis. The need for them is behavioural, not analytical. There is ample experience that a comparative value calculation is neither feasible nor reliable. This is due particularly, but not exclusively to the tendency to ignore or underestimate the extra costs of diversified operation. They are apparently not amenable to realistic quantification. The overwhelming evidence of overdiversification since 1960 points to the powerful human tendency to underestimate them. This was discussed earlier in this chapter. The need for an antidote to that tendency is the common thread that runs through all three filters.

To sum up, all three filters correct for this bias towards neglecting or playing down the extra costs of diversified operation. In addition, the contractual filter protects against uncompetitive feather-bedding, the best-owner filter against optimism, complacency and inertia, and the robustness one against unpleasant surprises and reluctance to change course.

The arithmetic of the criteria

How are the criteria applied arithmetically? The illustrations in Tables 14.1 and 14.2 are for the sake of simplicity restricted to the better-off test and the best-owner filter.

Table 14.1 *Arithmetic of deciding whether to add offering F*

NPV to the cluster, of			F's NPV to BAO	Action	Reason
G	G+F	F	F*		
−3	+3	+6	+5	add F:	F passes both test and filter.
−3	+3	+6	+7	divest G:	F fails filter
−3	−1	+2	+1	divest G:	F+G fails test
+5	+3	−2	−4	retain G:	F fails test
+5	+6	+1	−1	add F:	F passes both test and filter.
+5	+6	+1	+3	retain G:	F fails filter

Notes:
1 The F column derives F's npv to the cluster, from the difference between the first two columns.
2 The F* column reports the npv of F to BAO, its best alternative owner.

The illustrations assume that:

- the other two filters cause no problems, where required,
- the proposal is to add or retain as the case may be, offering F, because it will add value in combination with existing offering G,
- that a decision to retain or add F is not invalidated purely for lack of relatedness, discussed in Chapter 16.

The first illustration in Table 14.1 concerns a decision about the proposed addition of F. The figures in Table 14.1 each represent a net present value (NPV) of G, G + F or F. The first three columns show the NPV to our cluster, the fourth shows F's NPV to its best alternative owner. The amounts may be read as thousands or millions of dollars. The unit does not affect the principle.

The second illustration in Table 14.2 is about the retention or divestment of F, not its addition. Here we need to define:

- C = value of Company C's entire cluster (or its relevant part), including F.
- C – F = the best value of C without F. That best value is either (a) after selling it to the highest bidder, net after transaction costs, or (b) after closing it down, with due regard to assets realized and to redundancy and other costs of closure, whichever is greater.
- F = C – (C – F) = F's value to Company.
- F* = value of F to best alternative owner.

The arithmetic will be as in Table 14.2.

Table 14.2 *Arithmetic of deciding whether to divest offering F*

C	C–F	F	F*	*Action*	*Reason*
15	18	–3	5	Divest F	F fails test and filter
15	12	3	5	Divest F	F fails filter
15	18	–3	–5	Divest F	F fails test
15	11	4	3	Retain F	F passes test and filter

Applying the test and filters

Theoretically, the four criteria can be applied independently of each other, and in any order of priority. If the proposal to add or retain offering F fails one of the first three criteria, or if a proposal to add F fails the robustness filter, F should be rejected. In practice, it is often useful to look at the filters first. It is often transparent that one of them, such as the contractual alternative, is failed, in which case a good deal of time and effort can be saved by not undertaking the other three. The better-off test, with its detailed cash flow projection, is usually the most laborious. It may best be left until last.

Summary

This chapter has set out the case for stringent selectivity in diversification. It also suggests decision criteria to apply that stringent discipline: the better-off test and the three filters. The case rests on the experience of the decades after 1960 which saw an epidemic of unsuccessful diversifications in the English-speaking group of countries. Risk diversification and size, in the sense of number of line management units or physical size, are undesirable objectives.

The next chapter discusses a special kind of company, the corporate catalyst, to which different rules apply. Chapter 16 then resumes the main exposition of corporate strategy by setting out the types of diversifications which are likely to pass the better-off test.

Notes

1. Especially Porter (1987), Shleifer and Vishny (1991) and Ravenscraft and Scherer (1987).
2. The research only captured the fate of acquisitions; however the spate of activity was directed at diversification of any kind, not just acquisitions.
3. A good example was the sample used by Ravenscraft and Scherer (1987), p. 130.
4. For reviews see Jensen and Ruback (1983), Krinsky *et al.* (1988).

5. Shleifer and Vishny (1991).
6. However, there are opinions to the contrary: Shleifer and Vishny (1991).
7. See also Appendix 13.1.
8. See Appendix 13.1.
9. A review of managerial incentives (as distinct from the rationale discussed here) for overdiversification is in Markides (1995).
10. See Chapter 16.
11. Evidence that size may make the largest decile of UK quoted companies less vulnerable, is found in Higson and Elliott (1993).
12. See Chapter 2.
13. See Appendix 3.2, Exclusion Four.
14. Porter (1987) helpfully stresses these often neglected and largely hidden extra costs.
15. Williamson (1975).
16. Shleifer and Vishny (1991).
17. These criteria adapt, restructure and enhance the criteria used by Porter (1987). There are a number of differences from Porter's statement, especially the removal of the industry framework retained by Porter. The emphasis in the better-off test on financial value in corporate strategy goes back to Penrose (1959).
18. See Chapter 17.
19. It differs from orthodox financial doctrine for investment or divestment appraisal only by requiring offerings to be related and by being coupled with the filters.
20. Porter (1987) makes this a separate test.
21. See Chapter 3.
22. See also Link Four in Chapter 16.
23. Porter (1987) proposed a similar separate test, called the attractiveness test. Porter's test requires the diversification to be in an attractive industry, and is not described further.
24. See box in Chapter 15.

15 The corporate catalyst

Introduction: pure dealers

This book is about that great majority of businesses that pursue their financial objectives by seeking profitable customers. This chapter exceptionally describes a different kind, categorized as **pure dealing** business.[1] Pure dealers earn profits from professional ('proprietary') speculation[2] or arbitrage, for example in financial or commodity markets.

A currency dealer in a bank may be dealing in the foreign exchange market for the express purpose of making speculative and arbitrage gains for the employing bank. So might a market-maker in equities or bonds, or a commodity dealer in zinc. Such trading is often called 'proprietary'. Their job in that capacity is not to win customers, just to trade at profitable prices.

Any of these dealers may *in addition* spend some of their time executing market deals on behalf of clients, in which case the clients are customers whom they wish to deny to their competitors. In *that* endeavour they are competing for customers in a commercial market: this is not proprietary or pure dealing.

Dealing for clients is however quite a complex process. The dealer (say) in foreign exchange is simultaneously concerned with two 'markets', in this case (a) the dealing market (e.g. in forward US$/£stg) and also (b) the customer market for the business of clients. This calls for a very sharp distinction, because the two markets trade quite different items at quite differently defined prices. The box illustrates this with a technical description of market practice.

Currency dealers deal with each other in the inter-bank market. The large players quote rates to each other with a very thin bid-offer spread. The quoting bank must quote a spread between buying and selling rates because by convention it quotes *without* knowing whether the enquirer wishes to buy or sell the currency. That is only disclosed if and when the rate is accepted. For example, an *interbank* US dollar/sterling rate may be quoted $1.4310–1.4320, which means that the quoting dealer will buy dollars at $1.4320 = £1, or sell them at $1.4310 = £1. The difference represents the bank's dealing margin, to cover transaction costs, risk and return on capital.

However, when the bank deals on behalf of a client, it will quote the client a wider margin than interbank, say 0.30 instead of 0.10 US cents, quoting $1.4300–1.4330 to the client. The extra 0.20c spread covers the bank's costs of dealing with the client, including the client's credit risk.

We can now distinguish the two prices which are being quoted in the two different markets. The bank is effectively quoting a mid-price of $1.4315 as the $/£ spot rate *in the foreign exchange market*, its dealing market, and a 0.30c spread as its *price in the market for the client's business*. If the client can get a better price from another bank, then the first bank will lose the deal to a competitor. If all banks are assumed to quote the same interbank mid-rate of $1.4315, then the successful bank must have quoted a margin of less than 0.30c. $1.4315 was our bank's rate in the dealing market, 0.30c its spread in the customer market. Its interbank quotation of $1.4310–$1.4320 is its dealing quotation.

A commercial bank, such as the one in the box, in most of its activities competes for customers against competitors. It is also however likely to have some pure dealing activities like the one illustrated, in which its dealers are employed to make money for the bank in the financial market concerned. This *speculative and arbitrage* business is deal- and price-centred. Each deal is separate. No customers, no 'market share'.

The notion that pure dealing has no market share takes market share to mean a proportion of a finite number of customers. The pure dealer has no customers. The dealer's counterparties are not customers, nor is the dealer a supplier. The two sides play an equal and opposite part in the transaction, which is well illustrated by the convention under which the market-maker quotes a two-way price, without knowing whether the enquirer wishes to buy or sell.

Market-makers in equities or other instruments may or may not be pure dealers. They will not be pure dealers if they have leading market positions, which boost their volume of profitable deals. In that case they have an interest in maintaining or increasing their share of that dealing market. If so, they are likely to treat their counterparties as though they were also customers, and perhaps to trim their bid-offer spreads so as to defend or increase their share of the market. That exception however only applies to the dealer with a large position in such a market. Most other speculators or proprietary dealers are neither dominant nor concerned with their share of the market, and are entirely price- and deal-centred. It is they who are pure dealers.

Pure dealing is not part of a continuing effort to attract and retain customers. That is not how counterparties are identified. In this activity the bank has no customers, no continuing market position, no competitors for those same customers to watch. Price alone makes the difference between gain and loss. That is the meaning of pure dealing. A bank is however likely to have a mixture of pure dealing and competitive businesses, if it also deals on behalf of clients, as illustrated in the box. The two capacities can be closely intertwined.

Dealers in corporate control: corporate catalysts

This chapter focuses particularly on one type of pure dealer, the dealer in the market for corporate control.[3]

The term 'dealers in corporate control' is here used to refer to companies like Hanson[4] in Britain and US in the 1980s. The characteristic activity of such a company is to acquire another company, often by a hostile bid, to restructure and break it up, and to sell its different parts off at a profit. It typically also however retains some of the acquired businesses and runs them profitably. Such dealers in corporate control are usually labelled as either,

- conglomerates, or
- 'corporate raiders' or 'asset strippers',

depending on whether attention is focused on their continuing cluster of businesses or on their purchases and sales of business assets with a view to capital profits. A better, and less emotive and biased term than 'raiders' is 'corporate catalysts'. It describes what they do.

The 'relatedness' issue

The role of the corporate catalyst is of considerable general interest to students of corporate strategy, but the central issue for this chapter is a statistical one concerning 'relatedness'.

There is an important long-standing, but difficult debate about the relative merits of 'related' and 'unrelated' diversification[5]. 'Related' has been variously defined, and a very specific definition is put forward in Chapter 16.[6] However, it is common ground that the diversification spree of the 1960s and 1970s was predominantly unrelated in practically any relevant sense of the term.[7] What is perhaps remarkable is that a number of studies – especially less recent ones – have found the evidence either inconclusive or even pointing towards the superiority of unrelated clusters.[8]

However, it may be significant that empirical findings which failed to support the case against unrelated diversification seemed to concern mainly the UK, rather than the

US.[9] A reason for this may be that the capital profits of US corporate catalysts do not seem to get into statistics of conglomerate performance on any significant scale.[10]

Two suggestions are being made here:

- that some of these counterintuitive results and difficulties may be due to the inclusion of corporate catalysts in the unrelated or 'conglomerate' category, and
- that this inclusion needs to be questioned for the purpose of comparing the results of related and unrelated diversification.

The issue is statistical and technical, but has considerable bearing on relatedness, one of the primary issues of corporate strategy.

Earnings per share growth of corporate catalysts

Empirical researchers tend to include dealers in corporate control in the category of 'conglomerates'. The financial performance of dealers in corporate control is often well above average. They also tend to grow quite rapidly, so that they have come to form a significant part of the conglomerate category. Their inclusion – in the UK at least – therefore almost certainly improves the overall performance of the conglomerate sector.

What needs attention however, is the extent to which the superior results of corporate catalysts are due not to the results of their continuing cluster of unrelated businesses, but to their capital profits from buying and selling business assets which they had never intended to retain and use. The dealer in corporate control buys assets relatively cheaply and then sells a substantial proportion of them to the highest bidder. These gains are pure dealing gains. However, not all assets are usually resold. The catalyst also retains some, boosting the size and profits of its continuing cluster of firmlets.

In the UK at least the effect of the dealing gains on reported earnings per share is twofold:

- The capital profits will swell the earnings, but are usually known to analysts. They and the stockmarket can therefore take separate note of the dealing gains and the trading profits of the cluster.[11]
- The cash surplus which these capital profits represent, can fund subtantial additions to retained businesses, whose earnings will then swell the earnings per share of the catalyst company.

It is this second benefit to earnings per share which may not have received enough attention. A catalyst's earnings per share can rise, not because the continuing offerings have become more profitable, but because the accretion of these earnings streams have been financed with no commensurate new issues of shares or debt. They have been financed with funds which attract little attention, seemingly acquired at negligible or no cost at all.

This account has focused on earnings per share, because continual earnings per share growth has been used by some catalyst companies as their stated financial objective.[12]

Should corporate catalysts count as conglomerates?

A **conglomerate** is a diversified company with an unrelated cluster of activities. Corporate catalysts tend to retain unrelated clusters, and are in that sense correctly classified as conglomerates.

However, one important concern in this Part Five is whether a related or an unrelated cluster is more likely to generate financial value for a company's investors. That examination may require the exclusion of corporate catalysts from the unrelated, conglomerate category.

There are two arguments for that exclusion:

- First, successful corporate catalysts owe their financial returns predominantly to their capital profits on divested assets, rather than to the profitability of their retained clusters.

307

- Secondly, there must be a question-mark whether the largest and most successful corporate catalysts' strategic intent is what the conglomerate argument assumes it to be. That argument compares the performance of the strategies of unrelated and related diversification. It assumes that the strategic intent concerns the continuing cluster. If the catalyst's strategic aim focuses instead on capital profits, is it sufficiently similar to be a valid part of this comparison?

For these reasons it is here proposed that the results of the conglomerate sector should for this comparison be assessed without the contribution made by corporate catalysts, wherever this is of significant size.

There is no reason to exclude the capital profits of all businesses. Asset disposals are a normal feature of business, and profits or losses from them are a normal feature of business results. Catalysts' capital profits need exceptional treatment because they,

- are the principal goal of catalysts' strategies, and
- tend to form a dramatically larger element of their financial results.

The culture of the corporate catalyst

In its pure form, the corporate catalyst is a company whose managers are firmly focused on the pure dealing market in corporate control, on financial gains in one transaction after another. This requires a sharply different corporate culture from that of commercial and industrial managers.

This cultural divide between industrial/commercial and catalyst managers is hard to exaggerate (see box). It implies very different attitudes towards people. The contrast has of course here been caricatured in black-and-white terms. In real life a company seldom falls completely into either category. Nevertheless, the gulf between the ethos of the dealer and that of the commercial manager is so wide that it is useful to classify whole companies as either catalysts or non-

The reluctance of commercial and industrial managers to redivest recent acquisitions

The attention of commercial and industrial managers centres not on individual deals, but on the continuing customer-serving business activity and its enduring prosperity. They are concerned with the continuity of their business and its workforce, and with success in the competitive markets of its offerings. They too are focused on profits, but not deal by deal.[13] Their strategic targets, in the language of this book, are profitable customers.

Commercial and industrial managers do not normally acquire businesses and their workforces for the purpose of profitable redivestment. This is not because they are more caring or philanthropic: that may or may not be the case. It is because leadership of an organization is much more difficult without a sense of mutual trust and continuity between managers and workforce. That sense of trust and continuity is impaired when a manager is known to treat businesses, with their workers, as items to buy and sell.

This threat to their authority as managers does not extend to the case where an acquisition which makes 'industrial' sense, requires the incidental acquisition of other activities, which are then redivested as soon as possible. Company A cannot normally acquire offering F on its own. What can be bought or taken over tends to be the whole or a part of a company which contains more than offering F. The redivestment of such incidental purchases is widely tolerated as unavoidable and culturally acceptable.

catalysts. This distinction is closer to reality than many others in the world of business.

It is not therefore suggested that catalysts never retain businesses, or that non-catalysts never buy or sell businesses. The dividing line, inherent in the definition of the corporate catalyst, concerns the predominant motive:

- Only the catalyst's predominant objective is to buy with an eye on redisposal. Non-catalysts do this only because what they need to buy is seldom available on its own.[14] They must in that case buy what they want along with other offerings, which they will then need to redivest. Divestments which are incidental to a business-motivated acquisition, by definition do not make them catalysts. What counts is the motive.
- Only the catalyst is by definition more interested in profits from redivestment than in the continuing operating profits of retained businesses.

Corporate catalysts and corporate strategy

To the extent that managing the composition of their clusters of continuing businesses is not their goal, corporate catalysts have no corporate strategies as here defined. Their dealing strategies are not in this strict sense corporate strategies.

Corporate catalysts apply a kind of better-off test to each decision to acquire a company, but of course they apply it deal by deal, with a focus on dealing gains. Their primary focus, as that of currency dealers, is on dealing prices, not on any competitive positioning. They should also apply the better-off test to their retained clusters, but there have been signs that they are relatively slow to divest those businesses which they fail to resell during the restructuring stage after their acquisition.

In the mid-1990s there was a fall-off in 'raider' activity. This may turn out to be a temporary market phase, or it may be due to regulatory changes, for example in a number of US states, and it was not then possible to see whether the decline was short or long term.[15] The decline was accompanied by some signs that corporate catalysts may have been switching more attention to their clusters of continuing businesses, and to making these more related than heretofore. If so, they were ceasing to be catalysts.

Corporate catalysts' retained clusters

Why do corporate catalysts retain any firmlets at all? One theoretical explanation might be that they 'warehouse' some firmlets, awaiting a more opportune time to sell them. The evidence suggests that this occurs, but not on a large enough scale to explain the bulk of what is retained.

Some of their retained firmlets are 'related' in the sense defined in subsequent chapters, for example to realize the benefits of economies of scale, but that again is not a prevailing characteristic. Their retained firmlets do however have some common characteristics. They tend to be what Goold and Campbell[16] call 'manageable' businesses, which are neither capital-intensive nor technologically complex, nor characterized by a long lead-time from business decision to market execution. They can therefore be called short-fuse businesses. For example they are more likely to be in building materials than in major construction contracts. They tend to be suitable for the financial control style.[17]

So what are corporate catalysts' main objectives in having continuing clusters at all? Two motives suggest themselves. The first is that they need some continuing earnings to fill gaps between bids. Takeover bids are a discontinuous, lumpy business. They cannot form a smooth continuous series. Targets are not always plentiful, prices are not always attractive, and catalysts cannot safely acquire companies during recessions when there are no purchasers offering attractive prices for what they wish to redivest. A major acquisition takes time to digest. Immediately after such a major acquisition, the catalyst's management resources and debt capacity may be too fully stretched to tackle the next one. While the catalyst pauses for breath, it needs day-to-day earnings.

A clue to the second motive is to be found in the very fact that catalysts are so widely classified as conglomerates.

Catalysts may understandably prefer the public image of industrialists running a continuing cluster rather than that of 'corporate raiders'. Although the catalyst performs a useful social function, that of unlocking underutilized assets for more productive use, the process disrupts lives and therefore does not always enjoy high public esteem. The continuing cluster with its conglomerate label distracts attention from the buying and selling of business assets.

Assessing the performance of corporate catalysts

It might be contended that the high returns earned by corporate catalysts justify the addition of firmlets to their retained clusters. Catalysts tend to collect and retain manageable or short-fuse[18] businesses. Unlike managers of other businesses, catalysts do not see the profits of those businesses as the prime source of their generation of financial value. The primary source is capital profits. The retained businesses do not therefore need to be 'related' as we shall define that term in Chapter 16. To the catalyst the relatedness issue is therefore of less consequence than to the non-catalyst. An investor considering a purchase of catalyst shares is likely to give much more weight to the company's scope for further takeover bids than to the growth prospects of its existing cluster.

The corporate catalyst's distinctive talents

The qualities required of a corporate catalyst's managers are an ability to spot undervalued assets, a flair for buying and selling them at a gain, a flair for restrucuring,[19] and a financial control style.[20]

In managing the retained cluster a corporate catalyst needs to be alert to:

- the better-off test, and
- restructuring.

312

Non-catalyst cluster managers must watch a number of additional issues, including the filters[21] and relatedness.[22]

Summary and conclusion

This chapter has looked at a special phenomenon, so far confined to the Anglo Saxon financial markets: the corporate catalyst. It is a company which creates financial and social value by buying underutilized assets relatively cheaply with the predominant motive of reselling them at a profit. It underpins, and operates in the market for corporate control. Its continuing cluster of businesses is not held for the primary purpose of creating financial value in its own right. That cluster's primary purpose is ancillary to the main task of buying and selling corporate assets. It provides continuing earnings in gaps between bids, and deflects some attention from the unpopular aspect of the main task.

Our reason for devoting a chapter to the corporate catalyst is to eliminate this type of company from the main discussion of competitive and corporate strategy. Even more important is the suggestion that empirical studies of the comparative performance of unrelated diversification, i.e. of conglomerates, should eliminate the performance of corporate catalysts, for an objective assessment of the value of unrelated diversification.

Notes

1. See Chapter 2.
2. 'Speculation' simply means dealing for gain against the view taken by the market as a whole. The speculator expects to beat the market. Successful speculation tends to smooth the ups and downs of market fluctuation. The expression is not here used in any pejorative sense.
3. Manne (1965).
4. The description fits Hanson as it operated in the 1970s and 1980s. Since 1990 Hanson has tended to operate more like a normal, customer-centred business, concentrating on managing its continuing cluster of offerings.
5. Capon *et al.* (1988) review its origins and methodology. Rumelt (1974) and (1982) followed Wrigley (1970) in developing the

product/market method of analysis.

6. See Appendix 16.2.
7. Bhagat, Shleifer and Vishny (1990), Shleifer and Vishny (1991). However, the various research trends noted in Appendix 16.2 and its notes need to be borne in mind. Manageability (see Link 6, Chapter 16), i.e. the absence of investment intensive, technologically complex and long-fuse features, is a common feature of the clusters of catalysts. However, manageability is not enough to make an offering 'related'.
8. Michel and Shaked (1984), Dolan (1985), Luffman and Reed (1982) and (1984), Grant and Jammine (1988).
9. Grant and Jammine (1988) p. 335.
10. The reasons for this appear to be that the capital profits are not normally realized in listed US companies. LBO specialists like KKR also appear to take some of their gains in the form of fees from vendors.

    As for the results of restructured businesses in the US, many of these do not for any length of time become consolidated subsidiaries of listed corporate catalysts. The Economist, 17 September 1994, page 107, confirms that this is the case with KKR.
11. The actual display in the income statement of such capital profits has changed from time to time. At one time they tended to be shown on a separate line; the latest standard requires them to be aggregated with ordinary results.
12. Arends (1996).
13. 'Deal' does not here include the one-off engineering contract of a plant contractor like Kellogg or Bechtel. These contracts are with customers for a service, not with others buying or selling businesses.
14. Examples are found in Bhagat, Shleifer and Vishny (1990).
15. Jensen (1994).
16. Goold and Campbell (1987a).
17. See Appendix 16.1.
18. In Chapter 16 a business is defined as being 'long-fuse' if there is a long interval between a major decision and its financial outcome.
19. See Chapter 17.
20. Appendix 16.1.
21. See Chapter 14.
22. See Chapter 16.

16 Valuable clusters of offerings: relatedness

Introduction

Chapters 3 and 13 have defined the task of corporate strategy as managing the company's cluster of offerings with a view to boosting its value. Chapter 14 provisionally – and negatively – described relatedness as a valid objective in contrast with risk diversification or size, and argued that unrelated clusters will not generate value. In its own right, it was argued, diversification has only one certain effect: it adds the significant costs of diversified operation. These costs are imposed by the existence of a head office. Risk diversification is no offset to those costs. Size, as we saw, can at certain thresholds reduce the cost of capital. Yet even that must not be treated as a commensurate offset to the costs of diversified operation, unless a diversification is related – as defined in this chapter – and also passes the criteria proposed in Chapter 14.

We are therefore looking for clusters which can add financial value and pass those criteria. If mere size and risk diversification do not create such clusters, then it is natural to look for clusters in which added offerings create value by virtue of links with the remainder of the company: in other words for *related* clusters. Hence the well-known distinction between **related** and **unrelated diversification**.[1]

We can now give 'related' diversification a positive meaning: it is the adding of one or more offerings which have one of a finite set of links with other parts of the company. That link is what confers on a candidate offering the value-generating potential for passing the criteria.

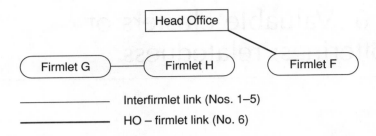

Figure 16.1 Two types of relatedness links

The candidate offering's relationship can be either:

- with other offerings or firmlets owned by the company, or
- with the head office.

In Figure 16.1 offering H is justified by its horizontal link with G, whereas offering F is justified by its vertical link with the head office.

Six such links have come to light. Of these six the first five are links between firmlets, and the last a link between a firmlet and the head office.

The six value-generating links

The six value-generating types of link are:

1 The *sharing* of efforts and resources between various offerings in the cluster: much the most common case.
2 Vertical integration; substituting an internal for a competitive contractual relationship with a customer or supplier.
3 Protective offerings such as:

   (a) those which ensure the supply of *complementary* offerings by internalizing their supply, or
   (b) the *'cross-parry'*:[2] a company launches offering F so as to give indirect protection to its existing offering G.

4 Links exploiting customer preferences.
5 Joining firmlets to improve *market power*.

6 Core clusters, in which firmlets benefit from a head office as an informed critic.

The common thread that runs through all six links is their purpose of making the company significantly more valuable by internalizing relationships. This is invariably a response to or an exploitation of some market imperfection, or the deliberate creation of such an imperfection. The imperfection is often, but not always one of circularity.[3]

As already said, the links are needed to give the candidate offering the value-building potential for passing the criteria. The link needs to generate value which is significant, and could not be achieved without the element of internalization.

Interestingly enough, these six relationships hardly depend on whether the parts of the cluster are in the same industry. This marks a considerable step away from conventional discussions of the relatedness issue.

For the sake of clarity and consistency, the following discussion of the links will refer to the proposed new addition to the cluster as firmlet F, and to any existing cluster member that may be affected by the addition, as firmlet G.

Link One: Sharing efforts and resources

The first case for adding offering F to offering G so as to link F and G under common ownership, arises where F and G can add significant value to one another by sharing resources and current efforts which help them to attract profitable customers.[4]

The value gained from this link can take broadly three forms:

- a significant reduction of unit costs, brought about by economies of scale,[5] or perhaps by exploiting by-products, such as glycerine from the manufacture of soap, or
- a significant improvement in absolute costs, for example if a key resource improves production technology in the offering thus enabled to share it, or

- a significant improvement in the offering's quality and appeal to customers: Sara Lee's transfer of food manufacturing and marketing skills to garments is a case in point.[6] The link here extends the scope of a valuable resource to a wider set of customer markets.

The potential gain to F or G must be significant, and obtainable only if F is owned by Company C. In other words, it could not be achieved with F either owned by some other company X, or independent. If the resource shared by F were merely C's canteen, this would not meet the requirement. C is not unique in having a canteen. Nor would C's chief executive's time qualify as a resource to be shared, unless C's chief executive happened to be of a rare type uniquely needed by F. This case is part of the 'dominant logic' issue discussed later in this chapter. If the resource were easily obtained by

Seagate Technology of Scotts Valley, California, makes hard-disk drives, a fiercely competitive, but technically exacting offering. In the early 1990s prices of PCs were plunging. In little over a decade the size of a drive had fallen by two-thirds, its data storage had grown 1,000-fold. In the July–September quarter of 1993 Seagate reported a small, and declining, net profit of $36m on $774m sales. However, it alone among its competitors was not reporting a loss. In 1989 Seagate had decided to become a technological leader. It made a well-targeted acquisition of Imprimis Technology. In 1991 it decided that mastery of a core set of skills was not enough: it must also learn to apply them to more and more offerings. It became a supplier of products for handling text, graphics, audio and video; to supply everything from mass-storage devices to the software for managing databases and networks. A classic example of exploiting a key resource over enough offerings to achieve needed economies of scale.[7]

F without being owned by C, the proposal to add F would in any case fail two of the filters.

Link Two: Vertical integration

The second link, vertical integration, is the merging under single ownership of an offering's customer or supplier, with the object of internalizing what would otherwise be an arm's length contractual relationship. Internalization can add value:

- in a thin market, by securing the continuity of the link which might otherwise be precarious,
- again in a thin market, by denying it to competitors: the acquisition of pubs by breweries could be an example,
- by ensuring quality where the internal customer's tight specification or difficult process requires the extra degree of control conferred by an internal link: an example might be a dental practice in a remote area employing its own dental mechanic.

Vertical integration has often been unsuccessful, even disastrous. The internalization of a link removes the discipline of the market, i.e. the incentive to be competitive. Vertical integration is of course just what the contractual filter of Chapter 14 sets out to check. The drawback of vertical integration is its destruction of the competitive incentive inherent in the contractual link. For that incentive to be preserved under vertical integration, both parties would need to remain free to deal with parties outside the group. That would run foul of the psychology not only of internal, but also of external relations. Internal parties tend to substitute internal politics for tight management. Outsiders for their part are less willing to buy from a business owned by a competitor.

This is exactly why the contractual filter requires a high degree of inadequacy in the external contractual market, to justify the internalization of a vertical link. Whenever a competitive contractual relationship would achieve equivalent benefits, there is no possible way that an internalized link could add further value. For example, there may be little benefit in an auditor's use of in-house software packages. Vertical integration is valid only where there is no sufficiently competitive market to sustain the contractual alternative, i.e. where the auditor cannot buy suitable software in the market.

Economies of scale could of course justify a link which coincidentally happens to be vertical, just as they could justify a non-vertical link. However, in that case what adds value is the sharing of effort or resource (Link One), not the vertical link. Moreover, economies of scale too would fail to justify the diversification if there were an adequate contractual market in the underemployed efforts or resources.[8]

Link Three: Protective offerings

In Link Three offering F is added merely in order to give some indirect protection to offering G which is already in the cluster.[9] F has no strategic purpose in its own right. Its job is to make a critical contribution to the viability or robustness of G. The criteria apply as set out in Chapter 14.[10]

Examples of Link Three are both complementary goods and the cross-parry. Offering F is here defined as *complementary* to G if it meets the following conditions:

- G would be useless to customers unless they can also purchase F.
- F has no significant substitutes, for example because it has a specification customized for G.

Kenwood water filter cartridges would pass this test, as other maker's cartridges would not fit the Kenwood filter. Complementarity is only a short step away from F and G being components of a single offering.[11]

The addition of complementary offering F needs to pass the best-owner filter. It will fail this unless the market for F, like that for Kenwood cartridges, is very imperfect and circular.[12] If there were many substitutes suitable for use with G, F would tend to fail that filter.[13]

This can be illustrated by a Betamax video recorder. This recorder G is manufactured by Company A. A might need to acquire Company B which makes videocassettes, in order to ensure the availability to G's customers of offering F: Betamax cassettes. Otherwise the Betamax recorder would have no value to customers. Similarly the Gillette Sensor would not have been a viable offering without an assured supply of replacement blades. This would not have been true for traditional safety razors, which were of uniform design that any blade used to fit.

The cross-parry[14] is the other type of defensive offering. It is illustrated by Michelin and Goodyear. Tyres are not a global offering; the competitive configuration tends to vary from country to country, sometimes from area to area, because tyres are costly to transport, and best made relatively close to the customer. Consequently the competitors may not be identical from place to place. Michelin's most profitable offering was automobile tyres in the European market. Goodyear's was its offering G in the US home market. However, in the early 1970s Michelin attacked that US market. Goodyear decided that its best countermove was to diversify into a protective offering F to threaten or attack Michelin's source of cash flow, the European market. As it happens, Goodyear did not succeed in stopping Michelin's attack on the US market, but at least it slowed it down.[15]

Link Three tends to apply in conditions of circularity, where each competitor has to take account of the potential countermoves of other dominant players. Link Three also shares some characteristics with the non-strategic 'loss leader' tactic. The loss leader F is not intended as a direct value-builder in its own right, but as a significant indirect promotion for G. F as a protective new offering is a pawn in a game of chess in which G is the queen.

In all valid protective diversifications what necessitates the internalization, is a restricted or circular market for the item to be internalized. Otherwise the addition of offering F would be unnecessary.

Link Four: Exploiting customer preferences

Link Four meets or exploits customer preferences which make it profitable to join two offerings in the same cluster. The circumstances in which this can occur, are:

(a) where significant groups of customers prefer to buy F and G from the same supplier, e.g. the case of the electrical retailer in Appendix 3.1 who both sells and repairs appliances,[16]
(b) where extra demand would be stimulated for offering G by the existence or convenient availability of offering F, and where it takes an internal link to ensure that availability.[17]

Example 1: G, a novel in book form, will attract more readers if there is also F, a film version. Similarly films have been known to attract extra audiences if there is a 'book of the film'. In this case all that is needed, is that F exists.

Example 2: G, a supermarket, attracts extra customers if there is a petrol station F in its car park, and the petrol station may also be better patronized because it is convenient for shoppers at the supermarket. In this case F's adjacent location is the attraction, not its mere existence.

The link will in each case pass the better-off test if,

- there is sufficient market failure for common ownership to be needed,
- the diversification improves the present value of the cluster as a whole, discounted at the cost of capital of the proposal to diversify.

Link Five: Improving market power

The conditions for the fifth link can occur both in customer markets, where the link aims to increase the degree of monopoly, and in buying markets, where it aims at greater monopsony. In the monopoly-seeking case the offering to be acquired is a competitor with a significant share of our existing offering's market. Its acquisition would aim at a greater degree of monopoly and thus better margins.[18] This could be achieved by a local newsagent buying its nearest rival, by the local sole practitioner accountant merging with the only local competitor, or by a local railway company buying a local bus undertaking. If there are also scale economies, they are coincidental.

The model of the private market does not make the notion of market share obsolete. An offering has a share of its private market and can seek to improve that share. In any case, the real world also contains some public and quasi-public markets.[19]

Buying market share aims at better, more monopolistic margins. In principle, this tends to run counter to public policy and to attract action under legislation against restrictive practices. However, such regulatory action is seldom practicable where the scale is small, as in small-scale local retailing.

This form of relatedness need not be very transparent. A supermarket chain might purchase an underused local cinema and redevelop it as a health and leisure centre to prevent it being bought by a rival supermarket chain. The motive is again protection of market share. Shareholder value has been improved. Whether the best-owner filter is passed by retaining the new centre, is a separate issue.

The second set of conditions in which this link can arise concerns the company's buying rather than its selling markets. The link aims at greater monopsony, which is the mirror image of monopoly. The owner of 50 per cent of all cinemas in an area could increase its bargaining power with film distributors if it were able to step up its percentage to 90 per cent.

Link Six: Strategic planning style

Where an offering is at least one of the following:

- investment-intensive,
- technically complex,
- long-fuse, i.e. there is a long interval between major decisions and their financial outcome,

then it is best monitored by a technically competent head office, not directly by the stockmarket.[20] We call a business or firmlet with one of these characteristics 'long-fuse'. Goold and Campbell[21] call a business which *lacks* them 'manageable'.

Strategic decisions concerning such offerings are often large and lumpy. As their effects also take years to become apparent, the market is unlikely to have an opportunity to check bad investment decisions before major losses have been incurred or funds wasted and lost. What such an offering needs, is a funding authority which is both technically versed in the problems of its business and closer at hand than an impersonal and distant market.[22]

Link Six is therefore unique in requiring the head office itself. Links One to Five require it merely as a roof of common ownership for interfirmlet links. What Link Six justifies is not so much the diversification as the head office. Of course, in justifying the head office, it indirectly justifies the diversification too, as a head office is unlikely to be economic for a single firmlet. This head office–firmlet link goes with a management style called 'strategic planning'.

Strategic planning and the core cluster

The 'strategic planning' concept is part of the framework identified by the work of Goold and Campbell.[23] These authors were researching the different control styles operated by different head offices, and found that the most effective style, i.e. the best degree and manner of centralization or decentralization, varied with the nature of the businesses owned by different companies. Goold and Campbell's 'businesses' were profit centres such as divisions, but their findings are equally appropriate to our firmlets.

Our interest is in what Goold and Campbell call the *strategic planning* style. This was the only style among those identified by them, in which the head office is an active participant in the task of formulating competitive strategy for the offerings. This they found to be appropriate for investment-intensive, technically complex, or long-fuse businesses, for reasons already described.

The concept of the need for a technically aware close critic runs counter to modern financial theory with its model of efficient financial markets with rational expectations. The efficient and external markets of this model are better critics of decisions to add, retain or divest than an internally governing head office. Goold and Campbell's findings however suggest that this efficient market model is less appropriate where there is technical complexity or a long fuse. The efficient markets model works well with 'manageable' offerings, but technical complexity and long fuses impair stockmarket efficiency.

The style required of a head office in such cases is called **'strategic planning'**, because the head office managers must sufficiently participate in the task of formulating the offering's competitive strategy to make informed judgements of investment and other major proposals. They must also have a degree of expertise in the technological and competitive structures of the firmlet's business. This applies most obviously in fields like biotechnology, chemical process plant operation and advanced electronic systems. As it can hardly be economic for such expert head office managers to control just one or two offerings, they will usually need to acquire a cluster of offerings requiring the same specialized knowledge, i.e. with similar technological and competitive problems, and that type of cluster is called a **core cluster.**[24]

Do all firmlets need a head office?

Advocates of the 'transaction costs' theory have suggested[25] that the case for the head office as a closer, better informed 'internal capital market' (and thus critic) applies generally, i.e. not just to firmlets which are investment-intensive, technically complex, or long-fuse. The grounds are again that the stockmarket is too slow, too remote, too impersonal. If this argument were to be extended,[26] it would of course legitimize almost any unrelated diversification that preserves a firmlet from the unthinkable state of independence!

The question however is not whether the stockmarket has shortcomings, but in what conditions the head office is a superior substitute. First, it is wrong to compare the head office with fragmented small investors. The market's discipline comes predominantly not from them, but from the potential hostile bidder. Secondly, it is easy to be critical of the stockmarket without heeding the qualities which this substitution requires of head office managers. Even if *good* head office managers are more effective at disciplining the businesses,[27] what discipline ensures that the head office managers themselves are *and remain* effective?[28] Good managers will always achieve good results, but bad head office managers may tolerate bad business results for far longer than the stockmarket would, were it in direct control of the businesses. Moreover, good head office managers do not always stay good. Only with a tail wind of outstanding management will the conglomerate or unrelated structure impose an effective discipline.

'Manageable' firmlets have no major needs for investment, no long lead times and no technological complexity. The head office must be able to obtain good results by appointing effective managers, setting tight budgets and monitoring performance against those budgets.[29] It needs no intimate understanding of firmlets' competitive strategies or investment projects. By the same token this short-fuse cluster does not on the face of it need to be a related one. Surely this describes just what the stockmarket is best suited to monitor directly, without an interposed head office?

We do well here to remember yet again the significant extra costs of diversified operation, and our rejection of either size or risk diversification as a valid reason for placing a firmlet under a head office.

In short, tail winds apart, there appears to be no case for concluding that a head office as such adds value to an unrelated cluster or a 'manageable' firmlet.

Top management skills as a constraint: The 'dominant logic'

Tail winds in our present context are any significant favourable factors outside the control of the incumbent top management team. There are many types of tail winds, like for example an uncompetitive market rigged in the company's favour, say by regulation.

There is however a school of thought, of which Prahalad and Bettis[30] are prominent exponents, which ascribes the success of some apparently unrelated diversifiers to superior skills of the top management team.

The particular skill which Prahalad and Bettis identify, is the ability of the top team to conceptualize the management task. Different competitive fields have different 'dominant logics', i.e. different patterns for top managers to conceptualize. Some competitive fields have similar dominant logics and may well therefore be within the grasp of a single management team to command. The authors suggest that this similarity of cognitive demands should perhaps become an additional test of relatedness. Other competitive fields, they suggest, are more dissimilar, and in this sense unrelated. In their view it takes a more highly skilled team to conceptualize a more variegated, i.e. less related cluster. The team can either conceptualize so widely from the outset, or it subsequently learns to broaden its scope.

The view taken here is that relatedness should be defined as requiring one of the six links. The conceptualizing skill may in some cases qualify as a resource shared in Link One. This will only however be the case where (a) it is rare and decisive to the success of the offerings, and where at the same time (b) the offerings need to be in the same cluster in order to create value, i.e. that the same result could not be achieved by contract or other means. This suggests a degree of market failure in this particular resource. It may well be harder to find a manager able to direct a biotechnology company than one to run a liquor store.

On the other hand managers do need to be able to conceptualize all the dominant logics required by an entire cluster. If an offering falls outside that ability, it is in an important sense 'unrelated', and its inclusion in the cluster would destroy value, not generate it. On the other hand the mere fact that it falls within it, is not enough to make it related.

This ability is thus a necessary, but not a sufficient condition of passing the better-off test. It incidentally also fails to make two offerings related, unless it also meets the above conditions (a) and (b) to bring it within Link One.

It would take unusual ability for a management team to conceptualize what is in this chapter treated as an unrelated cluster. Such unusual ability should be seen as a tail wind. There are several reasons for this. First, it is unlikely that the top team was selected or assembled with this objective in mind. Secondly, the corollary is that a team which wants to broaden the scope of its cluster and earn its cost of capital, must learn new conceptualization skills of a high order. However, to achieve such a radical acquisition of extra skills is likely to be impossible without replacing at least a substantial part of the top management team. If the team members are willing to contemplate their own replacement, their selfless devotion is of course to be admired and encouraged. However, as the task will be carried out by others, they will not benefit from reading a book like this.[31]

This book is therefore addressed to incumbent teams who wish to improve their own, rather than their successors' performance. Diversification proposals by such a team, it is submitted, will pass the better-off test only if the team sticks to challenges within its own scope. That should restrict them to related diversification. Top management skills are therefore here taken as largely[32] given, not as a controllable variable.

To sum up, grasp of the dominant logics of all parts of the cluster is a condition of passing the better-off test, but is not of itself a relating link. That grasp is not by itself enough to make the offerings related or pass the test. If certain further conditions are met, it can however constitute Link One[33].

The need to understand the offerings

The strategic planning and core cluster case is characterized by the need for head office managers who are expert in a complex area of business. It does not of course follow that managers of other head offices, controlling clusters of the other five related types, do not need to understand their offerings and the markets and technologies in which they compete.

The addition of any offering to a cluster cannot be justified unless there are grounds for expecting benefits greater than the extra costs of the head office structure. Those extra costs will evidently be greater if the head office managers are unfamiliar with the specific operating and commercial issues facing the offerings. To minimize these further extra costs, head office managers need at least some grasp of those issues. The more general cases of Links One to Five differ from the strategic planning case first in degree and secondly in technical complexity. For shorter-fuse offerings the understanding is easier to acquire and does not need to be as intimate. Food retailing or house building are easier to understand than biotechnology.

No offering is likely to prosper under a head office which fails to understand its critical characteristics. A small group with lumpy and complex long-fuse decisions needs its head office to understand them in enough detail to become a real participant in the decisions. The much larger shorter-fuse remainder needs either no head office or a head office with a broader, less technical and less detailed grasp of those features.

Value from related diversification

The contention here is that relatedness is a necessary condition for a diversification to pass the better-off test. Even that is not enough to justify the diversification: it must also pass the three filters.

None of the six related categories add value unless there is some market imperfection serious enough to cause the benefits of internalization to outweigh the costs.

In our examples we have concentrated mainly on the better-off test. Before an offering's addition or retention is justified, however, it must also pass the filters. For example, the health and leisure centre which has replaced the under-used cinema may fail the best-owner filter: it might be still better off under some other ownership, or independent. In that case it may need to be divested as though the company were a corporate catalyst.

The links and the filters

With one exception, the links and the filters are not interrelated. The exception here is the antithesis between the contractual filter and vertical integration, both concerned with the supplier-customer relationship. That apart, each proposal to add an offering should be checked for the presence of significant supplier-buyer relationships, significant alternative owners or adverse competitive scenarios. Any of these indicate that one of the filters needs to be applied.

How necessary is relatedness?

It may be objected that the doctrine advocated in this Part Five is stringent. To justify a diversification, it needs to be demonstrated that it is related, and passes the other stringent conditions of the better-off test and filters. Moreover, the objectors will no doubt point to successful and brilliantly managed companies which have not complied with all these criteria.

That, however, is just the point. As already said above, a book like this is not written for brilliant managers. They do not need it: therein lies their brilliance. An unrelated or any other kind of diversification will succeed with the tail wind of excellent management.

This has been well expressed by Ravenscraft and Scherer[34] when they stress 'that making mergers while drunk with power greatly increases the risk of mishap, that merger trips should be planned carefully, with adequate attention to the known hazards, and that double-bottom 18-wheeler conglomerates should be operated only by the extraordinarily skilled.'

Creative, defensive and other corporate strategies

We are now reaching the end of this search for valid corporate strategies. Corporate strategy has been defined as a company's management of its cluster of offerings. However the offerings do not have to be lifeless figures like cards in a pack from which the manager of a cluster picks his or her selection. The benefit of diversification is usually due to some market imperfection; an imperfection which may or may not amount to circularity. That imperfection can often be deliberately created or aggravated to the detriment of competitors. The brewery buying pubs and the underused cinema demonstrated that conditions which favour diversification, are not always environmental, and passively accepted by the firmlet. One part of this phenomenon is what we have[35] called the 'transformer' firmlet. Winning firmlets are often *created* by a corporate strategy.

Centre of stage is here occupied by key resources. Key resources give a company unique competitive opportunities. They enable it to create uniquely profitable offerings, and to make them and any newly added offerings more profitable by enabling them to exploit the same resource.

One simple example is economies of scale. A company may well begin by building up a resource or advantage which itself can create economies of scale for offerings, irrespective of whether the offerings are already in the cluster or to be added. In a multiple retailer this might be a buying skill, in a pharmaceutical company an R&D capability or a special skill in selling to public sector health authorities. In all these cases it is likely to include the ability to weld this skill together with more ordinary marketing or operating skills. Once the corporate capability or competence has been built up, offerings can be added to the cluster which exploit this resource. It thus becomes a shared resource, a source of synergy. In other words, in this case the conditions for

331

synergy are created first, and later additions to the cluster derived from them. Acquisitions may in fact play a part in building up resources and capabilities.

A creative approach might equally apply to a core cluster. A head office with a core cluster might seek to acquire further offerings within its span of competence which need strategic planning and pass the better-off test and filters.

Again, the creative process can apply to vertical integration. When Alcoa and Reynolds in the late 1960s developed a new aluminium can making process, they tried to turn over this process to can manufacturers. When none of them were willing to incur the costs of the change, they integrated forward and set up their own lines. Market failure saw to it that the diversification added value.[36]

By contrast, the process can be a defensive necessity. If competitors have achieved major cost and price reductions by their own economies of scale, a company's existing firmlet G might need to be restored to competitiveness by the addition of firmlet F: both F and G are then made competitive in their respective markets through joint economies of scale. The company must either divest G or acquire F.

Of course, a corporate strategy need not be either creative or defensive. In the most common case existing firmlets are assembled to exploit synergies in the cluster. There is no single formula for the successful management of a cluster.

Summary: value generated by the head office

It is mainly since about 1980 that it has been so fashionable to ask whether the head office adds value. The question might have been more clearly and accurately formulated if it had asked what an individual firmlet might gain from being part of a company. The recent trend has in any case been to question the benefit of head offices.

In the context of corporate strategy the essential functions *of a head office* consist of:

- managing or structuring the composition of the cluster,
- making key resources available to additional offerings,

- financing additions to the cluster,
- acting as critic of a core cluster's strategic decisions.

The critic function is of course part of the funding function. It is not however the norm to have that function located inside the company; the core cluster case is the exception.

The increasingly influential view is that businesses are better off without a head office. This is the 'small is beautiful' view. The view taken here is that a head office is beneficial in the strategic planning case and justifiable where diversification is related by one of the other five links. The onus of proof must always be on those who seek to show that an offering is more valuable in a cluster than on its own.

This onus of proof, it appears, cannot be discharged for unrelated diversifications, i.e. without one of the six links. Outside the six links, it is suggested, the better-off test cannot be passed.

Most importantly, offerings must not just pass the better-off test to justify inclusion in a cluster. They must always pass the filters as well. For example, the company must be satisfied that the benefits of adding or retaining an offering could not have been achieved by competitive contractual relationships.

* * *

Appendix 16.1

The three styles of Goold and Campbell

A full understanding of the core cluster case requires a summary of the work of Goold and Campbell.[37] These authors set out to study the styles used by companies to manage different business units. From our point of view these are effectively clusters of firmlets. They therefore studied how a head office adds value not by the way it selects offerings for its cluster, but by how it directs a cluster. In their sample of 16 UK companies they found evidence for the following conclusions, expressed here in terms of 'companies' and 'firmlets':

- companies used three main styles for directing the firmlets they owned,
- these differences in style influenced what type of firmlets they owned,
- because some kinds of firmlets were unsuitable for one or other of the styles.

The three main styles are:

(a) **Strategic planning**: here the head office participates in setting (competitive) strategy in the company's firmlets. This style requires a **'core'** cluster.

(b) **Financial control**: here the head office merely appoints the management, sets stringent financial performance targets – usually for up to one year at a time – and then monitors the unit's financial performance against those targets; apart from that it gives the managers a wide measure of autonomy. This style requires a cluster in which the head office does not need to concern itself with its firmlets' competitive strategies; typically a conglomerate cluster of **'manageable'**[38] firmlets.

Firmlets are 'manageable' if they score low in all three of the following attributes:
- the amount of investment required,
- the lead times between major decisions and their results,
- the degree of technical complexity.

(c) **Strategic control**: In the 1987b paper this is described as a halfway house where the company owns a mixed cluster of 'core' and 'manageable' firmlets, requiring a mixture of strategic planning and financial control styles. This is achieved by having an intermediate layer of divisional managers, some in each of the two styles (a) and (b). Strategic control is differently defined in other papers.[39]

Goold and Campbell's work has some bearing on the composition of corporate clusters: that is our concern.

Appendix 16.2

The principle of relatedness

This book seeks to define what links between an offering and the rest of the company can make that company more valuable. That adding of value is the only common characteristic of the six links put forward in this chapter. In all other respects the links are diverse. There is no attempt here to reduce the concept of relatedness to any one principle.

This fairly practical and value-centred approach was also Porter's,[40] but a number of academic theorists and researchers have long looked for some general principle of relatedness, as well as for a useful empirical proxy or set of proxies.

Since 1970[41] research at first used the US Standard Industrial Classifications (SIC) as indicators of relatedness. This may capture value-building relatedness, without however appreciably refining relatedness into an underlying principle. This is because many an industry has some common idiosyncratic characteristics not just in its market structure, but also in its input or operating logistics.

More recently[42] research has switched to a narrower set of explanations, revolving around resources,[43] especially the resource of senior managerial skills. The insight behind this is that managers cannot successfully direct business areas whose problems and opportunities lie outside their skills and experience. A pharmaceutical chief executive with a thorough grasp of the economics of research into drugs and of the buying practices of public health authorities, may be less versed in the problems and opportunities of the rag trade.

This switch to researching management skills may well have been stimulated by the recent interest in corporate capabilities or competences.[44] Corporate competences are a narrower set of skills which set whole companies apart.

However, the managerial skills which have attracted more recent research are a much wider set and cover all those skills which are specific to the running of different ranges of business activities. It is sometimes suggested, for example in the 'dominant logic' framework, that such competences might make any such ranges of activities 'related'.

These ideas overlap with some of those put forward in Chapter 16. On the other hand this recent research tends in most cases to be at some distance from the concept of relatedness developed in the chapter, or indeed from the whole value-building concept of the better-off test.

First, success does not appear to be measured against the cost of capital. The suggestion is that top teams with this skill have more successful unrelated clusters (unrelated as defined in this book) than those without it. In principle they might in that case merely fall somewhat less short of earning the cost of capital. Secondly, relatedness is not examined in terms of individual offerings. Again, it does not apply any of the three filters, or eliminate the corporate catalyst from unrelated diversifiers.

Our Link One has a bearing on this more recent research into relatedness. Top management skills can be a shared resource in the sense of Link One if they are sufficiently rare, sufficiently necessary to the success of the diversification, and shareable only in conditions of single ownership. Porter[45] made the point that this type of link can occur anywhere in the value chain. Recent research has completed the picture by stressing that the competitive fields must also be within the span of the managers' skills and experience. Nevertheless the top managers' ability to conceptualize the task of managing an offering is not by itself enough to make that offering related. It is just that their inability to do this would make the offering one that we must call 'unrelated'.

Link Six, the core cluster, is a different matter. It applies to relatively few offerings with long-fuse or technologically complex economics. It does need managers with a deep understanding of these offerings, but as critics on behalf of investors. The skills required for Link Six may or may not be identical, but the purpose of the link is quite different.

None of this affects the main thrust of Chapter 16. Managers will do well to be wary of unrelated diversification, and treat only those diversifications as related which take the form of one of the six links. No single quality or characteristic encapsulates the essence of relatedness.

Notes

1. Some empirical studies have found high returns earned by 'unrelated' diversifiers (e.g. Michel and Shaked, 1984; Luffman and Reed, 1984). We have two reservations here. First, some of these studies have unhelpfully tended to take 'related' as 'belonging to the same industry classification'. Secondly, we have suggested in Chapter 15 that the 'unrelated' samples used in these studies would have looked less successful if they had excluded corporate catalysts. There is scope here for further empirical work. On the principle of what relatedness is, see Appendix 16.2.
2. Porter (1980); Porter has since called it 'multipoint competition', as have others.
3. See Chapter 7.
4. Chapter 10 discusses resources and their various categories.
5. The reader is reminded that, as mentioned in Chapter 3, the distinction between economies of scale and scope is not significant in this framework.
6. *The Economist*, 14 November 1992.
7. *The Economist*, 13 November 1993.
8. The criteria which justify vertical integration are more fully explored by Oster (1990), Chapter 9.
9. This is the simplest assumption. Alternatively it might be contemplated to acquire both together.
10. 'The four criteria' refers. 'The arithmetic of the criteria' may also be helpful.
11. See Chapter 3.
12. Chapter 7 defines and discusses circularity.
13. The acquisition of F is unlikely to fail the contractual alternative filter, because it is G's customers, not G that need to be able to buy F. On the other hand an unnecessarily internalized F would tend to fail the better-off test because it would lack the more intense competitive incentives of its substitutes.
14. Porter (1980) p. 84, Hamel and Prahalad (1985).
15. Hamel and Prahalad (1985).
16. If the conditions of Link Four apply, then sale and repair are not a single offering. It is implied that other groups of customers buy

the two offerings from separate outlets, so that the prices of the two offerings are determined separately. Of course, if the joint customers, who treat the two as a single offering, came to predominate to the point where prices were jointly determined, the two offerings would become a single offering.

17. The case clearly differs from that of complementary goods, where the degree of complementarity is so total that neither offering is useful without the other.

18. It was explained in Chapter 14 that this aim could not be achieved by a competitive contract, contract being defined in this book as a vertical deal between supplier and customer.

19. The concept of the quasi-public market was described in Chapter 4.

20. The case for direct ownership of a business by financial markets is the efficient markets hypothesis, which strictly applies only to a stock market. The case for long-fuse businesses needing a head office can however be extended to unlisted businesses whose critical financial institution is its principal bank or banks.

21. Goold and Campbell are the authors of the framework described in the next section.

22. Chandler (1991).

23. See Appendix 16.1.

24. Goold and Campbell's expression is 'core portfolio'. The word 'portfolio' is avoided here because of its technical, risk-related meaning in financial theory.

25. Teece (1982) and Williamson (1975), but see the critique by Hill (1985) and Demsetz (1991).

26. Williamson in fact acknowledges that there are limits to this contention. In any case, it must be remembered that the transaction cost school's primary purpose is not prescriptive, but a valuable contribution to an understanding of why multiproduct 'firms' have become so prevalent in the twentieth century. For a critique, see Hill (1985).

27. Goold, Campbell and Alexander (1994).

28. Salter and Weinhold (1978), Hoskisson and Turk (1990).

29. Chandler (1991).

30. Prahalad and Bettis (1986).

31. This issue is more fully explored in Chapter 21.

32. Minor incremental upgrading or updating of skills is not of course excluded.

33. See also Appendix 16.2.

34. Ravenscraft and Scherer (1987).

35. In Chapter 9.

36. Bower *et al.* (1991): Crown Cork and Seal case.

37. Goold and Campbell (1987a, b), Campbell and Goold (1988), Goold, Campbell and Alexander (1994).

38. Also called 'short-fuse' in this book.
39. See also Chandler (1991).
40. Porter (1987).
41. Intensive research into relatedness began with Wrigley (1970) and Rumelt (1974).
42. Helpful reviews of this most recent research are found in Barney and Zajac (1994) and Robins and Wiersema (1995).
43. The 'resource-based' *theory* discussed in Part Four is concerned with how *offerings* defy success-aping forces. The 'resource-based' *insights* used by writers in the context of corporate strategy,

  - use resource differences between companies to explain why one company as a whole – not individual offerings – performs better than another,
  - do not seek to explain the overcoming of any success-aping equilibrium forces or the sustainability of value-building by offerings.

  Chapter 10 has argued that the model of pure competition with its equilibrium forces only applies to offerings, not to corporate performance in its own right.
44. Especially the frameworks put forward by Prahalad and Hamel. Corporate competences are discussed in Chapter 11.
45. Porter (1987).

17 Developing successful corporate strategies

Introduction: Managing the cluster is not glamorous

This chapter reviews the tasks of corporate strategy for the practitioner, before summing up Part Five.

Students and some others may be tempted to form a somewhat glamorous picture of corporate strategy. In this picture the task constantly grabs the headlines in the financial press and on television with takeover bids, 'white knights', management buy-outs and proxy fights. That picture covers a very small proportion of the task.

The less exciting truth is that corporate strategy is needed day by day in nearly every business, from the smallest to the largest. The chemist shop adds photographic film processing, the brewer sells or franchises its public houses, the multiple clothes retailer decides to serve meals; the construction company decides to close down its property development business: all these are adding or divesting offerings, and all are practising corporate strategy.

Moreover, a large majority of additions to the cluster are in-house start-ups of new offerings rather than acquisitions of existing businesses.

The least glamorous and least discussed task is that of constantly questioning the retention of existing parts of the cluster. No offering is permanently valuable in a given cluster, and most failures of corporate strategy are those of hanging on to offerings or wider areas of business which are no longer earning their keep: their cost of capital. Inertia, i.e. failure to let go, failure to question the existing cluster, has undoubtedly caused more corporate failures than failure to develop new offerings. Self-criticism and timing are the critical attainments. Managers should grasp every opportunity to make their companies smaller and leaner.

Corporate strategy is therefore seldom a discontinuous, dramatic activity. It is a continual, painstaking task, with no let-up. The head of every independent business must think as a head office, and continually ask whether the cluster can be improved by additions or deletions – it nearly always can be! The necessary questions require an element of humility: what value does this offering add to my company and is my company its best owner? Would it be more valuable under some other ownership and head office? Would the company be more valuable if it were smaller?

Analysing proposals for additions

This section describes the analysis of proposals to add offerings, and the next section the analysis of whether to retain or divest. Both closely follow conventional financial management doctrine, tempered only by the links of relatedness and by the filters. Material differences between the two processes will become apparent.

The analysis of a proposal to add offering F should involve the following steps:

- Check that the addition falls within one of the links of relatedness: otherwise the better-off test cannot be passed.
- Estimate the net effect of the addition of F on the company's entire annual cash flows over the appropriate number of years. This includes F's own cash flows and any favourable or unfavourable effects on cash flows elsewhere in the company. The effect on other offerings of customer reactions[1] must here be taken into account.
- Estimate and allow for any option value inherent in F, i.e. the value of any opportunities to invest in further competitive strategies in the future; opportunities which would not exist without the offering now being evaluated.[2]

- Estimate – however broadly – the extra costs of diversified operation (Chapter 14).
- Estimate the cost of acquisition (price and transaction costs)
or internal investment.
- Estimate the once-off restructuring costs.
- Estimate the risk-adjusted cost of capital of the proposal.
- Using all the above information, complete the better-off
test, i.e. calculate the opportunity effect of the proposal on
the financial value of the company as a whole. For this
purpose ascertain the net present value of the proposal
from the sum of the incremental cash flows, discounted at
the cost of capital. The calculation must take account of
any impact which the proposal may have on the entire
company's investment rating and cost of capital, and also
tax or other technical financial effects.[3] If this value is positive, the better-off test is passed. The test cannot of course
be passed if there is insufficient protective armour to
ensure that the offering will maintain its required financial performance until the cost of capital is recovered.
- Check that the proposal passes the three filters: contractual alternative, best-owner and robustness. All four
criteria must be passed.

Analysing whether to retain or divest offering F

There are three reasons why this process is so different:

- *The time difference*: Suppose that offering F was planned in
year –3, launched year 0, and that we are now in year +3
analysing whether to retain it. Some of the most important uncertainties at year –3 are now historical fact. Its
competitive positioning against customers and competitors, the cost structures, the financial performance to date:
all these are now known with the precision of hindsight.
- *The future period*: The task is not to ascertain the value built
by offering F over its life, but whether it will continue
value-building *from the present date* in year +3. Will it add
value for another three months, three years, or not at all?
Even if it will only add value for another six months, we

should not divest now. This is why retention decisions do not need the robustness filter. The forward look is shorter and less uncertain.

- *Interdependence*: Offering F may have become too interdependent with the rest of the company to be divestable on its own. Its divestment might make other offerings G and H unviable. This could have supply side reasons like shared resources, or demand side reasons, customers who would stop buying offerings G or H if the company ceased to supply F. An example might be a hotel unable to divest its conference business without also losing much of its banqueting and other turnover with business clients.

The analysis must, as always, be in opportunity cost terms, against the best alternative course of action. This might for example be simply to discontinue the offering, or to sell it to a competitor, or to replace it with an updated and improved version.

Assuming that what might be divestable is firmlet F rather than a grouping F + G + H, the analytical procedure might take the following sequence:

- Estimate net cash flows lost by divestment: F's gross profits plus the gross profits of which other offerings in the cluster would be deprived.
- Allow for any net effect on the cash flows in the remaining cluster. Some other offerings may for example gain extra customers.[4]
- Estimate and allow for any option value inherent in F.
- Estimate company overheads to be saved. For example, if F is a significant part of the company, it may be possible to save personnel, overhead or space costs.
- Estimate savings in costs of diversified operation. This is very hard to quantify, but some rough assessment is important.
- Estimate the once-off costs of divestment, such as redundancy, real estate agents, restructuring costs.
- Estimate the capital released by the divestment, either by liquidation or sale. This calculation must take account of

the effect of tax and the possible use of tax-minimizing structures.

- Ascertain the cost of capital and calculate the net present value of the divestment. This calculation will take account of the effect of any technical financial changes, such as for example gearing or leverage, on the cost of capital and the appropriate discount rate.[5]
- Finally check whether the divestment would have a knock-on effect on the investment rating and thus the cost of capital of the rest of the company.

Up to this point, the better-off test is no more than orthodox financial analysis. However, if the analysis up to this point validates the retention of the offering, it must then be subjected to three further tests, for relatedness and two of the filters:

- F must be related to the rest of the cluster by one of the links. This test could have been applied earlier, but the above analytical process can bring to light a relatedness which has been overlooked. This test completes the better-off test.
- F must then finally be subjected to the contractual alternative and best-owner filters. Again, it may save time to apply these before the analysis, if the filters are evidently going to point towards divestment.

Restructuring acquisitions[6]

Nothing said here is to deny that acquisitions are an important and hazardous part of the craft of corporate strategy.

An obvious first point is that practically all acquisitions need to be restructured. It is in reality seldom practicable to acquire a free-standing offering. A takeover bid by definition is for a company; a negotiated purchase might merely buy some profit centre, some bundle of assets. In each case it is likely that what is acquired is more than what the purchaser really wanted or needed. The purchaser may often be after one or more offerings, but in other cases it may be after some key resources. What is rare, is the opportunity to acquire just what is wanted and nothing else. The acquirer must then opportunistically, but with minimum delay divest the un-wanted assets or offerings.[7]

Secondly, even if the purchaser were fortunate enough to acquire exactly what passes the better-off test and filters and is to be retained, it is almost certainly not in the correct state in which it will pass them. If for example a new offering's value lies in the inputs which it can share with existing members of the cluster, then physical locations, management reporting responsibilities and operating systems and routines may have to be rearranged so as to achieve that.

The restructuring process can include redivestment of an offering if that is its best destination. Restructuring covers a wide spectrum of measures including:

- sorting out which offerings are to be redivested or retained in the continuing cluster,
- merging or splitting resources,
- redeploying key resources to serve offerings joining the cluster,
- replacing ineffective management,
- taking out surplus costs or assets,
- repositioning or reconfiguring firmlets so as to forge syner-gistic links with sister firmlets.

The last of these points applies not merely to the supply side, where efforts and resources are reallocated to offerings, but also to the demand side, where existing offerings in the cluster may for example have to be repositioned if a new offering will induce customers to switch away from them. The goal of corporate strategy is to maximize the value of the cluster as a whole, not that of individual offerings.[8]

Restructuring of an acquisition is a discontinuous, one-off process. As here defined, it does not include the subsequent running of the firmlet as part of the cluster. It excludes that even where features introduced in the restructuring phase, such as tight management and cost control, are intended to continue. Restructuring is a break between old and new routines.

Restructuring is thus a discrete, limited creation of value. However, a good related acquisition often requires an additional longer-term process of value creation.[9] This longer-term effort welds two or more businesses together, brings capabilities to bear on the partner that has not yet enjoyed their benefits, and generally ensures that the potential benefits of the merger are achieved. Corporate strategy has to focus very directly and persistently on the aim of value creation.

Summary: corporate strategy

The reader is now asked to look back over the whole of Part Five, not just this chapter. Corporate strategy is:

- the management by a company of its cluster of offerings,
- making decisions to add, retain or divest offerings, i.e. competitive strategies,
- a necessary function of the head office,
- directly concerned with adding financial value.

All decisions in corporate strategy need to be taken with the aim of earning no less than the cost of capital. This applies both to a decision to retain an offering and to a decision to add one. For this reason the addition of an offering in the corporate cluster needs to pass four stringent criteria, and a decision to retain it the first three:

- The better-off test requires that an offering should only enter into or remain in a cluster if it adds value to the company.
- The best-owner filter requires that the company is the best possible owner of the offering.
- The contractual alternative filter precludes a diversification or retention whose benefits could alternatively be attained by a contractual buyer–supplier relationship. The diversification or retention is justified only if the relationship needs to be internalized.

346

- The robustness filter further requires the benefit to be durable enough to recover the cost of capital of the diversification despite worse than expected circumstances and despite managerial reluctance to cut losses.

The criteria cannot be met unless the offering is a related one, within one of the six valid categories of relatedness.

Corporate strategy, by virtue of managing the cluster in accordance with these principles, assists competitive strategies by bringing together resources, other efforts and sales volumes which will make exploitation of those resources competitive. This is a consequence of the big asymmetry of business strategy.

Finally corporate strategy gives a company an opportunity to become a sustained value-builder without running into a success-aping process which will erode that creation of value.[10] This requires a flair[11] for managing the cluster, for choosing the right offerings to add, retain or divest, and for judging the timing of additions and divestments.

Notes

1. See Chapter 14, towards the end of the Section 'The better-off test'. The addition of F to the cluster may attract customers away from other offerings in the cluster.
2. Kester (1984) pp 153–160. The fundamental insight that an investment in offering A may open the door to a further investment in subsequent offerings B, C, D etc. is of course at the back of the concept of serial innovation, discussed in Chapter 11.
3. See also Appendix 3.1.
4. See Chapter 14, towards the end of the section 'The better-off test'. Just as the addition of F to the cluster may attract customers away from other offerings in the cluster, so F's divestment may gain customers for them.
5. See also Appendix 3.1.
6. Copeland, Koller and Murrin (1990) in Exhibit 2.3 (p. 35) present an interesting model of how restructuring can improve value.
7. Bhagat, Shleifer and Vishny (1990) present a most interesting and thorough study of redivestments after hostile bids in the US in the 1980s. Among other interesting findings, it emerges that the proportion of divestments to what is spent on acquisitions, is no unequivocal indicator of motive. For example, a non-catalyst like

Quaker Oats can bid for Anderson Clayton (p. 35) and sell off everything except the Gaines dog food business which was the motive for the bid.

The authors also make the vital point that where the motive is non-catalyst, the capital profits on divestments can substantially reduce the acquisition cost of the desired diversification. This can be a major influence on the viability of any given diversification proposal.

8. See also in Chapter 14 under 'better-off test'.
9. Haspeslagh and Jemison (1991). The authors apply the term 'value capture' to what is here called 'restructuring', in contrast with 'value creation'.
10. See Chapter 10.
11. Chapter 10 specified that this flair is neither a key resource (because it does not enable any one offering to overcome success-aping attempts) nor a pure management resource.

Part Six Distant and International Strategies

One of the popular issues of business strategy concerns:

- how far afield *customers* are targeted: what makes a business from Denver, Colorado, target customers in Little Rock, Arkansas, Switzerland, Namibia or Canada?
- how far afield operations extend: what makes that same business from Denver *operate* in some of those places?

Answers to these questions lie in both the demand and the supply dimension. They include issues of:

- the nature of the markets,
- local preferences or idiosyncracies,
- operating economics and logistics, including those of sheer spatial distance such as transport costs, and also
- political barriers, or requirements imposed by governments such as taxes and tariffs.

Only the last of these categories operates at the frontiers of sovereign states.

Part Six, like the rest of this book, examines these issues from the point of view of the offering. Viewed from this angle, distant and cross-frontier markets and operations do indeed have some distinctive features, but they may be less significant than is sometimes believed. In a world of differentiated offerings, distances and frontiers leave the essential characteristics of competitive strategy, and to a lesser extent those of corporate strategy much as they have been described earlier in this book.

Chapter 18 examines the geographical span of markets. Chapter 19 looks at distant and cross-frontier operations. Chapter 20 then discusses what structures, routines, skills and capabilities companies need to operate across frontiers.

18 The geographical span of markets

The hierarchy of business decisions

This chapter aims to clarify what is meant by such phrases as 'global market' or 'international market', within the framework put forward by this book. In other words, it discusses the geographical extent of markets.

That is a topic in its own right. It receives attention from both writers and practitioners. Its issues are nevertheless not free-standing ones. The view taken in this book is that a business takes its fundamental decisions at a hierarchy of three interlocking levels:

- The top level of decisions is what profitable customers the business wishes to serve – that priority applies across frontiers, as well as within countries.
- At the second level it has to be decided how and where to operate. For example in one location or country, in several, or in many? Decisions at this level are constrained by the production and delivery logistics of each offering, and therefore by the decision taken at the top level.
- The third level concerns issues like how to operate in several locations with very different cultural and political environments. These issues arise from the decisions taken at the second level.

For example, Boeing's top level decision is to offer aircraft like the 777, for which the world is a single market. At the second level the logistics and economics of airframes dictate manufacture in very few locations, and serving the whole world from those very few locations. Third order issues mainly concern political relations with the often publicly owned or governmental customers. By contrast, a manufacturer of automobile tyres like Michelin has offerings which together also sell to the whole free market world, but with transport logistics which make it uneconomic to manufacture at any great distance from customers. Michelin therefore at the second level of issues needs to have its tyres manufactured in perhaps 50 to 100 countries or locations around the world. That means that Michelin is intimately concerned with third level issues of how to adapt to many cultures, how to deal with both customers and workers and local communities and authorities.

All but the most localized offerings raise these three levels of issues, with the second subordinate to the first and the third to the second. This hierarchy must be borne in mind in discussing the geographical extent of markets.

Geographical space, offerings and markets

In the framework put forward in this book, competitive strategy positions an individual offering in its market. That market is normally a 'private' market,[1] not coextensive with that of any substitute. Corporate strategy on the other hand manages a company's cluster of offerings.[2]

The example of the Dorchester Hotel in Chapter 4 showed that distance in space can be among the determinants of the extent of a market. This occurs when that distance matters to customers. If therefore an Amstrad personal computer with its standard software is a single offering[3] in the whole of the United Kingdom and the Irish Republic, then its positioning in the market extending over the two countries is a matter of competitive strategy. If on the other hand it is two different offerings, one in each country, then Amstrad's decision to market the PC in both countries is one of corporate strategy. It concerns more than one offering.

Markets: a resumé

The following reminder about markets may be useful:

- Our concern is with customer markets, not pure dealing markets such as markets in traded commodities or financial instruments (Chapter 2).
- A single offering is what has a single price, or rather a price determined in a single process[4] (Chapter 3).
- A market is a price-determining mechanism; its boundaries are set to encompass those competing substitutes which significantly influence customers' choices, and thus the price (Chapter 4).
- Most customer markets in the modern developed world are *private* to each offering. This means that offering A will have its own unique list of competing substitutes. That list in most cases partially overlaps with the substitutes of any competing offering, such as B. A *public* market by contrast consists of a set of offerings, each of which competes with every other member of the set and with no non-members (Chapter 4).

To sum up, if markets are private, each offering has a unique market which does however partially overlap with the markets of its substitutes. This was illustrated in Figure 4.4, reproduced here as Figure 18.1.

Markets and geography

This basic model of the differentiated modern world is fully applicable to the geographical or country dimension. The American Express card is marketed to the entire world of free markets. However, in France and Japan for example it may have different lists of competitors, and in each of those two countries a different competitor may be its closest rival. The two countries are therefore separate markets. Moreover, in the light of the discussion in Chapter 4 they are private markets.

The Boeing 777 on the other hand is best regarded as a worldwide single, 'global' offering. Although many global

353

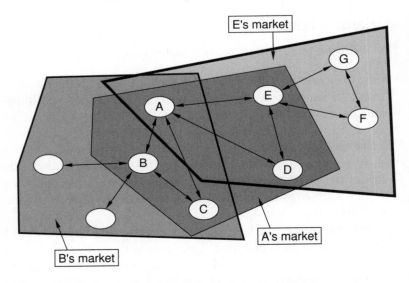

Figure 18.1 *Private markets of offerings A, B and E*

markets are private, the market of the 777 might perhaps be considered a public worldwide market, for its group of significant substitutes like Airbus 330 are probably all in competition with each other throughout the world, and not with any substitutes outside that group.

The issues raised by geography

We are here enquiring into the impact, if any, of:

(a) geographical distance,
(b) political frontiers.

In this chapter we ask these questions about markets, i.e. where to seek customers, e.g. by exporting. In Chapter 19 we shall then look at where in the world companies locate their operations, i.e. where they produce or add value[5] to their offerings.

If we had asked these questions in 1950, we might have had to write separately about a number of relatively isolated countries and regions. Since then the world has shrunk to a point where it is fashionable to talk about 'global' markets, global cars, global strategies, and even global industries and companies.

The word 'global' may in fact be less unambiguous than is widely believed. A global market is presumably one that extends over practically the whole world of free commercial markets. Some countries like North Korea in the mid-1990s or East Germany before 1989 are so insulated from international markets that they are not part of the world system. The world therefore here comprises all those countries which conduct most of their trade at free market prices.[6]

The shrinking world

The twentieth century, and especially its second half, has seen strong and accelerating changes in the world economy:

- Technological advances in communications have shrunk the world in a number of ways. Cheaper and faster transport, new mass media and electronic communications, all these have made offerings accessible over ever-increasing distances. As the market for an offering approaches the ultimate point of being truly global, so the distinction between that offering's home and export markets disappears. The world becomes its home market.
- As logistical barriers came down, the new worldwide competitive forces progressively gained the upper hand against artificial regulatory and other barriers which had isolated individual countries from external competition. In finance this is typified by the wholesale euromarkets, which have to a large extent unified the banking systems and bond markets of the free world. Barriers remain, but they are dwindling in number and height.
- Wherever competition heated up in this way, higher cost producers have gone to the wall, and real incomes have risen. This did not of course occur for example in Africa where governments successfully isolated uncompetitive economies from these trends.

- Rising real incomes in their turn make for a more diverse economy, i.e. an economy with a greater proportion of differentiated offerings. This trend towards more differentiation tends to counteract the trend towards greater worldwide standardization which results from the globalization of markets. Differences between countries and regions have declined, differences between the preferences of individual customers within each and every country have grown.

How global or local are markets now?

Although the world has been shrinking, global markets are not yet the norm, and may never be the norm. Most offerings have markets confined to much less than the whole free market world. The local chemist's or hairdresser's market may have a radius of under a mile. The national newspaper like the *Daily Mail* or *Corriere della Sera* has a market restricted to its country, plus a few expatriates or travellers abroad.

On the other hand, the customers of an international marketing consultancy, a bulk chemical or a computer software system may well extend to a few dozen countries, but not to the hundreds of countries which make up the world of free markets. Language differences can cause different word processing software to be preferred in China, Japan or Russia. Hot and cold climates can also create different preferences for interior decorations, home laundry appliances or alcoholic drinks. On the other hand a given General Electric aero engine is a global offering with a global market.

It goes without saying that a *company* cannot have a global *market*. First, only offerings have markets, not companies. Secondly, what may appear to be one offering, may in fact be many offerings, requiring many different competitive strategies. Schweppes ginger ale may have a global sale, and even have an identical set of competitors in every country, and yet face different configurations of competitive positions among that set of competitors in 30 areas, some of them countries. In that case Schweppes ginger ale may be a single *generic offering*.[7] Nevertheless,

- it is not one, but 30 offerings, with 30 markets,
- no one of these has a global market as here defined.

Geographical distance as a dimension of differentiation

We must now introduce the concept of geographical distance as a dimension of differentiation. Chapter 5 discussed how offerings are differentiated generally. It adopted merchandise and support as the dimensions in which differentiation could most usefully be classified and analysed. The present context is concerned with the dimension of geographical distance. Moreover, we here treat distance in space as if it were the only form of differentiation, traded off against price.

The tourist in Singapore who wants to have a meal out, is limited in the distance that she can reasonably travel to that meal. Tokyo, Saigon, and even Kuala Lumpur are likely to be out of range. The acceptable distance depends on her transport logistics. Once a restaurant is within range, accessibility is merely one of the attributes that will influence her choice along with all the other attributes in the merchandise and support dimension[8]. Distance in space on the one hand and support and merchandise on the other are not mutually exclusive.

There seems to be little evidence that distance in space is unlike other forms of differentiation between offerings. This was of course what we learned from the illustration of the Dorchester Hotel in Chapter 4. Its competitive positioning depends to some extent on its location, but equally on how it compares with its competitors in the quality of its accommodation, service, or catering. Location is just one of many factors that shapes its merchandise and support differentiation. We have not so far found any significant gap between locational and other outputs. Location can of course be critical for particular types of offering, like a petrol station or a neigbourhood shop. In the same way however can the quality of the cuisine be critical for a restaurant, or its credit rating for a bank.

The tradeoff between local preferences and price

Preferences around the world can sometimes converge. Examples are Mont Blanc pens, expensive perfumes, designer dresses and Ferraris. In other cases preferences remain diverse. Where that is the case, the competing business must of course decide how and to what extent to adapt its offering to local preferences. Interestingly, what at first sight might appear to be inputs, can here turn out to be outputs. If local public or private sector customers prefer offerings produced locally, or produced in working or hygienic conditions which meet local standards, then the choices of local customers might be swayed by these features, which are in that case outputs.

The choice between a cheaper standard offering and a dearer one, more closely adapted to the preferences of a narrower group of customers, is of course nothing new to the reader. The more standardized offering can normally exploit greater economies of scale, and thus be offered at a lower price. Customers in that case face a tradeoff between a cheaper offering and a more differentiated one closer to their individual preferences. There must always be a price gap just large enough to leave a customer indifferent between the two choices. When the Honda motor-cycle first swept the British market with its strong loyalty to local brands, the price saving was no doubt a major factor.

The standard offering is normally cheaper even across distances, but that is not universally the case. Houses in hot climates, e.g. in Sicily, tend to have shutters and no curtains, but shutters are not usual in cooler climates like that of the UK. Consequently shutters are relatively dearer in the UK than in Sicily. However at a higher cost a native of Sicily could fit shutters to his or her house in Birmingham. An Italian supplier of shutters would find it much costlier to supply shutters to a customer in Birmingham. Shutters are not cheap to transport, and there are too few customers for them in Birmingham to yield economies of scale. Whether that customer will actually pay the extra cost, must depend on how high that extra cost is. Chapter 6 called that tradeoff the price sensitivity of customers for the offering.

It is this tradeoff which determines the geographical extent of the market for the cheaper offering. Therefore whether a market for a geographically standardized cheaper offering is global, depends on whether its unit cost has fallen to the point where it can find customers in the whole free market world. That does not mean that no-one will buy its more locally adapted and in that dimension more closely targeted substitutes. There will always be some customers with different price sensitivities who will buy those substitutes.

An internationally standardized offering can be said to have a global market, if there is no part of the free market world where it will not find buyers, and provided that its triangular positioning is uniform across the globe.

The role of costs

This chapter examines the geographical size of markets, which is ultimately determined by customers. However, we again and again encounter the evident fact that customers' choices are powerfully affected by prices, which in their turn are to some extent influenced by costs. We therefore now review the issues raised by costs, before resuming the main argument of this chapter.

The central issue is of course the tradeoff between the competing pulls of (a) local preferences and (b) costs saved by overriding those preferences. In competitive conditions lower prices depend on savings in unit costs. Such savings can arise,

- from economies of scale achieved by standardization and concentration of supply, or
- from reductions in transport or other transaction costs of delivering an offering to a customer across distances or cultural and other barriers.[9]

359

Economies of scale

Economies of scale are the most prominent strategic determinant of unit costs. Flow production techniques reduce unit costs and by the same token raise breakeven points. Television receivers are a frequently quoted example of an offering in which the economies of scale have since say 1960 risen dramatically. With a given number and configuration of competitors, markets tend to burst out of national or local boundaries as soon as breakeven volumes exceed the buying capacity of a single country or region.

Assuming n competitors and fixed equal market shares, the bursting point would be reached when 1/nth of the country's buying capacity is exceeded by a given competitor's breakeven volume. This model is oversimplified. It assumes for example a public market with little differentiation among the competitors, yet it does serve to illustrate why a need for economies of scale can force a business to 'export or die'.

Now let us assume that customer preferences in an export territory are different; different enough to require modifications. We further assume that the modifications reduce the economies of scale and raise the breakeven price. In this very common case outcomes have been of both kinds. Washing machines illustrate the case where local differences have been known to prevail; automobiles and TV receivers are examples where the standardized, cheaper offering often overcomes local preferences.

Different geographical areas end up buying different types of washing machines, e.g. cold wash in hot climates and vice versa. They are separate markets, and washing machines are a generic offering.[10] In each such separate market the washing machine is a different offering.

In automobiles and TV receivers, a single standardized offering crosses frontiers. Wherever customer preferences and competitor configuration do not change at a border, the market is wider than one country.

Whether markets end up global, regional or fragmented and local, depends on the interrelation between the intensity of local preferences[11] and the economies of scale.

Transport and other transaction costs

Generally, where something is costly to transport, like Michelin's automobile tyres, it is more economic to produce it close to the customer, close to the point of sale. How close, is determined by a tradeoff between transport costs and the scale economies of producing in a single location.

Can a market in such a case be global? In principle we cannot exclude that possibility. In practice, however, competitive positions in each region will be influenced by the local productive capacity of each supplier. Even in the improbable case of an identical list of suppliers in each such region, their competitive positions are unlikely to be uniform across the world, and customers would perceive them to be differently positioned. The input logistics have modified the outputs!

Transport costs are one of several categories of *transaction* costs. Other kinds of transaction costs are especially important in intangible offerings. Consultancy services from Britain can be costly to deliver to Brazil with its very different culture. Similar costs would arise in offering insurance, banking services or executive recruitment to Brazil. For the UK service to be useful in Brazil, it must contain important elements which are equally applicable in Brazil. The translation of those common elements into Brazil's language and business environment is costly. The service must ultimately be delivered by a UK or a Brazilian national. That national will be a foreigner in one of the countries. In such a case the UK-owned supplier may have substantially higher costs than its local competitors who have no language cost to overcome. It may in that case have to charge substantially higher fees than its local competitors and also higher than its fees in the UK, its home country. These price differentials are enough to separate the Brazilian from the UK market in this consultancy service.

Transaction costs are of course of many kinds, including customs documentation, or the translation of documents; in fact all costs caused by language, cultural, regulatory or fiscal barriers. A van driver who crosses frontiers, must learn to deal with the foreign country's traffic, insurance and health regulations: the cost of learning is a kind of transaction cost, even if the cost declines with experience gained on successive trips.

Factor costs varying between countries

Whereas savings in transaction costs may widen the geographical span of markets, reductions in factor costs have no such effect.

International economics[12] has always stressed that factor costs vary between countries. Wage levels and productivity vary from country to country because international markets in labour are far from perfect, and conditioned by fiscal and regulatory differences between countries. People are not as mobile as offerings. Only a minority migrate to where they can earn higher wages. When the urge to migrate rises to substantial levels, destination countries tend to restrict immigration.

Materials are cheaper in countries where they are plentiful, provided markets fail to establish a single world price, perhaps due to high transport or transaction costs.

Financing costs also vary between countries, for example with savings to income ratios, unless financial markets are free to arbitrage the differences away by exporting and importing capital.

All this is well established, and differences in factor costs have an influence on where offerings are most economically produced: on the international division of labour. What is not always understood is that differences in factor costs do not imply country-bound markets. If Zambia and Chile produce raw copper more cheaply than Australia, it does not follow that the market in copper is not global. It is. Differences between factor costs influence where things are produced, not where they are sold.

This concludes our digression on the issues raised by costs. Economies of scale can often widen the geographical span of markets, transport and other transaction costs will on balance reduce that span, but varying factor costs in different places do not of themselves affect it.

Are countries 'markets'?

The discussion has not so far specifically treated the frontiers of sovereign states as actual or potential boundaries of markets. This may surprise some readers. Managers and writers commonly speak of countries as markets, almost as if the two terms were synonymous; as if Singapore or Peru were 'markets', or as if the European Union could meaningfully be a 'single market'. An example was the goal of '45 per cent of EU market' in the box in Chapter 1.

The separation of the territory of a sovereign state from other markets presupposes some political cause. Government affects the conduct of business in many ways. It can create barriers for example by fiscal means like tariffs or subsidies, or through direct or indirect regulation. However, its sharpest impact is on those offerings which are sold to public sector buyers, or which concern those parts of the economy which are closest to public policy and administration: utilities, defence, public order, health, education, environment, media, banking and finance.

Governmental intervention can affect the demand for offerings by 'dirigiste' policies. It can do this mainly by limiting the freedom to enter markets and set prices. Motives vary from favouring locally owned private or state-owned enterprises, to protecting local employment, suppressing price inflation, restricting imports and conserving foreign exchange. The most extreme case is the command economy, in which the pricing system and the interplay of demand and supply are replaced by bureaucratic decisions.

The very common usage which equates countries with markets no doubt corresponded with reality just after World War II, when its two implied conditions were largely met. First, many countries were isolated from each other by exchange controls and by protectionist devices like tariffs, quotas and import licensing. Secondly, competitive markets were still to a much greater extent public rather than private, because offerings tended to be homogeneous rather than diverse.

These conditions have rapidly disappeared in the advanced economies, especially during the 1970s and 1980s. This does not mean that political frontiers have completely ceased to act as market boundaries. Political barriers to the entry of various offerings are still to be found. They are most prominent in countries with strong cultures like Japan, and for offerings bought by the public sector.

Countries continue to be separate markets for some public utilities, for defence equipment, for offerings like pharmaceuticals bought by public health services, and sometimes for agricultural or other products where they are regarded as politically sensitive: rice in Japan is again a prominent example.

For most offerings however, the extent of markets is determined by the economic forces described earlier, customer preferences and supply issues like transport costs. For that majority of offerings markets can be of any geographical extent: they can extend to more or less than one country, or to the whole free market world. Political borders will define the boundaries of markets only,

- where the state imposes barriers of the various kinds just discussed, or
- where political borders coincide with differences in customer preferences.

A change in the list of competitors also of course constitutes a market boundary, but that change will only occur at a political border due to some political cause.

The role of political barriers

Customer preferences in their turn can vary between countries for either politically conditioned or other reasons. Many writers make this distinction. Table 18.1 lists some barriers of each type.

Barriers in the right-hand column are created by political authority and vary with jurisdictions. Those in the left-hand

Table 18.1 *Role of political frontiers in affecting customer preferences*

Non-political barriers	Political barriers
Culture	Regulation
Climate	Taxes and duties
Ethnic attributes	Currency
Religion	Public procurement policy
Terrain	Political system
Language	Financial system
	Law

column are not created by political institutions. They may of course cover an area which coincides with a jurisdiction. The frontiers of such areas are not necessarily those of sovereign states. Some right-hand column barriers exist between US states or similar jurisdictions, as for example between England and Scotland. By the same token some of them may be eliminated within a block like the European Union.

The usefulness of this distinction between politically conditioned and other preferences is often overestimated. It is a matter of shades of gray, not of black and white. A communist state colours the mentality of its citizens, even when they go shopping for food. In a free society like that of Belgium or Canada on the other hand, sales or value added taxes may be the most political of the influences affecting consumer behaviour.

In any case, not all customers are consumers. Many customers are business purchasing officers, whose buying practices may not diverge dramatically from those of a public corporation or local authority.

However, differences which can occur at frontiers, *can* also occur elsewhere. There can be dramatic variations of climate within a big country like Russia, or within countries with both Atlantic and Mediterranean coastlines, e.g. France and

Spain. Geography can affect consumer preferences at least as much as political boundaries.

Customer preferences influence what competitors offer, and vice versa. Different geographical areas may naturally have different customer profiles. At the same time, competing businesses often take the initiative. They differentiate their offerings so as to shape markets differently in different places. Wherever this changes the configuration of competitive positions between one place and another, offerings and markets are different and separate.

In none of these respects are political borders the only places where preferences change. Markets can be both smaller and larger than countries.

The effect of exchange rates

Currencies can act as powerful barriers to global markets. Moreover, currency areas always have political boundaries, because it is states that issue currencies through their central banks. To the extent that exchange rates fluctuate, cross-frontier commercial markets are impeded in determining a single price.[13] A few minutes of exchange rate market fluctuation can cause price discrepancies to the point where buyers may have an arbitrage opportunity to buy in the country whose currency has become cheaper.

When currencies float, a more than countrywide commercial market requires a price in a single currency. Oil, aircraft and electronic components are universally priced in US dollars: their markets are more than countrywide. Single currency pricing is not however feasible in fast moving consumer items. Supermarket checkouts tend to operate in the domestic currency only.

This is of course the principle behind the pressure for single currency areas in Europe and elsewhere.

Circularity or oligopoly

Chapter 7 defined circularity as a condition present whenever a strategy needs to take account of the potential

366

countermoves of specific important competitors. Its classically pure form is oligopoly, where competition is restricted to a handful of dominant competitors. Its effect is a degree of indeterminacy: prices could for example end up high or low.

There are many instances of oligopoly in international business, where markets around the world are contested by a few dominant competitors. Computers, aircraft, tractors and washing detergents are well-known examples. However, circularity as such has no general influence on the geographical size of markets: that is determined by the factors already discussed, the competitive configuration and the tradeoff between local customer preferences and unit costs.

Summary

The chapter has discussed the geographical span of markets, as defined in this book. The rise in prosperity of a shrinking developed world causes markets to both grow and shrink in geographical size. We have found that geographical distance matters, but does not change our understanding of the nature of markets.

Some offerings become cheaper and more standardized across the world, others become more geographically diverse, meeting more localized customer preferences. Whether offerings become cheaper or more locally adapted, depends on customers' price sensitivity, their tradeoff between these two benefits.

Countries or jurisdictions are not automatically markets. Political frontiers can be market boundaries whenever they are either barriers to competition in their own right, or the places where other barriers such as language or culture happen to be located. Frontiers thus make a difference, but it does not follow that we can equate market boundaries with political frontiers.

On the supply side the size of markets is affected by economies of scale and by transport and other transaction costs. In this context they consist of all costs caused by delivering offerings across distances, cultures, languages, currencies and so on. Differences in factor costs do not affect where offerings are sold, only where they are produced.

Worldwide markets can be characterized by circularity, i.e. by oligopolistic features, but these do not necessarily affect their size.

Notes

1. See Chapter 4.
2. See Chapter 13.
3. Defined in Chapter 3.
4. Strictly, whether something is a single offering or two, is a matter of whether prices are jointly determined. Applied to the distance or cross-border dimensions, we can say that the Amstrad PC is a single offering in the UK and Ireland if fluctuations in the punt/ pound exchange rate do not significantly, or more than fleetingly, disturb that joint determination process. This leaves room for minor or temporary price differences caused by such factors as currency movements. The language of the 'single price' is there- fore shorthand for jointly determined prices. What matters, is that a significant price *change* in one country will be echoed in the rest of its market.
5. 'Add value' is here used in the sense of incurring cost and performing some operation in-house, which enhances what a customer is willing to pay for. It does *not* here mean creating a positive net present value, which is how Kay (1993) uses the expression.
6. This single-price definition is not incompatible with Porter's (1980: Chapter 13) description of a global industry (equated with a market). In the terminology of this book, Porter's global industry is one in which the strategic positions of competing offerings are fundamentally affected by their worldwide positions: failure to coordinate competition worldwide risks competitive disadvantage.
7. See Chapter 9.
8. We do not here subclassify differentiation by two dimensions like merchandise and support. When an offering like a retail service is very distant from a customer, distance itself is its predominant attribute. As it gets closer to the customer, it finally merges into merchandise or support. The retailer who arranges free delivery so as to make the offering more accessible, differentiates support, the one who opens a shop close to the customer differentiates merchandise.
9. 'Transaction cost' is here used in its normal managerial meaning, of an out-of-pocket expense arising from a sale or purchase. This

is different from the way the expression is used in 'transaction cost' economics, which is concerned with the differential efficiencies of managing processes within a company or contractually between companies.

10. Chapter 9.
11. In other words, by the slope of the demand curve and the relative weight placed on price by customers.
12. For example, Heffernan and Sinclair (1990)
13. Kenyon (1990).

19 Locating operations around the world

Introduction

This chapter examines the logic of where the operations which produce, sell and deliver an offering are geographically located.[1]

Trading and operating

The distinction between (a) exporting to customers in distant locations and (b) operating there, is of course fundamental. 'Operating' in a particular place means any continuing effort by the business to add value through its own employees at a local workplace. Operations can be located anywhere in the value chain[2] and might for example be a factory, warehouse, research establishment, distribution or sales office, or an after-sales servicing facility.

Decisions about where to sell and where to operate can be quite separate. Businesses often find it profitable to operate in countries or places where they have no customers, or to export to many countries or places where they do not operate. Thus German banks used to find it profitable to use Luxembourg subsidiaries to fund their loans to German customers. Again, textile manufacturers in high-wage and high-rent Hong Kong save costs by locating or even subcontracting manufacturing processes to Guangdong province of the People's Republic of China, for sales to European customers.

Why operate in distant locations?

Just as markets are undergoing an evolution driven by supply and demand factors, so is the choice of operating locations. There are four types of reasons for operating in a particular location, reasons which can outweigh any countervailing economics, two each on the supply and demand sides.

(a) High transport costs: unit costs are minimized by operating close to customers.
(b) Low local labour or other costs: this is the case for offshore or third country manufacture.
(c) Strong local preferences by customers: they can make it more profitable to have operations, especially downstream ones like selling, stocking and after-sales service, close to customers.
(d) Strong preferences by customers for offerings produced either locally or in specific third countries (e.g. fashion garments made or styled in Italy). Bias towards local manufacture can be especially pronounced in public sector customers, but it often extends to the general buying public. They may have greater confidence[3] in locally produced offerings, or a patriotic or regional preference for them.

Adapting to local conditions and preferences

Customers may have views about *how* offerings are produced as well as *where*. They may prefer a local modus operandi, such as the employment of local labour, or compliance with local religious, humane or cultural preferences, health, safety or quality standards.

Policies which either add value locally, or modify local operations so as to meet local preferences, are sometimes called 'multidomestic'.[4] Such adaptive, multidomestic policies can be aimed at either market characteristics or social and political considerations. In the first case, the requirements of local customers are better met by performing some operations close to them; in the second by operating locally, or by operating

371

locally in a manner which makes the business more acceptable to the local community. Examples might be the employment of local people or the visible adoption of local health, safety, quality or environmental standards.

Chapter 18 noted that the extent of customer markets was usually discussed on the assumption that sovereign states are 'markets'. We also found that this identification of countries with markets could be misleading. It would be equally misleading to think about the location of operations purely in terms of political frontiers. The issues of operating across distances, cultures and the like, can equally apply to areas or regions which are either smaller or larger than independent countries. Few of these issues would be greatly modified for example by the fragmentation of countries like the Soviet Union, or by the creation of the European Community's single 'market'.

What determines the location of operations?

We have already discussed the main influences on where it is best to locate value-adding operations that make up the final offering. The general principle is that in *competitive* conditions operations will be located in the most profitable places. Otherwise competitors are likely to erode the profits of our offering by optimizing their operating locations, then reducing their prices, thus driving our returns below the cost of capital.[5] The most profitable locations are not necessarily those where unit costs are lowest. We saw that it can be profitable to locate operations where either customer preferences or the fiscal or regulatory environment suggest a location which does not minimize costs, but nevertheless maximizes profit, especially after-tax profit.[6]

The competitive pressures which force companies to locate their operations in the most profitable places will be weaker in many other cases, for example where there is differentiation or oligopolistic circularity. In such conditions locations may be found in places other than the most profitable. However, the strength of competitive pressures is always a matter of degree: there will always be some pressure.

Subject therefore to the intensity of those pressures, the location of operations is likely to be determined by the supply economics of:

- economies of scale,
- transport and other transaction costs,
- differences in factor costs in different places,

but also by the demand side factors of:

- local preferences, or
- political and social influences

which tend to favour locally adaptive inputs.

Location, geographical distance and strategy

So far in Chapters 18 and 19 we have examined the logic of where customers and operations are located. How does all this help us to formulate business strategy?

Competitive strategy will look at the geographical extent of each offering quite simply as part of the problem of targeting profitable customers. Here and now there may be little choice about the spatial extent of one's market, if there are steep barriers. Postage stamps and haggis, for example, might be expected to come up against such barriers.

On the other hand over different time-frames a company's options and incentives may vary. A wider market may for example be more profitable in the longer term, but not immediately. It may pay to tackle a narrower area first, and more distant customer groups at a later stage. The likely responses of potential competitors must of course be carefully weighed.

Geography does not, however, characterize the essential nature of competitive strategy. For any proposed new offering the potential market, i.e. its potential customers and competitors, must be clearly identified in all its dimensions, of which the geographical extent is only one. It makes no difference in principle whether that extent be the whole free market world or the local shopping centre.

Geographical expansion is more often a *corporate strategy*. One of the central concerns of corporate strategy is the company's key resources,[7] and in many cases a company has a key resource consisting for example of:

- a skill in addressing distant customers, or
- a production facility in a particular location, or
- more generally a distinctive ability to operate outside its home country, or
- a brand with pulling power over a large part of the world,

which give it a capacity for sustained value generation[8] in further offerings both in its home country and elsewhere in the world. That wider exploitation of these key resources is of course part of its corporate strategy. The key resources affect its international posture, just as that posture may have created some of the key resources.

A high degree of skill and experience in serving distant and foreign customers, and in managing operations across distances and frontiers, can be a corporate competence, a key resource which will build extra value in offerings which require that resource. It may cover such skills as a feel for other cultures, an ability to master languages, currency fluctuations, worldwide financial markets, different fiscal and regulatory regimes, to manage human resources in different cultures, climates and economies.

For a given cluster of offerings, corporate strategy may well need to look at where operations are best located, so as to optimize the resources needed for a number of offerings. These resource decisions will in turn of course affect the best composition of the cluster of offerings.

Corporate strategy may also choose to create learning resources[9] by adding distant or foreign facilities to the cluster for the express purpose of acquiring skills and knowledge which will add value to the company's offerings.

All the criteria set out for corporate strategy in Part Five must of course be applied. To take just one example, if the benefits of a geographical diversification could equally be

374

achieved by the contractual route, that route should be followed.

Summary

Chapter 19 has looked at the logic of the location of operations and at the strategic implications of what Chapters 18 and 19 have had to say about location of customers and operations. The thread which has run through both these chapters is that geographical issues make little difference to the general framework of business strategy. This runs counter to the received view.[10] There are three main reasons for this. First, the conventional approach, which treats international business as a separate topic, does not always distinguish sharply between competitive and corporate strategy. Secondly, there is the widespread tendency to speak of countries as 'markets'. Thirdly, conventional approaches do not treat competition as occurring between offerings. This last is the more important source of misunderstanding.

On the other hand geography is a significant issue in its own right in *corporate* strategy. This is because corporate strategy has resources as a central concern, and location of operations is very much a resource. It is also closely intertwined with a potentially decisive resource, the skill of dealing and managing at a distance and across frontiers.

The main conclusion however is that distance and frontiers are a much smaller strategic issue than is widely believed.

Notes

1. All these issues are discussed in the literature of international business. The difference here is that the offering is here the unit of analysis, not the 'firm' or the 'industry'.
2. Porter (1985).
3. This motivation can also of course work in reverse, when customers have a preference for anything imported. This generally occurs where there are import or exchange control restrictions. These restrictions systematically ensure that local production is uncompetitive, as it is protected from international competition.

The preference for imports can however be irrational. There have been many examples of this in India.
4. Hout, Porter and Rudden (1982).
5. This is the equilibrium or success-aping assumption of the efficient markets model. In that model, if entry is free, and if we fail to optimize, competitors will seize the opportunity to offer a cheaper or otherwise more attractive offering, forcing us to lose sales or to squeeze our margins by matching their price reductions.
6. This discussion is conducted in the accounting language of 'profit', as a short-hand way of referring to the building of financial value. Chapters 2 and 8 discuss the distinction.
7. See Chapter 10.
8. Defined in Chapter 10.
9. Ghoshal (1987).
10. Krugman (1991) questions the received view. He finds that political boundaries are not free-standing issues, or wholly separate from other competitive issues.

20 Distant and international strategy: implementation and structure

Introduction

Chapters 18 and 19 examined the issues of geographically distant customers and operations. This chapter reviews some consequences for business organization and structure.

One of our themes has been that distance and frontiers make no dramatic difference to business strategy. Differences have of course been noted. Languages, cultures, currencies, legal, regulatory and fiscal systems vary in different jurisdictions. Extra documentation, controls and duties and 'non-tariff' barriers like discriminatory quality controls can impose extra costs on the movement of goods or even services at political frontiers. However, all these leave the fundamentals intact. The task of competitive strategy is still to target profitable customers, and that of corporate strategy to manage the cluster of firmlets or offerings.

Management structures, on the other hand, are rather more affected by the impact of distance and frontiers. The belief that the significance of the cross-frontier dimension is less than fundamental, is perhaps reinforced by the fact that writers on international strategy tend to devote more space to implementation and structure than to markets to contest.

The strategic relevance of organization structures and corporate culture

The role of organization structure in the topic of trading and operating across distances and frontiers has thus received a great deal of attention. The view taken here is as follows:

- A decision to trade or operate at a distance must normally make a difference to a company's organization structure. However, this impact is not always of strategic significance. Day-to-day intelligence, logistics and control have to be the dominant influence on structures.
- If a new business strategy makes a major difference to the geographical spread of markets, cultures and operations, it normally requires changes in the company's basic structure and culture. These changes may be very difficult, and must be carefully weighed in the decision to adopt the strategy.
- Lesser new strategies may entail less dramatic changes in the geographical extent of markets, and thus in basic cultures and operations. They may not require changes in the basic structure. If so, these strategies will be constrained by the company's existing basic structure. Minor structural adjustments, like the creation of a new subordinate headquarters in a new country, may of course be required.

All this can be seen as a resource-based topic. It is a little closer to the topic of corporate resources than to the configuration of customer markets. The company's organization structure and corporate culture may in a few cases even be a key resource. More often it is likely to be a pure management skill[1] which can be upgraded or modified only at a cost. It will often be a constraining influence on what strategic change is economic.

Political frontiers have more influence on management structures than distances within or across them. This chapter will therefore focus a little more on barriers arising at political frontiers.

Ghoshal's framework

A very insightful framework showing how companies structure for international business is that of Ghoshal, Bartlett and others.[2] Their main thesis concerns the change in the skills now needed by the truly worldwide company. Up to (say) the mid-1980s, companies chose either central control, with local operations following some central pattern, or more decentralized local control, encouraging each local operation to manage its business in a locally adaptive way.

As the world shrinks, and as both economies of scale and local adaptation become competitively more important, companies have to learn *both* tricks. Moreover, they must learn to impose them not in some mechanically uniform manner like a matrix structure, but in a subtly variegated way which optimizes the competitive edge of each offering, each location. A valuable feature of the framework is its stress on learning. A company can use a distant operation in (say) India or Silicon Valley to learn about production techniques, customer profiles, climatic conditions and so on, and transmit that knowledge throughout the worldwide organization if appropriate.

The company which has mastered this skill of simultaneously combining global integration with local responsiveness is called the 'transnational' company.[3] Like for example the flair for corporate strategy, this capability for transnational operation is a high-level resource, not a key resource. The transnational company is contrasted by the authors with their other models, called global, multinational and international.

Ghoshal's (and others') structural dimensions

The authors use a diagram which plots the cost advantages of global integration (vertical axis) against the 'differentiation benefits of responding to national differences in tastes, industry structures, distribution systems, and government regulations' (horizontal). This paradigm is applied by the authors at many levels. The four examples illustrated[4] are industries within the economy, competitors within an industry, functions within a company, tasks within business units. At the first (industries) level, consumer electronics is shown to have low differentiation and high integration advantages, packaged foods the reverse, telecommunications scores high in both dimensions and cement low in both.

In one of the papers[5] Ghoshal helpfully introduces *risk management* as one of the major concerns of selling and operating across frontiers. Certainly the need to manage the risks of currencies, exchange controls, changes in trade policies, country default, and political risks like confiscation or flag discrimination, are of central concern to managers, and have a powerful influence on the structures and skills needed to implement strategies in this field.

This type of framework gives useful insights into international management structures. It is less important to the task of formulating business strategy in the sense of targeting profitable customers. This is because the framework does not make customers' choices of offerings its starting point. It is not however unimportant even to this competitive task, because it provides many insights into the resources which confer a competitive edge in international business.

Issues

In the following discussion the term 'standardize' is used in an unusually wide sense. It here stands for giving priority to unit costs, rather than to local preferences, sensitivities or conditions, in deciding the location of operations. In a majority of cases a priority given to unit costs implies a geographically standardized offering which achieves better economies of scale, but in other cases the decisive factor could be factor costs or transaction costs.[6] Such a priority is correct whenever the resulting price reduction will result in better profits than the alternative local adaptation. That alternative is here referred to as 'localize'.

Distant customers and operations raise the following two issues for implementation and structure:

- Localize versus standardize,
- Centralize versus decentralize: central coordination versus local autonomy.

Of these two topics the first affects where activities are *located*, the second where they are *controlled*.

A centralized, i.e. centrally controlled activity, is not always best located in the multinational's parent country or in the country of sale. Its best location may well be in a third country. Manufacturing may be most efficient where raw materials or labour are cheapest, R&D where specialized skills are most plentiful, storage tanks in customs-free zones of ports and so on. By contrast, offshore production facilities in tax havens or free ports are seldom ideal locations for the central management of a company.

The localization and centralization issues both contrast concentrating forces with dispersing ones. Dispersing pressures stem from local idiosyncracies, which include customers' preferences, political sensitivities, or sometimes more advanced technologies. Concentrating forces tend to be cost pressures, or the shrinking of the world into unified markets, or again the need to confront global competitors with global strategies.

In addition to these two main issues there is a third:

• The need for a local presence not for *supplying*, but for *sourcing* either materials or experience of local conditions and technologies: this last process is called 'learning'. Learning can be very important in some classes of business. This is why many non-US companies at one time sought a presence in 'Silicon Valley' and why many Japanese commercial and investment banks established their branches in London. Their functions may later have changed, but their original purpose was to learn.

Political influences

Chapter 18 examined the extent to which markets can be affected or geographically constrained by public authorities, both central and local. This can be a decisive influence on the setting and implementing of competitive strategies.

From time to time a multinational has to consider whether and how to operate and structure itself in a relatively dirigiste country. The overriding problem for the company here is not so much how to structure itself in such a country, but whether:

- to operate there at all,[7] or
- to exploit the country's artificial constraints by entrenching its own position at the expense of its main international rivals or,
- to invest in local production capacity with or without local partners or,
- to prepare contingency exit plans against future deteriorations in the climate or a change of regime.[8]

Governmental intervention or discrimination can be legal, regulatory, fiscal or administrative. The multinational needs a close understanding of all these dimensions. In many cases it needs both well-informed advisors and well-connected friends or partners. It may need them as much to avoid pitfalls as to influence official decision-takers. Successful manipulation can be more harmful than unsuccessful attempts, especially in African countries where regimes change suddenly.

The problem of dealing with dirigiste authorities does not lend itself to much generalization, because there is no limit to the variety of possible forms of intervention. The principal need is for alertness, sensitivity, good intelligence, and rapid response to intelligence.

Ringing the changes

We have identified two main structural issues, localization and centralization; where to locate activities and where to take decisions about their location and control. However, just what is meant by 'activities'?

Activities need to be broken down into their constituent parts as in Porter's[9] value chain. The value chain breaks down the operations of a business into discrete activities like purchasing, manufacturing, distribution, selling, service, R&D, human resource management. A multinational company needs to choose the location and centralization or decentralization of each of these separately, but with an eye on how they are mutually linked. In a software house for example a link might occur between R&D and service.

The multinational may for example concentrate production in some places, R&D in others, centralize pricing policy, and decentralize policy on 'downstream' activities like distribution and service. This would have the effect of controlling outputs (other than price) closer to the customer. A single manufacturing plant for worldwide sales does not necessarily have to be controlled centrally.

The choices are therefore numerous and complex, and few companies can afford the luxury of a tidy pattern. A US petrochemical contractor may use a centrally developed process, but

- execute the application engineering locally in India where the process plant is being built,
- rely on an Indian civil contractor,
- subcontract the chief item of hardware, the compressor, to a German, French or Canadian company, depending on the cheapest tender, and
- supply the project management team from its UK subsidiary.

Such a set of choices would maximize the customer interfaces handled by Indians.

A Swiss pharmaceutical manufacturer may have plants in a number of countries. It may also have a shareholding in a Portuguese vineyard in order to learn cork technology from it. It may have distribution subsidiaries in many customer countries to handle not only distribution logistics, but above all to gain the maximum confidence of local public health authorities. It may again have research activities in some of these countries so as to get close to local state-of-the-art drug specifications and developments. The ability to meet all these challenges in whatever way suits each set of circumstances is what Ghoshal and colleagues call 'transnational'.

Japanese manufacturers of videorecorders concentrate production facilities wherever labour and other costs are lowest. Originally Japanese car manufacturers were very successful with the same policy of manufacture centralized, in their case in Japan, but then went for local manufacture,

prompted both by changing cost patterns and by local protectionist countermeasures. Distribution arrangements are in
many cases franchised.

Coordination is often most tightly centralized in markets
that cover a wide geographical area, i.e. where price and cost
are more important than local customer preferences. In such
cases prices must be coordinated worldwide because
customers are free to shop around and arbitrage differences
between prices for the same offering in different places and
countries. Companies must be careful not to adopt strategies
requiring such coordination if they lack that skill.

The dynamics of international competition

Much of what has been said in this chapter so far, applies to
the task of management generally, not strictly just to strategy.
Strategy concerns decisions about tomorrow's competitive
positioning and tomorrow's cluster of offerings, not tactical
responses to today's changes in the competitive environment. However, decisions about resource dispositions, about
centralized or decentralized coordination, and about the
location of activities are strategic in the sense that they affect
the feasibility of strategies and their chances of success.

Whether markets are global or multidomestic, companies
need the appropriate kind of local presences and well informed
intelligence about where markets are going or could be made
to go in the period for which strategies are being formulated.

World markets can change rapidly, for example from
multidomestic to global. However, even where change is
rare, it can come swiftly, dramatically and unexpectedly. The
events which have recently toppled IBM from its dominant
position in computers, or those which led to a revolution in
the motor-cycle and automobile markets, are good examples.

Conclusion

Managers of all companies need a wide range of skills, and
the open-mindedness and flexibility to adopt an unrestricted
variety of management styles and structures, across their

384

businesses, within a given business, and across time. There is no single stance, like centralized or decentralized, locally responsive or standardized, which will universally, invariably or permanently suit an international company, let alone a complex one.

Part Six has left us with a view of the world which is not dramatically different from that of the single country. Markets have geographical boundaries which can vary between short walking distances and the entire globe. The more complex the geographical area is, the more complex must be the response of the business to that complexity, and this applies to both the demand and the supply side, to outputs and inputs.

Complexities do increase at political frontiers, in all those matters which differ between one sovereign state and another. Yet these differences can be less than other differences like climate, language, or culture. These too can and do change at places other than political frontiers. Companies must pay attention to all features which affect their business. Differences between countries have sometimes had disproportionate attention.

Notes

1. Chapter 10.
2. Ghoshal (1987), Bartlett and Ghoshal (1987), Ghoshal and Nohria (1993). Ghoshal (1987) clarifies that the integration-responsiveness framework was originally proposed by Prahalad (1975), and developed and applied by a number of authors including Doz, Bartlett and Prahalad (1981), and Porter (1984).
3. Bartlett and Ghoshal (1989).
4. Ghoshal (1987) p. 429, using a diagram reproduced from Bartlett (1985).
5. Ghoshal (1987).
6. Costs arising in individual buy or sell transactions.
7. In the context of selecting a competitive strategy or offering, the point is part of the wider issue discussed in Chapter 7 under the heading 'Oligopoly and strategy implementation'.
8. Prominent examples are the departure from India of both Coca-Cola and IBM in the 1970s. Coca-Cola was unwilling to lose control of its formula, IBM of its product and manufacturing policy.
9. Porter (1985, 1986).

Part Seven   Organizing for Formulating and Implementing Business Strategy

Part Seven consists of a single chapter. It briefly reviews the extent to which business strategy interacts with management structures and communications. This book is not about organizational theory. Part Seven makes certain assumptions about this important topic, and discusses the implications of the framework presented in the earlier parts.

One view taken here is that organization structures are quite correctly in the main dictated by day-to-day rather than strategic needs.

21 Operating and organizational aspects of business strategy

Introduction

This single chapter raises a topic which can and does fill entire books. Its limited purpose is to suggest in brief outline how the competitive and corporate strategy frameworks in this book are translated into action within the ordinary structures and practices of business management.

The chapter discusses two types of issues. One is the chain of command for various functions related to business strategy, i.e. who should do what? The other issue is the degree of decentralization, already encountered in a narrower context in Chapter 20.

Interest is focused on two interlocking tasks. One of them is the task of strategy formulation itself. Who selects competitive and corporate strategies, and how does that responsibility link with the general organization structures of a company?

The other task is that of implementing each strategy, once it has been adopted. Who is responsible? How does implementation relate to the day-to-day task of organizing and running the company? How is implementation monitored internally and externally, and how does this link with control procedures like budgeting?

For this purpose we introduce two terms, which will help to clarify these issues:

• The **'inter-unit structure'** concerns the chain of command between a company's head office and its profit centres. This includes the interposition of intermediate line management levels like divisions.

- The 'interpersonal structure' concerns the – often informal – chain of command between a company's chief executive and the relatively small number of decision-takers in the formulation, approval and execution of individual competitive and corporate strategies.

The message of this chapter is that neither the inter-unit structure nor the implementation of specific competitive or corporate strategies are mainly *strategic* topics. The issues raised by the implementation of strategies are not dramatically different from those of day-to-day business management. The inter-unit structure should be tailored to the composition and configuration of a company's activities. Strategies will affect the activities, but any discussion of the inter-unit structure must mainly concern the link between activity and inter-unit structure, not the strategy–activity link. The strategy–activity link in its own right has little bearing on the inter-unit structure.

The reorientation which this book suggests is towards the micro-scene of the individual offering competing for profitable customers, and away from the structural problems of the corporate colossus. This reorientation is as much for the small corner store as for the heavyweights. Its recommendations are intended equally for both.

The ground covered by this chapter is part of what Goold, Campbell and Alexander[1] call 'parenting' (see box). If parenting is something wider than the functions of the head office, it is also wider than the structural and organizational questions raised in this chapter. The job of allocating capital among the profit centres and offerings is purely for the head office, but other resources may be allocated or sometimes coordinated centrally by managers who are part of the parent, but not part of the head office.

Is the company's inter-unit structure a prime strategic issue?

This chapter will surprise some readers not with what it covers, but with what it omits. It will not discuss how a large,

---

'Parenting'

The authors define the parent as the 'corporate hierarchy of line managers, functions and staffs' outside the businesses that could exist independently. Thus defined, the parent is something wider than what this book calls the head office, whose minimum functions consist of just finance, corporate strategy and line management tasks like appointing senior operating management and monitoring performance against budgets, targets, or milestones.[2] Parenting functions are wider than these and cover any support that a head office may give to operating units. The authors' central theme is the company's 'parenting advantage', the quality that makes it the best possible parent for its businesses. and is akin to our best owner filter.[3] The authors' view of corporate strategy is similar to that put forward in this book, but it places much more emphasis on vertical – head office to firmlet – links than on horizontal ones between firmlets.

---

complex conglomerate should arrange its inter-unit structure: whether for example that structure is best arranged in multi-divisional or centralized, functional form.

There was a time when the inter-unit structure was treated as the principal strategic issue. That however was when it was unquestioningly assumed that companies would in fact continue to get bigger. This was thought to be either desirable or at any rate inevitable. It was also taken to be the meaning and essence of business strategy. Companies' main objective was assumed to be size.[4] The heyday of this doctrine was the 1960s. The 'strategic' objective was for the company to grow in size either by increasing its share of its existing markets or by entering new ones. Competition was not at that time a central concern. Companies consequently became large and complex. Inter-unit structures had to be found which accommodated and managed a growing range of activities. The multidivisional structure, with a head office ever more remote from customer markets, became a popular model.[5]

When markets became more competitive, and companies like General Motors and General Electric faced challenges from Japan and elsewhere, competition replaced size as the focal point. The growth model gradually gave way to a 'portfolio' model, in which size was no longer the unquestioned objective. However, it was less clear just what the portfolio was diversifying. Was it risk (and if so, what risk?) or was it cash-generating and cash-absorbing profiles? Developments in financial theory put a question-mark over these concepts.

In the 1980s the tide finally turned. Research had shown that size was no passport to success, and had cast doubt on the economic value of unrelated diversification. Small became beautiful, and it became fashionable to divest, to demerge, to seek management buy-outs. Strategy ceased to be preoccupied with inter-unit structures.

The assumptions[6]

As this book is not about organizational theory, we make the following eight assumptions which belong to that field:

1 Top management not a variable

Many modern writers set out to define desirable changes in the skills of top management.[7] Some changes are part of the process of change in the technologies and environments of a company's existing mix of businesses. Others would enable the top management team to undertake a much wider mix of businesses.[8] One end of the spectrum therefore concerns the updating of individual and collective skills which most top management teams would as a matter of routine expect to undertake all the time. At the other end are more radical expansions and changes of skills which might well require a change of people in the top team. This book treats the incumbent top management as given. In other words it treats that team as a constraint on strategy, not as a variable. It does not explore what strategies might be feasible if the top team were changed. There are several reasons for this assumption.

First, behavioural topics are outside the authors' field of study. Secondly, managers are not normally interested in strategic change which would require their own replacement. In any case, skills which can be acquired by an incumbent team may well also be imitable: in that case they do not qualify as key resources for sustained value-building.[9]

2 Decentralization (inter-unit structure)

Companies are assumed to seek a decentralized structure whenever their size and degree of complexity make a monolithic structure uneconomic. In such a structure every commercial activity is the responsibility of a line manager. The line manager is in full day-to-day control, with no back-seat driver at head office, as long as he or she delivers results. The line manager is close to customer markets and to the operations that serve those markets, close enough to be in personal touch and sensitive and responsive to changes in those environments. In a company which is not small enough to be manageable by a single line manager, each of these line managers will be in command of a profit centre.

3 Profit centre autonomy (inter-unit structure)

The objective is maximum autonomy of profit centre managers and minimum interference in their day-to-day decisions, so as to give them the greatest possible sense of profit responsibility, together with authority and motivation to discharge that responsibility.

4 Inter-unit structure follows activity, not strategy

The inter-unit structure is shaped not by strategy, but by the list and configuration of the company's activities. Strategy will of course powerfully influence and modify that list and configuration. The changes in activities caused by strategy will in their turn often, though not invariably, prompt changes in the inter-unit structure. Of these two links:

- strategy → activities,
- activities → inter-unit structure,

only the first is strategic. The second is a feature of day-to-day management and only indirectly strategic. It is therefore the former link that concerns us.

A civil construction company will have a very different inter-unit structure from a soft drinks manufacturer or advertising agency: very different activities and operating profiles, hence different structures. Again, advertising agencies with quite different competitive strategies will nevertheless have similar inter-unit structures. Same activity, same structure. Lastly, when Singer disbanded its in-house servicing department for sewing machines, and substituted a network of franchises, this significant shrinkage in its internal activities may well have resulted in a changed inter-unit structure. A change in scope of activities can prompt a change in structure.

5 Strategy formulation is the responsibility of the top few (interpersonal structure)

In the formulation of competitive and corporate strategies as defined in this book only top and senior management are decision-takers. This is not to deny the need for the participation, i.e. for the involvement and commitment of the entire workforce. Ideas must flow up as well as down the line; the aim is the widest, yet firmly committed ownership of each strategy's objectives and implementation path. Nevertheless, responsibility for decisions rests firmly at the top.

6 Strategy implementation is not separate from day-to-day management (inter-unit structure)

Implementation of strategies as here defined is not separate from day-to-day management; on the contrary, it has to be integrated into day-to-day management.

7 Profit centres need maximum autonomy, and should therefore interact as much as possible through market mechanisms (inter-unit structure)

Where resources are shared between profit centres, the corporate centre will intervene at the time when the strategy which causes the interdependence, is initiated. The centre will then seek to avoid day-to-day intervention so as not to weaken the line managers' sense of total responsibility for their profit centres. Few costs are greater than those of diluted managerial responsibility. The means of avoiding top level intervention is the use of internal subcontracting or other market mechanisms, so as to harmonize the interests of each profit centre with those of the company as a whole.

Key resources generally grow with use, and should not therefore, except in the very short term, cause allocation problems. The sharing of non-key resources does not need to be restricted within the company. On the contrary, internal suppliers and users should compete for them in external markets. Neither key nor non-key resources should therefore normally cause capacity constraints.

8 The same profit centre formulates and implements strategy (inter-unit structure)

In the interests of continuity in the task of satisfying customers, responsibility for strategy formulation and implementation is allocated to the same profit centre.

In this set of assumptions we have not distinguished between competitive and corporate strategy, but in what follows it will be clear that the formulation of corporate strategy is one of the few tasks for which *responsibility* cannot be decentralized, even if the *task* may in some cases need to be delegated.

'Strategies' and 'plans'

Two basic terms are central to our topic: 'strategy' and 'plan'. They were discussed in Chapter 1 for the purpose of defining 'strategy' as something deliberately intended for the future. A specific competitive strategy is for an offering or firmlet, whereas a specific plan is for a profit centre. Profit centres usually contain a number of offerings, but their scope can be narrower as well as wider than that of an offering. A specific corporate strategy is of course the addition, retention or divestment of one or more offerings.

Managers normally treat a **'budget'** as the intended financial path and destination of an *entire profit centre*, division or company over an imminent or current period. A **'plan'** is taken to mean the same thing, but for subsequent periods. Both words therefore refer to the income and expenditure of an entire unit, and not to specific ventures or offerings. In this book on the other hand a competitive strategy means an initiative concerning one specific offering. A decision by the company to add, retain or divest an offering is a specific corporate strategy.

Although in some contexts it is permissible to classify a strategy as a form of plan, in this book they are different things. What a 'strategy' charts, is not the future course of a profit centre, whereas that is precisely what a 'plan' does, as that word is here used.

The unit of strategy

There is a widespread tacit assumption that a management unit, such as a profit centre, is also the competing unit. In our terminology, that assumption would imply that profit centres are firmlets. That is not impossible: a single offering may be the sole activity of a profit centre or even a company. In those exceptional cases the design of the inter-unit structure is relatively simple.

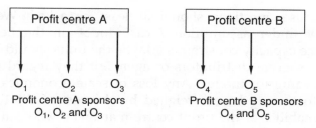

Figure 21.1   *Many offerings per profit centre*

However, as we saw in Chapter 3, that is not a normal state of affairs. Normally a profit centre contains a number, possibly a large number of offerings, as in Figure 21.1. In that normal case one line manager has responsibility for that plurality of offerings and competitive strategies. Where an offering is delivered by several profit centres, the responsibilities can become even more complex. This more complex case will be discussed below.

A decentralized management structure must evidently give line responsibility to profit centres. A profit centre is any unit with responsibility for (a) the efficient use of corporate resources (b) a profit budget, and (c) plans for the future beyond the budget period.

Assumption 7 earlier in this chapter gave profit centre managers as much day-to-day autonomy and responsibility as possible. Where they need to share resources, this should as far as possible be done by arm's length contracting. A favourite example is where several profit centres have to share a sales force (a) to reap economies of scale, and (b) to avoid adverse reactions from customers visited by too many salespersons from the same company. The collective interest of the company is said to be in potential conflict with the sum of the individual units' interests. Each wishes to be in charge of its own sales force.

In such cases it is worth investigating whether the units concerned should not be in the same profit centre, or whether perhaps the sales force should be turned into a separate profit centre supplying a service to the various manufacturing units at competitive charges.[10] If units have common customers, then those questions should at least be asked. We have already under assumption 7 cast doubt on the need for resource capacity constraints. Maybe the units should be free to use external distributors or agents, if they regard that as better value for money. Any loss of scale economies in the sales force may be outweighed by the cost of diluting the accountability of the profit centre managers, who can blame the imposed in-house sales force for shortfalls in sales.

There may in the end be residual cases where a physical day-to-day allocation system is needed which to that extent restricts the autonomy of the profit centres concerned. This solution should only be adopted where the high costs of diminished autonomy and responsibility are outweighed by the needs of the case.

However, even in these exceptional cases, the allocation process should not be looked upon as an essential function of the company's head office,[11] not even if that is where the allocator happens to be located. A head office should not normally have operating functions of its own. If head office managers happen to perform operating functions, those functions should not be seen as integral to the head office.[12]

Who formulates a competitive strategy? The need for a sponsor

A unit cannot have budgets or plans unless it is responsible for costs and resources. Each competitive strategy on the other hand must be formulated by a personal **sponsor** who is close enough to the specific customers and competitors of an offering to assess a profitable positioning; profitable not now, but at the future time when the offering will be in place and competing. A sponsor might be described as the strategy's Mr or Ms Firmlet. The owner-manager of a very small business will of course combine the sponsor role. Similarly the exceptional profit centre manager who has only one or two offerings, may have a close enough familiarity with the markets of those offerings to act as sponsor. Most profit centre managers however would be too remote and too busy to be intimately familiar with each and every market in which their offerings may be competing. Profit centre managers need some understanding of their markets, but strategy formulation requires an extra degree of closeness. The normal case therefore requires a sponsor for each firmlet within a profit centre. Often a group of firmlets can share a sponsor. There is certainly a misfit between responsibilities for competitive strategy on the one hand and day-to-day operations on the other. That misfit is not avoidable; for what a business controls are its employees and operations, not competitive outcomes which largely depend on the actions of its customers and competitors.

In a nutshell, a competitive strategy needs to be designed and formulated by a sponsor sufficiently close to the market which the strategy will be contesting. The sponsor's task is to consider alternative profitable positionings in his or her specialist area of the galaxy, and to recommend the preferred one. This recommendation must be supported by the net present value, which must be positive when discounted at the risk-adjusted cost of capital of the competitive strategy concerned. The strategy must be a value-builder.

Who approves a competitive strategy?

(a) Modification of the cluster

Who can approve a new competitive strategy? The first principle is that the addition of an offering or firmlet is strictly a corporate strategy, and the prerogative of the chief executive. That final fiat must come from the head office.

In practice however there may be exceptions to the strict rule. Some decisions may not need to be taken at that top level. An example might be a competitive strategy which merely updates, modifies or extends a generic offering, in line with a declared corporate strategy. Approval may in such cases be given by a profit centre manager or at some intermediate level.

More illuminating is the case where a large intermediate headquarters, say the toiletries division of a pharmaceutical company, considers what range of offerings will most effectively confront the competition. It will develop a view on the best range, but every addition or deletion must still be subject to the CEO's approval. The head office alone confronts the financial markets, and the head office alone can look at the proposed changes and check that they are desirable and build value for the corporate cluster as a whole. A particular new offering may be harmful to another division's offerings or to the company's overall risk profile and cost of capital. The toiletries division will submit recommendations to the CEO, but the CEO must have the ultimate power of decision.

(b) Releasing the resources

Secondly, before a new competitive strategy reaches the final approval stage, its use of resources must be approved by whatever level is responsible for allocating the resources. If all the resources are used and controlled exclusively by the sponsoring profit centre, then the manager of that profit centre needs to approve it. The sponsor cannot approve the resources unless he or she happens to be that profit centre manager.

Often however the proposed strategy needs resources used or controlled by other profit centres as well. In that case, approval must be obtained either through the normal contractual channels between profit centres or from whatever next higher level (e.g. divisional or corporate) can approve the use of all the resources. In the contractual case if profit centre A sponsors and profit centre B subcontracts, A obtains B's formal agreement. The head office does have the job of requiring the sharing of resources at the formulation stage. This should not however be its day-to-day task at the implementation stage. The point was noted earlier.

However, any new competitive strategy may utilize an existing resource, and resources may in the short term at least have some capacity constraint. It is therefore necessary that each decision to adopt a strategy is checked to ensure that the intended resources are available. Unknown to each other, various sponsors in the company may simultaneously be recommending strategies which need the same resource and which *collectively* would more than exhaust its spare capacity. All decisions therefore need the concurrence of those levels in the company, profit centre, division or corporate, at which the relevant resources can be controlled and allocated.

This is not necessarily a matter of whether capacity is available: yes or no? It is better seen as a matter of cost. For example, a major process plant may be a constraining resource. If it has spare capacity, any proposal to take up such spare capacity should value the opportunity cost of using it at zero. However, if simultaneous proposals over-absorb its spare capacity, then one option is to increase the capacity by one means or another, with the effect that a very considerable extra cost will arise, because the extra cost will be that of a step function. Even if capacity can be bought in from outside the company, it may be of lower quality or cost more: this would still constitute a step function. The evaluation of whatever competitive strategy would cause that step function to be incurred, must then treat it as a cash outflow in computing the strategy's return on capital. The result may lead to the rejection of the proposed strategy. In that case the effect is as if the resource had simply been treated as not available. However, if the proposal retains a positive value, despite the heavy cost of the step function, then it should go ahead.

The sponsor of a new competitive strategy therefore needs to consult the holders or allocators of resources in the company before as well as after making the recommendation, so as to ascertain whether the resource is available and at what opportunity cost.

The responsibilities are therefore hierarchically structured in such a way that the sponsor prepares alternative competitive strategies and recommends a selection among them. Decisions to adopt strategies are then taken at whatever level between profit centre and head office controls the resources needed for the strategy, with ultimate approval of a new offering being reserved to the chief executive as part of corporate strategy.

Complex structures: one offering, several profit centres

Offerings are sometimes unavoidably produced by several profit centres. The best inter-unit structure for such cases may vary from case to case, but in most cases the best place to locate responsibility for competitive strategy is the profit centre which lies furthest downstream, as in Figure 21.2, i.e. closest to the customer. A generally recommended structure is one in which the other profit centres subcontract to the downstream centre, preferably on competitive terms.

Two examples will illustrate the problems. First the sewing machine manufacturer with its own customer service organization. The choosing customer treats the availability, quality, and terms of servicing as features which influence his or her buying decision. The availability and quality of service arrangements are an output of the sewing machine offering.

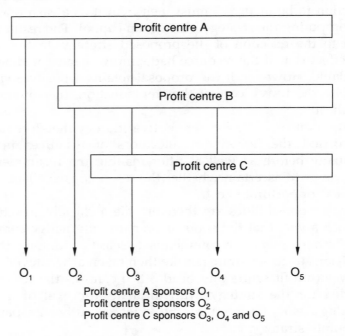

Profit centre A sponsors O_1
Profit centre B sponsors O_2
Profit centre C sponsors O_3, O_4 and O_5

Figure 21.2   *Offerings produced by varying numbers of profit centres*

In-house servicing is not in this case a must. Many manufacturers like Singer in our earlier example rely on franchised external service organizations. Such organizations are often tightly controlled, if only through their dependence on the manufacturer for parts. Others however may decide to keep the service organization in-house, perhaps for even tighter quality control.

The in-house servicing organization is likely to be a separate profit centre, but even in this internal relationship the manufacturing profit centre may exercise some control through the provision of parts. The two profit centres can in that case be left free to negotiate. It is best to leave both sides free even to terminate the arrangement and forge external relationships with other manufacturers or service organizations. The competitive incentives of such an internal market should ensure harmony with the financial goals of the company.[13]

The second example is that of complementary offerings in Link Three in Chapter 16. Betamax videorecorders were not a viable offering until there was an assured supply of betamax videocassettes. To make sure of that, the recorder manufacturer had to acquire a cassette manufacturer, and it appeared that no-one had an incentive to enter or remain in making Betamax cassettes. Here again the operating logistics are so dissimilar that it may well be best to have the two offerings in separate profit centres.

The difference between the two examples is that there is a lively market in appliance servicing, but almost total market failure in Betamax videocassettes. Singer had a choice whether to own or franchise its service organization; the Betamax manufacturer had no such choice. Its two offerings were Siamese twins. Again, even if Singer had kept its service in-house, it could have left each firmlet free to seek external trading partners. In the Betamax case there was no such option. The ultimate rule which applies to all offerings takes on a special importance for Betamax recorders and cassettes: an offering cannot be discontinued altogether without corporate strategy approval of divestment by the chief executive.

However, that rule does not dispose of all difficulties. Cassettes might force Recorders to go out of business by raising its price of Betamax cassettes to an uncompetitive level. Even so it remains the best solution to leave the two sides free to negotiate. Cassettes has no more incentive to put Recorders out of business than if Recorders were an external customer. By the same token it may pay Recorders to subsidize Cassettes so as to keep Cassettes viable. Ultimately the two Betamax businesses may both have to close down if their commercial success declines to the point where they are no longer viable. On our basic assumption that profit centres are left as free as possible to take responsibility for their own decisions, there is no justification for intervention or coordination by the head office. If the business is economic, it must be economic for the two offerings, taken together. Their freely negotiated decisions are the best arbiters.

Summary: formulating competitive strategy

The account just given applies equally to an individual competitive or corporate strategy. The adoption or abandonment of an offering or firmlet falls into both categories.

The principles for formulating a given competitive strategy are simple enough. A competitive strategy needs to be designed by a sponsor close to the market, but approved or selected at a profit centre or higher management unit where resources can be allocated in the corporate interest. The locus of each decision depends on how widely each resource is used and at what point in the structure it is controlled. This must logically occur at a profit centre or at the corporate head office or at an intermediate line management level.

Where a competitive strategy would use significant resources in more than one profit centre, the responsibility is harder to allocate. In such cases it should be as far downstream, near the customer, as possible, and dealings with the other profit centres should be internal arm's length subcontracts, franchise deals or whatever is appropriate. Alternative external contracting should be permitted wherever possible. The inherent uncompetitiveness of internalized relationships should be minimized as far as possible.

The profit centre approves the designing and shaping of a competitive strategy. Before the profit centre decides on a competitive strategy, it needs to obtain approval for any resources not under its own control. The chief executive approves the adoption, retention or divestment of an offering as part of the cluster.

The principles are simple enough, but the practicalities can be complex, because resources are manifold, of different internal scope, controlled at a variety of points in the company, and resources needed for any given offering can be few or many.

Managing and structuring corporate strategy: the principles and the complexities

In so far as corporate strategy approves individual competitive strategies, we have already dealt with it. In the sense of controlling the cluster, corporate strategy presents an even simpler pattern. Control of the cluster is a corporate responsibility of the chief executive. In the framework of this book every decision to add, retain or divest an offering or firmlet is an element in that task of controlling the cluster.

Once again the principle may be simple, but the task is complex. The complexities do not end for example with the decision to add a specific offering to the cluster: some of them continue into the subsequent implementation stage. The complexities are the following:

- Those responsible must decide the nature of the cluster and in what principal ways it is to be related. Chapter 16 described the links.
- They must establish the risk-adjusted cost of capital for each offering with a view to subsequently monitoring attainment of a positive net present value, discounted at that cost of capital.

405

- They must ensure the existence of mechanisms for the optimal procurement and allocation of resources shared between profit centres.

We have so far noted that the corporate strategy aspect of the adoption of a specific competitive strategy is its approval as part of the cluster. Corporate strategy may however also come into the picture in its resource-allocating role. This brings us back to what we have called the big asymmetry of business strategy. The decisive reason for approving or rejecting a competitive strategy may in some cases be its exploitation of key resources available to the company.

Making the corporate strategy task manageable

The chief executive's responsibility for corporate strategy can in some large or complex companies be daunting. In that case it can be reduced to a more manageable commitment by the following principles:

- Having as many resources as possible controlled and shared within one profit centre only, as long as this causes no waste of spare capacity.
- Restricting the number of offerings to a manageable level. This is in harmony with the insight that small is beautiful.
- Delegating to line managers or staff specialists the analytical and logistical tasks, such as identifying capacity constraints.
- In suitable cases, making decisions about generic offerings, delegating sub-decisions about replacements or extensions of individual offerings to profit centre managers.

However, the ultimate responsibility for the decisions and choices in the cluster of offerings is that of the chief executive, and cannot be delegated, as it allocates the company's capital.

When a new competitive strategy has been adopted

When a new offering or firmlet has been decided upon, what tasks remain which are not simply part of the day-to-day management of the company and its profit centres?

In principle, there are two tasks, one internal and one external. The first is to monitor the implementation by the company itself. The second is to watch the competitive environment, to see to what extent the reactions of customers and competitors vary from those assumed in the proposal to adopt the strategy. The two tasks overlap in that both can point to the need for internal management action. However the second, external monitoring task can result in decisions to modify the strategy itself, even before its full implementation. If the market is moving altogether away from the section of the galaxy addressed by the strategy, then the strategy may have to be aborted. If on the other hand, the change in the news merely shifts or tilts the demand curve for the proposed new offering, then all that may be needed is a change in the chosen price/volume set. This will modify the strategy. The new offering will be a repositioned version of the old. Its price or differentiation will be different, for example as a result of a stepping up or reduction of the degree of support differentiation.[14]

In any case, who in the company should hold this watching brief of the market environment? We have already given the answer earlier: the responsibility should rest with the profit centre which sponsored the strategy, and within it with the individual sponsor who successfully recommended its adoption.

The profit centre must however obtain higher authority for modifications of the strategy. This is needed for any changes in (a) the use of resources held elsewhere in the company, and (b) cluster management: corporate strategy. But what of the internal monitoring task?

Internal monitoring of the implementation of a new competitive strategy

Many managers and even writers seem to believe that the implementation of a competitive strategy should be monitored against the projections in the proposal. The principle is clearly beyond reproach. Competitive strategies are investment projects, and every such project should be followed up, and deviations between intentions and achievements allocated to their causes, external or internal.

The only difficulty is that this cannot normally be done by means of accounting records. For deciding whether to adopt a competitive strategy, projections of future cash flows are produced. These are discounted at the appropriate cost of capital to their net present value. The decision depends at least partly on the attractiveness or adequacy of that net present value.

However, the cash flows which are produced for this calculation, must be defined in *incremental*, and not in absolute terms. They measure the *difference* between the entire company's cash flows that would occur (a) with and (b) without the proposed new strategy. In these financial terms it is not possible to post-audit the implementation of the strategy, because there is no verifiable way of producing (with hindsight) what would have happened without the strategy. The original projections of what might happen without it, will soon lose all interest or relevance, and the hypothetical past is unverifiable.

This impediment would exist, even if financial results were obtainable for individual offerings as distinct from profit centres.

In short, the comparison of actual with intended effects cannot be produced in accounting terms. The correct way to monitor a project is to set out milestones, most of them in physical terms, to be attained at various forward dates. Dates for finished design, for installation of production line, for establishment of distribution channels, units made, units sold, assumed unit prices, market share percentages (carefully established for a private market[15]), all these can be pre-established and compared with actual achievements at the implementation stage.

A case study which shows a valiant attempt at not only monitoring the implementation of competitive strategies in this way, but even structuring a whole company with this purpose in mind, is the EG&G case.[16] The company in that case did its best to monitor by milestones and by financial performance, creating profit centres which are as close as possible to individual firmlets, i.e. offerings.[17]

The responsibility for this internal monitoring of implementation should clearly again lie with the sponsoring profit centre, but within that centre it is advisable to locate it with the sponsor of the strategy, the strategy's Mr or Ms Firmlet. The success of the strategy needs this continuity. It will improve that sponsor's realism in setting milestones for other strategies to be sponsored in the future. It is also vital that sponsors should not look upon sponsoring as a discrete paper task which ends at the point of approval. Their motivation should be to sponsor successful strategies rather than successful applications for approval. The continuing participation of the sponsor is thus needed both for the success of the strategy, and as a beneficial learning process for the sponsor, who will gain experience for sponsoring future competitive strategies.

Implementation of adopted corporate strategies

The implementation of corporate strategies is a relatively straightforward matter. First, responsibility is that of one person, the company's chief executive. Secondly, implementation of each addition and divestment is a discrete one-off task which normally extends over a limited period. It can be specifically delegated. That leaves as continuing tasks:

- the continual review of the existing cluster of offerings,
- updating corporate budgets and plans, as decisions are made to add or divest,
- monitoring the implementation of past decisions to add or divest.

All these are the responsibility of the chief executive with whatever help he or she arranges to obtain from subordinate managers and staff.

Companies with a multitude of offerings

A difficulty could arise where a company has too many offerings for one person to have the necessary ability to form an overview of the cluster. It may well be wise, and consonant with the 'small is beautiful' view, to question whether this itself may not be an indication that the company is too large and complex for its own and its investors' good.

However, let us assume that the aggregation of offerings in a company increases its value. Then the chief executive may well have to form a small team of senior colleagues to share the overview of the cluster, each taking a part of the cluster and identifying candidates for addition and divestment. They can then as a group take the necessary decisions.

What is not recommended, is to divisionalize the task, i.e. to delegate cluster management to divisional heads. It is essential that ultimate decisions are taken by people whose jobs depend not on parts of the cluster, but on the whole, and who are not emotionally or otherwise biased in favour of any part of the cluster.

Roles of general managers and staff

Some years ago, when perceptions of strategic management were concerned with very different issues, it was thought that 'planning' was a matter of filling sheets of paper with financial figures, which essentially extrapolated past performance into the future by means of certain growth assumptions.[18] In those days the task of building up these dossiers was naturally treated as a task for specialized planning staffs.

This book clearly sees strategy as a very different task. Decisions are very much the responsibility of general managers. They concern the future direction of the business in its competitive environment. Competitive strategy is for

410

the relevant profit centre manager, corporate strategy for the chief executive of the company. Both may seek help. Indeed it seems essential in most cases that the manager responsible for competitive strategy works closely with an internal sponsor of each strategy. Again, both the chief executive and intermediate managers of resources may need to obtain some staff help with resource capacity measurements and commitments. This need must depend on what key and other resources can become constraints on corporate and competitive strategies. The complexity here will vary from company to company. Detailed reconnaissance and record-keeping can be left to staff assistants: decisions and choices cannot.

If decisions are for the place where the buck stops, the ideas, suggestions and recommendations can and should come from all parts of the company, not excluding the shop floor.[19] Strategic ideas come from all levels; only decisions are made by line managers up to the chief executive. The best line managers are undoubtedly those who communicate and listen.

Summary: structuring for strategy

The company's inter-unit structure is not a prime strategic issue. It exclusively depends on its operating profile, its activities. What matters to business strategy, is the interpersonal structure, which allocates the senior managers' responsibilities for strategy.

The pattern which emerges in this chapter shows that corporate and competitive strategy are not in separate watertight compartments. This is (a) because every decision to adopt a competitive strategy also affects the composition of the cluster and (b) because some of the key and other resources needed for a competitive strategy are corporate and can be under the direct control of the head office. Nevertheless, different rules tend to apply to them, and responsibilities generally fall into the pattern shown in Table 21.1.

Table 21.1 *Overview of responsibilities for competitive and corporate strategy*

	Corporate strategy	Competitive strategy
Adopted by	Chief executive	Sponsoring profit centre[1] manager, advised by sponsor
Implemented by	Chief executive's appointee	Sponsoring profit centre[1] manager, and sponsor
Monitored by	Chief executive[2]	Sponsor

1 The sponsoring profit centre should normally be the most down-stream one, but the number and nature of resources required, and where they are held and controlled, may also play a part in its selection.
2 Outturn of corporate strategy is externally monitored by the principal financial market of the business, e.g. the stock market for listed companies.

Notes

1. Goold, Campbell and Alexander (1994).
2. See Chapter 13.
3. See Chapter 14.
4. See Chapters 13 and 14.
5. Chandler (1962) documented the growth of companies and how this growth was accompanied by the rising popularity of the multi-divisional or M-form. The transaction cost framework seeks to explain why diversification occurs at all, rather than why there was such a flood of diversification in the decades up to 1980. See Appendix 16.2.
6. Readers, especially those familiar with organizational theory, may wish to be reminded that the definition (Chapter 1) of 'business strategy' in this book is not one of the usual definitions.
7. The issue is fully discussed in Prahalad and Bettis (1986).
8. Prahalad and Bettis (1986) p. 495.

9. See Part Four.
10. As it is often neither feasible nor desirable for the sales force to serve external clients, a competitive level of charges can be ascertained by finding out on what terms the internal suppliers could find external distributors.
11. Discussed in Chapter 13.
12. See box on 'parenting' earlier in this chapter.
13. The principle here is analogous to that of the contractual alternative filter, Chapter 14.
14. See Chapter 5.
15. See Chapter 4.
16. Christensen *et al.* (1982). See also Gage (1982).
17. The achieved approximation is close rather than complete: complete success would of course amount to the squaring of a circle. However, the EG&G experiment is certainly interesting.
18. Chapter 1 discusses Mintzberg's critique.
19. This is one of the points helpfully stressed by Mintzberg.

Endpiece: Business strategy for a new century

What this book has tried to do

Business strategy covers a lot of ground, and this book has covered much of it. Its distinctive themes have been:

- The strong focus on the choosing customer, in a world of increasingly variegated offerings.
- The individual offering as the unit of competition in that world. The company is important, but is not itself what customers choose. Where offerings are so diverse, the industry is less and less relevant as the arena of competition.
- Inspired management by the head office of its cluster of offerings as a source of financial success. Sustained value-building can come from corporate strategy. It need not just come from the competitive success of offerings.
- Financial success as the overriding aim. That aim is not seen as diluted by any obligation of business to stakeholders other than owners. Those stakeholders have important moral rights, which society will protect by regulatory and moral pressures. Those pressures will change the terrain in which business must battle for financial value. They do not affect the raison d'être of a given business.

The directions of change

At the end of the second millennium the human race is wrestling with a number of difficult challenges. The most pressing threats come from tribalism in its widest sense, from the unreadiness of so many nations for the responsibilities of pluralistic government, and from new weapons of mass destruction. Between them they constitute a potentially cata-strophic mixture. Tribalism here means any form of tension and mutual fear which continues through generations, and divides groups characterized by religious, social, ethnic, cultural or other traditional differences.

Optimism rests on the undoubtedly rising popularity of pluralist prosperity among the masses. That means a yearning for the fruits of competitive markets and for the individual rights that can be safeguarded by democratic institutions. This general trend towards voter- and customer-driven structures will continue to meet resistance wherever there is tribalism and distrust of democracy and markets, but it seems unlikely that the resisting forces will in the long run prevail.

There are of course those who wrongly believe or pretend that pluralism denies social virtues like solidarity. The late twentieth century is reacting against the over-powerful state, not against the communitarian values of social cohesion. Pluralism means empowering individuals to have a say in what is to be produced tomorrow or in how they should be governed. It is inconsistent, and even incompatible with out-and-out individualism, with the view that everyone is free to ignore the interests of all others.

The challenge may become more global

If that assessment turns out to be correct, then the greatest scope for change exists in precisely those societies where the ascendancy of the ballot-box and the market is not yet complete. That concerns mostly developing countries like India, China, and nearly the whole of Africa, most of Latin America, but also Eastern Europe.

If this change to pluralism does materialize, it will of course boost this book's focus on choosing customers, on competing offerings of ever greater variety. The prevalence of differenti-ation will spread from the existing free-market economies, perhaps even to Afghanistan, Bangladesh, Albania, Yemen,

416

Sudan, Zaire and Cuba. Success will be in sight when Indian life assurance companies and Chinese banks vie with one another in the support dimension, as described in Chapter 5.

The culture will be different

Wherever this change to the market economy has yet to come, the cultural shock may well be traumatic. In Russia in the mid-1990s it is touch and go whether the shock can be absorbed. One day the business manager has to cultivate buraucrats and regulators: the next day it is customers. The difference is not so great for those specialized in selling to few and large customers. However, most offerings depend on being chosen by consumers or by a multitude of small businesses. Their customers tend to be faceless and fickle, and courted by many rivals. Before the shock, it was largely a matter of fostering a few critical relationships, where personal loyalty is at least a possibility. Afterwards it is much more shifting sands. In this new world, a business will find its most powerful armoury, and its only prospect of continuity, in its own excellence, in its own distinctive or key resources.

For whom are we working?

In the mid-1990s the stakeholder debate rages on, unresolved. In fact, it has been called a dialogue of the deaf. The debate is not new. In many developed countries like Japan, Germany and France the idea that business exists to make money had never taken root. However, in English-speaking countries like the US and UK, with their highly developed stockmarket systems, this was at least part of a well-established culture.

However, the 1980s and 1990s 'downsizing' spree made even the Americans and the British take a deep breath. Was job insecurity an acceptable way of life? Was the provision of reasonably secure livelihoods any part of the function of business, or was labour, even managerial labour, just another commodity to be bought and sold? And of course, this sneaking doubt about the stakeholder rights of employees coincided with a fresh wave of preoccupation with green issues. So a new doctrine was born: the doctrine that business was answerable not just to one set of 'stakeholders', the owners, but to several sets, including employees, customers, suppliers, and the environment. All of these had a stake in how the business conducted itself.

Chapter 2 has suggested a way of reconciling the two views. There is an inner area where good ethics, and looking after the other stakeholders, is also good business. Harming them will impose extra costs. There is also however an outer area where the two sets of interests conflict and where financial survival must prevail. A dead business cannot help any stakeholders. Where the survival of the business is incompatible with social objectives, it is up to society to impose and enforce rules within which business must be conducted.

It is also useful to distinguish between the business as an investment project and the managers and others who run it. The investment project is inanimate, and not an ethical agent. The managers are moral beings with value systems and personal and collective loyalties. The question 'for whom are we working?' makes sense for managers. The business on the other hand can only ask what its own purpose is: a very different question.

It seems likely that in the English-speaking countries the conflict will ultimately be resolved by distinguishing between the inner and outer areas. In the other countries, like Japan, Germany and France, there seems to be a growing awareness of the essential need for financial success. They too therefore seem destined to move towards the recognition that business needs a financial justification. Yet the debate may continue to be heated, as the two sides use very different models of the world. Until there is clarity on whether the question is about the personal loyalties of managers or about the purpose of the business, the answers will be hard to find.

It will be some time before the developing countries will become seriously interested in these issues. When they do, they too seem destined to resolve them as here suggested.

The rise of corporate strategy

For a century or longer up to about 1975 there was a dash for size. It was inspired no doubt by the rise of large-scale heavy industry. Strangely this dash for size caught on all over the world. The giant corporation became a model in developing countries as well as in the industrial ones. The first setback came with trust-busting in the US in the 1930s. The ironic reaction was that US companies decided to become conglomerates since the law stopped them getting bigger in their own industries. In any case, between 1960 and 1980 there was also a strong fashionable belief in the importance of market share, which seemed to reinforce the case for size, if not for conglomerates.

All these tendencies have now been reversed. Especially since the 1970s the trend has been away from large heavy industrial plants, away from size, and above all away from conglomerates, from unrelated expansion. Hotter competition is forcing companies to weed out their less successful operations. They have learned to focus on what each of them is good at, to divest the rest. They have learned the need to keep on questioning the validity of their clusters. Cluster management is coming into its own in the developed countries. It may well be that this will catch on in the rest of the world, as trade barriers and patronage recede and markets get more competitive. Part Four has argued that a flair for cluster management may well be a strong and persistent value-builder.

The shrinking world

This speculative tour of the significant issues has dwelt on trends in different parts of the world. The general impression is that the world is getting more alike, more open, more competitive, less regulated.

This is not to deny that deep cultural differences remain. Japan and societies with fundamentalist cultures are still largely male-dominated at a time when in the advanced Western countries women are rapidly advancing to equality or even ascendancy.

These deep cultural divides may ultimately disappear, but the process is unlikely to be rapid. Tribalism for example is very slow to decline in Northern Ireland, and there is little evidence of any decline in Quebec, former Yugoslavia, Iraq or Sri Lanka. In Africa it may even be on the increase. These deep-seated cultural barriers are sure to persist for decades or even centuries.

Yet the unifying forces on planet Earth are strong too. The strongest of them is the revolution in transport and communications. Electorates who can see on their own TV screens how prosperous people are in California and around Lake Geneva, will not for long put up with heavy trade barriers and exclusion from the benefits of free markets.

This book has largely treated international business as raising much the same strategic issues as domestic business. This is in contrast to the traditional doctrine calling for separate international strategies. There is still a vestige of a need for a separate look at what goes on across frontiers, but it is not much more than a vestige. If that makes international strategy a less exciting subject, or if it even caused downsizing in international business departments of business schools, there are plenty of new exciting topics to take its place, such as cluster management and the resource-based approach to sustained value-building. Pride of place will however surely belong to the need to take a customer-centred view of a more and more differentiated world of competitive offerings.

Glossary

Bold text indicates that the term is a glossary entry.

Agency conflict: A conflict between the interests of share-holders and those of (top) managers.

Appropriability: That quality of a resource which enables the company which owns it to retain the value of that resource against the bargaining power of inner team members, such as key suppliers or employees, who share in the creation of the resource. Sometimes used to denote vulnerability to an inner team member seizing most or all of that value from the company and other team members.

Aura: (as a subdimension of **merchandise differentiation**) concerns what the offering 'says' about the customer. See also **content**.

Best-owner filter: Requires that an offering should only be added to or remain in the company's cluster if the company is that offering's best possible owner, so that the offering could not be more valuable to another owner or independent.

Better-off test: The fundamental yardstick of whether the company should add or retain a specific offering in its cluster of offerings: will that offering make the cluster financially more valuable?

Business strategy: A significant intention about one or several offerings of the company in its commercial markets. It includes all stages: formulation, selection, adoption and implementation. Consists of both competitive and corporate strategy. It aims to make the company financially more valuable by selecting and retaining offerings with a positive net present value, after discounting at the cost of capital.

Capability: An ability and skill to use a number of **resources** in a co-ordinated and value-building manner.

CEO: The chief executive officer of a **company.**

Circularity: The essential quality of a market in a state of oligopoly: each member of the group of dominant competitors needs to take into account the likely or possible reaction of the other members before deciding on any competitive move.

Cluster: The collectivity of a company's offerings. To manage its composition is the task of corporate strategy.

Commodity-buy offering: An offering relatively undifferentiated in both the **support** and the **merchandise dimension**.

Company: An independent business entity, not owned by another business. It is not necessarily legally incorporated. It includes any subsidiary or affiliated companies. It thus also means the 'group' of companies.

Competitive strategy: A strategy to create a profitable offering, and its triangular positioning in relation to customers and competitors.

Conglomerate: A diversified company with an unrelated (see **related**) cluster of offerings. Not equated with a **corporate catalyst**. See also **relatedness**.

Content: (as a subdimension of **merchandise differentiation**) concerns what the offering will do for the customer. See also **aura**.

Contractual alternative filter: Requires that an offering should only be added to or remain in the company's cluster if its benefit to the cluster cannot be achieved by a contractual relationship with an external party.

Core cluster: A **link** of relatedness. Applies where offerings are so investment-intensive, or so technically complex, or so slow to put in place that an internal critic, closer than the external financial markets is needed to prevent uneconomic investment of capital. That critic needs to be a head office skilled in the specialized problems of a class of offerings. Such a head office will operate the **strategic planning style** and collect a core cluster of offerings in that class.

Cornerstones: The four qualities which a **key resource** must have. It must be (a) diverse (heterogeneous), (b) felicitous (build value after deducting the opportunity cost of acquiring or retaining it), (c) matchless (sufficiently armoured against imitation or substitution) and (d) inseparable (sufficiently armoured against loss to a competitor and against appropriation of its value by a closely related insider).

Corporate catalyst: A company which aims to create financial value primarily by profitably buying and selling existing companies or parts of such companies or their assets. Also called 'raider' or 'dealer in corporate control'.

Corporate strategy: A strategy to manage the composition of the cluster of offerings of a company. Consists of decisions to add, retain or divest offerings.

Cost leadership: A durable advantage over competitors in unit costs. This is a condition of **price leadership**.

Cost of capital (of a company, of an investment project, or of a proposed new offering): The risk-adjusted rate of return required by investors to invest in that company, project or offering. It is used as the rate at which cash flows are discounted to net present value in the evaluation of projects.

Customer segment: A group of customers with closely matched preferences. See also **segment**.

Differentiation: Both (a) a strategy of positioning an offering at a distance from its competing substitutes in order to make it less price-sensitive, and (b) the result of such a strategy.

Distance (of **differentiation**): The measure of how distant or close an offering is to one or more of its substitutes.

Diverse: See **cornerstones**.

Diversification: Adding additional offerings to a company's cluster, thus bringing them under the control of its head office. See also **risk diversification**.

Encroachment: The process of new offerings entering a *private* market because profits in that market are seen to exceed the encroachers' opportunity cost of capital. See also **entry**.

Entry (into an industry, a *public* market, or a part of an industry or public market): The process of new offerings entering a public market because profits in that market are seen to exceed the entrants' opportunity cost of capital. See also **encroachment**.

Equilibrium: A state in which none of the agents in a market stand to gain by shifting their positions. The shift can be in price, in offerings, or in resources used to produce offerings. The market is often that of an offering, but the set of markets in which a resource builds value can be wider than that of a single offering. Equilibrium can occur in pure or in imperfect competition. See also **general equilibrium**.

Ex ante: Describes how an event or a project looks before it occurs, i.e. an intention or expectation.

Ex post: Describes how an event or a project appears after it occurred, i.e. its realized out-turn.

Felicitous: See **cornerstones**.

Financial value: In this book assumed to be identical with **shareholder value**. Can alternatively be more widely defined, to include the value of lenders' and preferred shareholders' investment.

Firm: An ambiguous term variously used to describe anything from a whole company to an individual offering.

Firmlet: Synonymous with **'offering'**, but viewed in the context of the company's organization structure.

General equilibrium: A model in which the entire (world) economy is treated as the market in which both offerings and productive resources tend towards **equilibrium** prices. It contrasts with particular equilibrium models, e.g. individual industries as markets.

Generic offering: An occasionally convenient expression for a collection of **offerings** with minor variations in either space or time. Examples are (a) an offering sold in additional geographical areas or (b) one replaced with a very similar one, provided there is no material variation in either case in the way customers see the old and the new offering positioned against competing substitutes.

Global market: The market of a single offering (with a single triangular positioning in relation to customers and competitors) which extends over practically the whole world of free commercial markets.

Head office: The seat of the top management or CEO of a company.

Industry: A grouping of companies or business units with some commonality. This commonality may lie in the material used like steel, or in the offering, or in the technology or discipline used. Used as a statistical category, and is sometimes viewed as a market.

Inputs: All attributes of an offering, and all efforts and resources which go into it, provided they are *not* outputs, and therefore do not enter the customer's selection process. See also **outputs**.

Inseparable: See **cornerstones**.

Interpersonal structure: The – often informal – chain of command between a **company's CEO** and the relatively small number of decision-takers in the formulation, approval and execution of individual competitive and corporate strategies.

Key resource: A **resource** which, according to the **resource-based view**, meets the four conditions (**cornerstones**) to make it a **sustained value-builder**.

Links of relatedness: There are six links that can make an offering related to the remainder of the cluster of offerings. Five are links with other offerings: sharing of efforts and resources, vertical integration, **protective offerings**, customer preferences best met by common ownership, and market power. The remaining link is with the head office: **core cluster**.

Manager: Strictly any person who directs the activities of others. Used in business literature to denote a person who singly or with others directs and administers a business on behalf of its owners. Includes what is sometimes called an executive.

Market: A communication system enabling the interaction of buyers and sellers to ascertain and determine prices. See also **public market** and **private market**.

Market for corporate control: A market in which the management of companies and control of their assets and operations can change hands. The most important example is the takeover market.

Market segment: Subset of a public market, with a narrower, more specialized range of customer preferences. See also **segment**.

Market capitalization: The total number of shares issued by a company multiplied by its share price.

Matchless: See **cornerstones**.

Merchandise differentiation: Those differentiating features of an offering which are not classified as the **support dimension** of differentiation.

Offering: An item bought or sold, irrespective of whether it is a tangible good or an intangible service. An individual offering is separate from another offering of the same seller's if it is not identically positioned with the same set of customers and competitors. The prices of two separate offerings are not determined in the same process. See also **generic offering**.

Oligopoly: A market with few dominant sellers. See also **circularity**.

Outputs: The benefits and drawbacks of an offering which consciously or subconsciously influence customers' choices between that offering and its substitutes. See also **inputs**.

Plan: A project consisting of a goal and an explicit implementation path.

Price leadership: A durable capacity to attract customers away from competing substitutes by offering lower prices.

Can in conditions of **circularity** become an ability to influence competitors' prices. See also **cost leadership**.

Private market: A market which is 'personal' to a single differentiated offering, in the sense that its list of competing substitutes does not wholly overlap with the corresponding list of each of those substitutes. Private markets of competing offerings overlap, but are never coextensive. See also **public market**.

Product-buy offering: An offering relatively undifferentiated in the support dimension, but highly differentiated in the merchandise dimension.

Protective offering: A **link** of relatedness, where the offering concerned builds value not in its own right, but by protecting the viability of another offering in the cluster.

Public market: A market with publicly visible boundaries, containing offerings which all compete with one another, and none with offerings outside the boundaries. See also **private market**.

Pure dealing: Seeking to add financial value not by selling offerings to customers, but by either speculating or arbitraging in financial, commodity or similar markets. It is a deal- and price- rather than customer-centred activity.

Pure management resource: A **resource** or **capability** which makes the whole company distinctively efficient, but is too generalized to be identifiable as building value in any one offering.

Quasi-public market: A market which fails to meet the criteria of a **public market**, but which nevertheless has clear and publicly visible borders, at which there is a noticeable discontinuity in close substitutes. There are **private markets** within its borders, and some substitutes outside them, but the distance between the group of offerings within the border on the one hand and all substitutes outside it on the other, is substantially greater than any internal distances.

Rearranger offering: A new offering, the arrival of which changes the existing configuration of its **private market**, but without radically transforming that market and its surrounding landscape. See also **transformer offering**.

Related offering: An offering which has one of six specified **links** with the rest of the **company**. An offering which is in this sense unrelated to the rest, cannot pass the **better-off test**. See also **conglomerate**.

Relatedness (of an offering): Compliance with the conditions of being a **related offering**.

Resource: Any stock of unexhausted value from past **inputs**, capable of making an offering valuable. Its value need not be specific to any one offering. Can be an inanimate object, or skills of human beings, or collective skills of the company or of a part of the company. See also **key resources** and **resource-based view, pure management resources** and **capability**.

Resource-based view: A model of competitive strategy which looks for an explanation of observed **sustained value-building** in the heterogeneity of companies' resources. See also **resources** and **key resources**.

Risk diversification: The balancing or averaging out of risks by acquiring a portfolio of diverse risks.

Robustness filter: Requires that a new offering should only be added to the company's cluster if its benefit to the cluster is likely to endure for the greater of (a) the payback period needed to recover the net present value of the investment in the offering and (b) the lead time needed to divest or abort the offering.

Scale (or rankable) differentiation: The case where customers see competing substitutes as varying not along several different dimensions, but along a single dimension (e.g. 'quality'), making it possible to rank their distances or differentiation from some point of origin.

Scale economies: The reduction in unit costs due to extra volume, i.e. by spreading fixed costs over extra units. In the offering-based framework of this book it is not useful to distinguish between the economies of scale and those of scope.

Segment: A group of customers, or subset of a market, narrow enough to represent customers with closely matched preferences. See also **customer segment** and **market segment**.

Segmentation: Either (a) the act of analysing a market so as to identify **segments**, or (b) the creation of a segment on the initiative of a seller, or (c) the resulting state of the market = segmentedness.

Service-buy offering: An offering highly differentiated in the **support dimension**, but relatively undifferentiated in the **merchandise dimension**.

Shareholder value: The value of any particular shareholder's interest in the company. Shareholders are in this book assumed to be equity (ordinary or common) shareholders, those whose returns are directly related to the results of the company. See also **financial value**.

Short termism: A managerial state of mind which gives undue weight to immediate financial results and cash flow, i.e. more weight than is indicated by a discount rate representing the cost of capital.

Sponsor: A manager who formulates a new competitive strategy (i.e. offering or firmlet), acts as its advocate in the approval process, negotiates with those in the company who hold resources needed for the strategy, monitors its implementation and subsequent progress and developments in its market environment.

Stakeholders: A group of persons affected by the operations of a business. These are usually thought to include shareholders or other owners, employees, customers, suppliers, the adjacent community, or the wider public and its environment.

Strategy: A major plan to attain a stated objective. See also **business strategy, competitive strategy, corporate strategy**.

Strategic group: A more closely competitive subset of an industry.

Strategic planning style: A style of management by a head office needed for a **core cluster** of offerings. The head office needs to participate in the formulation of competitive strategies and act as internal critic for such a cluster.

Success-aping forces, pressures, etc.: Forces etc. that seek to exploit a disequilibrium, so as to emulate supernormal returns earned by others. In microeconomics the term 'rent-seeking' is more commonly used.

Support differentiation: Those differentiating features of an offering which customers perceive in the way the seller helps them in choosing, obtaining, and then using the offering. See also **merchandise differentiation**.

Sustained value-building/builder: The purpose of a successful competitive strategy, i.e. to select an offering which will sustain its **value-building**. The condition of 'sustained' is met if the offering can withstand threats to its value-building long enough to achieve a positive net present value. Synonyms like 'sustained competitive advantage' or 'persistent rents' are less unambiguously concerned with positive net present value.

System-buy offering: An offering highly differentiated in both the merchandise and the support dimension.

Transaction costs: (a) Narrow managerial usage: the direct costs of a purchase, sale or payment, e.g. bank charges on currency remittance, or costs of customs clearance. (b) Extended usage: the indirect costs of managing external procurement, e.g. negotiating contracts with outside parties, or internal procurement, e.g. internal command or communication inefficiencies.

Transaction life cycle: A model showing how an offering can be succeeded by other offerings which successively reduce the degree of differentiation and then again raise the degree of differentiation, or vice versa. The process can be iterative.

Transformer offering: A new offering the arrival of which radically transforms the configuration of markets in its part of the economy. See also **rearranger offering**.

Value-building/value-builder/building value: Describes the capacity (of an offering or project) to produce a positive net present value after discounting at the appropriate cost of capital.

References

Abell, D.F. and Hammond, J.S. (1979). *Strategic market planning*. Prentice Hall.

Amit, R. and Schoemaker, P.J.H. (1993). Strategic assets and organisational rent. *Strat. Mgt. J.*, **14**, 33–46.

Andrews, K.R. (1981). Replaying the board's role in formulating strategy. *Harv. Bus. Rev.*, May–June, 18–28.

Arends, A. (1996). Short-term shortcomings. *The Financial Times*, 9 February, p. 14.

Bain, G.W. (1956). *Barriers to new competition*. Harvard University Press.

Barney, J.B. (1986). Strategic factor markets: expectations, luck, and business strategy. *Mgt. Sc.*, **32** (10), 1231–1241.

Barney, J.B. (1991). Firm resources and sustained competitive advantage. *J. of Mgt.*, **17** (1), 99–120.

Barney, J.B. and Hoskisson, R.E. (1990). Strategic groups: untested assertions and research proposals. *Managerial and Decision Economics*, **11**, 187–198.

Barney, J.B. and Zajac, E.J. (1994). Competitive organizational behavior: toward an organizationally-based theory of competitive advantage. *Strat. Mgt. J.*, **15** (Special issue), 5–9.

Bartlett, C.A. (1985). *Global competition and MNC managers*. ICCH note 0-385-287, Harvard Business School Press.

Bartlett, C.A. and Ghoshal, S. (1987). Managing across borders: new organisational responses. *Sloan Mgt. Rev.*, Fall, 43–53.

Bartlett, C.A. and Ghoshal, S. (1989). *Managing across borders*. Harvard Business School Press.

Baumol, J. (1982). Contestable markets: an uprising in the theory of industry structure. *Amer. Econ. Rev.*, **72** (1), 1–15.

Baumol, J., Panzar, J.C. and Willig, R.D. (1982). *Contestable markets and the theory of industry structure*. Harcourt Brace Jovanovich.

Bethel, J.E. and Liebeskind, J. (1993). The effects of ownership structure on corporate restructuring. *Strat. Mgt. J.*, **14**, 15–31.

Bhagat, S., Shleifer, A. and Vishny, R.W. (1990). *Hostile takeovers in the 1980s: the return to corporate specialization*. Brookings Papers.

References

BIS (Bank for International Settlements) (1986). *Recent innovations in international banking*. Group of Ten study group.

Bower, J.L., Bartlett, C.A., Christensen, C.R., Pearson, A.E. and Andrews, K.R. (1991). Crown Cork and Seal case. In *Business policy: text and cases*. Seventh edition. Irwin.

Brealey, R.A. and Myers, S.C. (1991). *Principles of corporate finance*. Fourth edition, McGraw-Hill.

Brittan, S. (1995). *Capitalism with a human face*. Edward Elgar.

Brooks, G.R. (1995). Defining market boundaries. *Strat. Mgt. J.*, **16**, 535–549.

Buzzell, R.D. Gale, B.T. and Sultan, R.G.M. (1975). Market share – a key to profitability. *Harv. Bus. Rev.*, Jan–Feb, 97–106.

Buzzell, R.D. and Gale, B.T. (1987). *The PIMS principles – linking strategy to performance*. Free Press.

Campbell, A. and Goold, M. (1988). Adding value from corporate head-quarters. *London Business School Journal*, **12** (1), 48–58.

Capon, N., Hulbert, J.M., Farley, J.U. and Martin, L.E. (1988). Corporate diversity and economic performance: the impact of market special-isation. *Strat. Mgt. J.*, **9** (1), 61–74.

Castanias, R.P. and Helfat, C.E. (1991). Managerial resources and rents. *J. of Mgt.*, **17** (1), 155–171.

Caves, R.E. and Porter, M.E. (1977). From entry barriers to mobility barriers: conjectural decisions and deterrence to new competition. *Q. J. of Econ.*, **91**, 241–262.

Chandler, A.D. (1962). *Strategy and structure*. MIT Press. Reprinted 1991.

Chandler, A.D. Jr. (1991). The functions of the HQ unit in the multi-business firm. *Strat. Mgt. J.*, **12** (Special issue). Winter, 31–50.

Charkham, J. (1989). *Corporate governance and the market for control of companies*. Bank of England panel paper.

Charkham, J. (1994). *Keeping good company*. Oxford University Press.

Chi, T. (1994). Trading in strategic resources: necessary conditions, transaction cost problems, and choice of exchange structure. *Strat. Mgt. J.*, **15**, 271–290.

Christensen, C.R., Andrews, K.R., Bower, J.L., Hamermesh, R.G. and Porter, M.E. (1982). EG&G Inc. In *Business policy: text and cases*. Irwin, pp 325–358.

Coase, R.H. (1937). The nature of the firm. *Economica*, **8**, 386–405.

Collis, D.J. (1994). Research note: How valuable are organizational capabilities? *Strat. Mgt. J.*, **15**, 143–152.

Conner, K.R. (1991). A historical comparison of resource-based theory and five schools of thought within industrial organization econ-omics: do we have a new theory of the firm? *J. of Mgt.*, **17** (1), 121–154.

Copeland, T., Koller, T. and Murrin, J. (1990). *Valuation: measuring and managing the value of companies*. Wiley.

Craig Smith, N. (1990). *Morality and the market, consumer pressure for corporate accountability*. Routledge.

Crosby, P.B. (1979). *Quality is free: the art of making quality certain*. McGraw-Hill.

De Chernatony, L., Knox, S. and Chedgey, M. (1992). Brand pricing in a recession. *Eur. J. of Mktg.*, **26** (2), 5–14.

Demsetz, H. (1991). The theory of the firm revisited. In *The nature of the firm* (O.E. Williamson and S.G. Winter, eds). Chapter 10. Oxford University Press.

Dickson, P.R. and Ginter, J.L. (1987). Market segmentation, product differentiation, and marketing strategy. *J. of Mktg.*, **51**, 1–10.

Dierickx, I. and Cool, K. (1989). Asset stock accumulation and sustainability of competitive advantage. *Mgt. Sc.*, **35** (12), 1504–1511.

Dimsdale, N. (1994). The need to restore corporate accountability: an agenda for reform. In *Capital markets and corporate governance* (N. Dimsdale and M. Prevezer, eds) pp 13–49. Clarendon Press.

Dixit, A. and Nalebuff, B. (1991). *Thinking strategically: the competitive edge in business, politics and everyday life*. W.W. Norton.

Dolan, M.J. (1985). The case for the new conglomerate. Unpublished paper. Booz Allen and Hamilton.

Doz, Y., Bartlett, C.A. and Prahalad, C.K. (1981). Global competitive pressures v host country demands: managing tensions in multinational corporations. *Calif. Mgt. Rev.*, **23**, Spring, 63–74.

Economist, The, various issues.

Financial Times, The, various issues.

Franks, J.R. and Mayer, C. (1992). Corporate control: a synthesis of the international evidence. IFA Working Paper, London Business School, No. 165–192.

Franks, J.R. and Harris, R. (1989). Shareholder wealth effects of UK takeovers: implications for merger policy. In *Mergers and merger policy* (J. Fairburn and J. Kay, eds). Oxford University Press.

Friedman, M. (1935). The methodology of positive economics. Reprinted in *Readings in microeconomics* (1968) (W. Breit and H.M. Hochman, eds). Holt, Rinehart and Winston, pp 23–47.

Gage, G.H. (1982). On acceptance of strategic planning systems. In *Implementation of strategic planning* (P. Lorange, ed.), pp. 171–182. Prentice Hall.

Ghoshal, S. (1987). Global strategy: an organising framework. *Strat. Mgt. J.*, **8**, 425–440.

Ghoshal, S. and Nohria, N. (1993). Horses for courses, organizational forms for multinational corporations. *Sloan Mgt. Rev.*, Winter, 23–35.

Goold, M. and Campbell, A. (1987a). *Strategies and Styles*. Blackwell.

Goold, M. and Campbell, A. (1987b). Managing diversity: strategy and control in diversified British companies. *Long Range Planning*, **20** (5), October, 42–52.

References

Goold, M., Campbell, A. and Alexander, M. (1994). *Corporate-level strategy*. Wiley.

Grant, R.M. (1991). The resource-based theory of competitive advantage. Implications for strategy formulation. *Calif. Mgt. Rev.*, Spring, 114–135.

Grant, R.M. (1995). *Contemporary Strategy Analysis*. Second edition. Blackwell.

Grant, R.M. and Jammine, A.P. (1988). Performance differences between the Wrigley/Rumelt strategic categories. *Strat. Mgt. J.*, **9**, 333–346.

Hamel, G. and Prahalad, C.K. (1985). Do you really have a global strategy? *Harv. Bus. Rev.*, July–August, 139–148.

Hart, O. (1995). Corporate governance: some theory and implications. *Econ. J.*, **105** (May), 678–689.

Haspeslagh, P.C. and Jemison, D.B. (1991). *Managing acquisitions: creating value through corporate renewal*. The Free Press.

Hatten. K.J. and Hatten, M.L. (1987). Strategic groups, asymmetrical mobility barriers and contestability. *Strat. Mgt. J.*, **8**, 329–342.

Heffernan, S. A. and Sinclair, P. (1990). *Modern international economics*. Blackwell.

Higson, C. and Elliot, J. (1993) *Are acquired firms distinctive? The effect of choice on control*. IFA Working Paper 170–93. London Business School.

Hill, C.W.L (1985). Oliver Williamson and the M-form firm: a critical review. *Journal of Economic Issues*, **19** (3), 731–751.

Hirshleifer, J. (1980). *Price theory and applications*. Second edition, Prentice Hall.

Hofstede, G. (1991). *Cultures and Organisations*. McGraw-Hill.

Hoskisson, R.E. and Turk, T.A. (1990). Corporate restructuring: governance and control limits of the internal capital market. *Ac. of Mgt. Rev.*, **15** (3), 459–477.

Hout, T., Porter, M.E. and Rudden, E. (1982). How global companies win out. *Harv. Bus. Rev.*, September–October, 98–108.

Hunt, S.D. and Morgan, R.M. (1995). The comparative advantage theory of competition. *J. of Mktg.*, **59**, 1–15.

Jacobson, R. (1992). The 'Austrian' school of strategy. *Ac. of Mgt. Rev.* **17** (4), 782–807.

Jensen, M.C. (1988). Takeovers: their causes and consequences. *J. of Econ. Perspectives*, **2** (1), 21–48.

Jensen, M.C. (1989). Eclipse of the public corporation, *Harv. Bus. Rev.*, September–October, 61–74.

Jensen, M.C. (1993). The modern industrial revolution, exit, and the failure of internal control systems. *J. of Fin.*, **XLVIII**, 831–880.

Jensen, M.C. and Meckling, W.H. (1976). Theory of the firm: managerial behavior, agency costs and ownership structure. *J. of Fin. Econ.*, **3**, 5–50.

Jensen, M.C. and Ruback, R.S. (1983). The market for corporate control: the scientific evidence. *J. of Fin. Econ.*, **11**, 5–50.

434

Kaplan, R.S. and Roll, R. (1972). Investor evaluation of accounting information; some empirical evidence. *J. of Bus.*, **45**, April, 225–257.

Karnani, A. and Wernerfelt, B. (1985). Multiple point competition. *Strat. Mgt. J.*, **6**, 87–96.

Kay, J. (1993). *Foundations of corporate success*. Oxford University Press.

Kenyon, A. (1990). *Currency Risk and business management*. Blackwell.

Kenyon, A. (1996). The social responsibility of business: who are the responsible agents? *Bus. Ethics, a Eur. Rev.*, **5** (2), 81–86.

Kenyon, A. and Mathur, S.S. (1993). The meaning of strategy; the 'designed' versus 'emergent' dispute. *Eur. Mgt. J.*, **11** (3), 357–360.

Kester, W.C. (1984). Today's options for tomorrow's growth. *Harv. Bus. Rev.*, March–April, 153–160.

Krinsky, I., Rotenberg, W.D. and Thornton, D.B. (1988). Takeovers – a synthesis. *J. of Acct. Lit.*, **7**, 243–279.

Krugman, P. (1991). *Geography and Trade*. Leuven University Press and MIT Press.

Kotler, P. (1965). Phasing out weak products. *Harv. Bus. Rev.*, March–April, 107–118.

Leonard-Barton, D. (1992). Core capabilities and core rigidities: a paradox in managing new product development. *Strat. Mgt. J.*, **13**, 111–125.

Lessem, R. (1989). *Global Management Principles*. Prentice Hall.

Lippman, S.A. and Rumelt, R.P. (1982). Uncertain imitability: an analysis of interfirm differences in efficiency under competition. *The Bell J. of Econ.*, **13**, 418–438.

Luffman, G.A. and Reed, R. (1982). Diversification in British industry in the 1970s. *Strat. Mgt. J.*, **3** (4), 303–314.

Luffman, G.A. and Reed, R. (1984). *The strategy and performance of British industry*. Macmillan.

McGee, J. and Thomas, H. (1986). Strategic groups: research and taxonomy. *Strat. Mgt. J.*, **7**, 141–160.

McGee, J. and Thomas, H. (1992). Strategic groups and intra-industry competition. In *International Review of Strategic Management* (D.E. Hussey, ed.), Wiley.

McKiernan, P. (1992). *Strategies of growth*. Routledge.

Mahoney, J. (1993). Who's responsible for ethical business? 1. Investors. Public lecture, Gresham College, London.

Manne, H.G. (1965). Mergers and the market for corporate control. *J. of Pol. Econ.*, **73**, 110–120.

Markides, C.C. (1995). Diversification, restructuring and economic performance. *Strat. Mgt. J.*, **16**, 101–108.

Marsh, P. (1990). *Short-termism on trial*. Institutional Fund Managers Association.

Marsh, P. (1994). *Market assessment of company performance*. In *Capital markets and corporate governance* (N. Dimsdale and M. Prevezer, eds) pp 66–98. Clarendon Press.

References

Marshall, A. (1890). *Principles of economics*. Ninth edition, Macmillan, 1961.

Mathur, S.S. (1984). Competitive industrial marketing strategies. *Long Range Planning*, **17** (4), 102–109.

Mathur, S.S. (1988). How firms compete: a new classification of competitive strategies. *J. of Gen. Mgt.*, **14** (1), 30–57.

Mathur, S.S. (1992). Talking straight about competitive strategy. *J. of Mktg. Mgt.*, **8**, 199–217.

Michel, A. and Shaked, I. (1984). Does business diversification affect performance? *Fin. Mgt.*, **13** (4), 18–24.

Mintzberg, H. (1987a). Crafting strategy. *Harv. Bus. Rev.*, July–August, 66–75.

Mintzberg, H. (1987b). The strategy concept 1: five Ps for strategy. *Calif. Mgt. Rev.*, **30** (1), 11–24.

Mintzberg, H. (1990). The design school: reconsidering the basic premises of strategic management. *Strat. Mgt. J.*, **11**, 171–195.

Mintzberg, H. and Waters, J.A. (1985). Of strategies, deliberate and emergent. *Strat. Mgt. J.*, **6**, 257–272.

Mitchell, M.L. and Lehn, K. (1990). Do bad bidders become good targets? *J. of Pol. Econ.*, **98** (2), 372–398.

Murphy, K.J. (1985). Corporate performance & managerial remuneration. *J. of Acctg and Econ.*, **7**, 11–42.

Nelson, R.R. and Winter, S.G. (1982). *An evolutionary theory of economic change*. Harvard University Press.

Oster, S. (1990). *Modern competitive analysis*. Oxford University Press.

Penrose, E.T. (1959), The theory of the growth of the firm. Blackwell.

Peteraf, M.A. (1993). The cornerstones of competitive advantage: a resource-based view. *Strat. Mgt. J.*, **14**, 179–191.

Porter, M.E. (1980). *Competitive strategy*. Free Press.

Porter, M.E. (1984). *Competition in global industries*. Colloquium paper, Harvard Business School.

Porter, M.E. (1985). *Competitive advantage*. Free Press.

Porter, M.E. (ed.) (1986). *Competition in global industries*. Harvard Business School Press.

Porter, M.E. (1987). From competitive advantage to corporate strategy. *Harv. Bus. Rev.*, May–June, 43–59.

Porter, M E, (1992). Capital disadvantage: America's failing capital investment system. *Harv. Bus. Rev.*, September–October, 65–82.

Prahalad, C.K. (1975). The strategic process in a multinational corporation. Unpublished doctoral dissertation, Graduate School of Business Administration, Harvard University.

Prahalad, C.K. and Bettis, R.A. (1986). The dominant logic: a new linkage between diversity and performance. *Strat. Mgt. J.*, **7**, 485–501.

Prahalad, C.K. and Hamel, G. (1990). The core competence of the corporation. *Harv. Bus. Rev.*, May–June, 79–91.

Price, F. (1990). *Right every time*. Gower.

Rappaport, A. (1986). *Creating shareholder value: the new standard for business performance*. Free Press.

Ravenscraft, D.J. and Scherer, F.M. (1987). *Mergers, sell-offs and economic efficiency*. The Brookings Institution.

Robins, J. and Wiersema, M.F. (1995). A resource-based approach to the multibusiness firm: empirical analysis of portfolio interrelationships and corporate financial performance. *Strat. Mgt. J.*, **16**, 277–299.

Rumelt, R.P. (1974). *Strategy, structure and economic performance*. Harvard University Press.

Rumelt, R.P. (1982). Diversification strategy and profitability. *Strat. Mgt. J.*, **3**, 359–369.

Rumelt, R.P. (1984). Towards a strategic theory of the firm. In *Competitive strategic management* (R.B. Lamb, ed.) pp. 556–570. Prentice Hall.

Rumelt, R.P. (1991). How much does industry matter? *Strat. Mgt. J.*, **12**, 167–185.

Rumelt, R.P., Schendel D. and Teece D.J. (1991). Strategic management and economics. *Strat. Mgt. J.*, **12**, Special issue, Winter, 5–29.

Salter, M.D. and Weinhold, W.A. (1978). Diversification via acquisition: creating value. *Harv. Bus. Rev.*, July–August, 166–176.

Schelling, T.C. (1960). *The strategy of conflict*. Harvard University Press.

Scherer, F.M. and Ross, D. (1990). *Industrial market structure and economic performance*, Third edition. Houghton Mifflin.

Schumpeter, J.A. (1934). *The Theory of Economic Development*. Harvard University Press.

Sheth, J.N. Gardner, D.M. and Garrett, D.E. (1988). *Marketing theory: evolution and evaluation*. Wiley.

Shleifer, A. and Vishny, R.W. (1991). Takeovers in the '60s and the '80s: evidence and implications. *Strat. Mgt. J.*, **12**, (Special issue), 51–59.

Slatter, S. (1984). *Corporate recovery*. Penguin Books.

Sparkes, R. (1995). *The ethical investor*. Harper Collins.

Sternberg, E. (1994). *Just business*. Little, Brown and Company.

Stewart, G.B. (1991). *The quest for value*. Harper Collins.

Sudarsanam, P.S. (1995). *The essence of mergers and acquisitions*. Prentice Hall.

Szymanski, D.M., Bharadwaj, S.G. and Varadarajan, P.R. (1993). An analysis of the market share-profitability relationship. *Journal of Mktg.*, **57** July, 1–18.

Teece, D.J. (1980). Economies of scope and the scope of the enterprise. *J. of Econ. Behaviour and Org.*, **1**, 223–247.

Teece, D.J. (1982). Towards an economic theory of the multiproduct firm. *J. of Econ. Behaviour and Org.*, **3**, 39–63.

Thomas, D.R.E. (1978). Strategy is different in service businesses. *Harv. Bus. Rev.*, July–August, 158–165.

References

Triffin, R. (1940). *Monopolistic competition and general equilibrium theory.* Harvard University Press.

Velasquez, M. (1988). *Business ethics: concepts and cases.* Second edition. Prentice Hall.

Walsh, J.P. and Kosnik, R.D. (1993). Corporate raiders and their disciplinary role in the market for corporate control. *Ac. of Mgt. J.,* **36** (4), 671–700.

Williamson, O.E. (1975). *Markets and hierarchies.* The Free Press.

Whittington, R. (1993). *What is strategy, and does it matter?* Routledge.

Wrigley, L. (1970). *Divisional autonomy and diversification.* Doctoral dissertation. Harvard Business School.

Index

DATE DUE

HIGHSMITH #45230

Printed
in USA